Improving Higher Education in Malawi
for Competitiveness in the Global Economy

A WORLD BANK STUDY

Improving Higher Education in Malawi for Competitiveness in the Global Economy

Michael M. Mambo, Muna Salih Meky, Nobuyuki Tanaka and Jamil Salmi

© 2016 International Bank for Reconstruction and Development / The World Bank
1818 H Street NW, Washington, DC 20433
Telephone: 202-473-1000; Internet: www.worldbank.org

Some rights reserved

1 2 3 4 19 18 17 16

World Bank Studies are published to communicate the results of the Bank's work to the development community with the least possible delay. The manuscript of this paper therefore has not been prepared in accordance with the procedures appropriate to formally edited texts.

This work is a product of the staff of The World Bank with external contributions. The findings, interpretations, and conclusions expressed in this work do not necessarily reflect the views of The World Bank, its Board of Executive Directors, or the governments they represent. The World Bank does not guarantee the accuracy of the data included in this work. The boundaries, colors, denominations, and other information shown on any map in this work do not imply any judgment on the part of The World Bank concerning the legal status of any territory or the endorsement or acceptance of such boundaries.

Nothing herein shall constitute or be considered to be a limitation upon or waiver of the privileges and immunities of The World Bank, all of which are specifically reserved.

Rights and Permissions

This work is available under the Creative Commons Attribution 3.0 IGO license (CC BY 3.0 IGO) http://creativecommons.org/licenses/by/3.0/igo. Under the Creative Commons Attribution license, you are free to copy, distribute, transmit, and adapt this work, including for commercial purposes, under the following conditions:

Attribution—Mambo, Michael M., Muna Salih Meky, Nobuyuki Tanaka and Jamil Salmi. 2016. *Improving Higher Education in Malawi for Competitiveness in the Global Economy.* World Bank Studies. Washington, DC: World Bank. doi: 10.1596/978-1-4648-0798-5. License: Creative Commons Attribution CC BT 3.0 IGO.

Translations—If you create a translation of this work, please add the following disclaimer along with the attribution: *This translation was not created by The World Bank and should not be considered an official World Bank translation. The World Bank shall not be liable for any content or error in this translation.*

Adaptations—If you create an adaptation of this work, please add the following disclaimer along with the attribution: *This is an adaptation of an original work by The World Bank. Views and opinions expressed in the adaptation are the sole responsibility of the author or authors of the adaptation and are not endorsed by The World Bank.*

Third-party content—The World Bank does not necessarily own each component of the content contained within the work. The World Bank therefore does not warrant that the use of any third-party-owned individual component or part contained in the work will not infringe on the rights of those third parties. The risk of claims resulting from such infringement rests solely with you. If you wish to re-use a component of the work, it is your responsibility to determine whether permission is needed for that re-use and to obtain permission from the copyright owner. Examples of components can include, but are not limited to, tables, figures, or images.

All queries on rights and licenses should be addressed to the Publishing and Knowledge Division, The World Bank, 1818 H Street NW, Washington, DC 20433, USA; fax: 202-522-2625; e-mail: pubrights@worldbank.org.

ISBN (paper): 978-1-4648-0798-5
ISBN (electronic): 978-1-4648-0795-4
DOI: 10.1596/978-1-4648-0798-5

Library of Congress Cataloging-in-Publication Data has been requested

Contents

Acknowledgments		*ix*
About the Authors		*xi*
Executive Summary		*xiii*
Abbreviations		*xxix*
Chapter 1	**Introduction**	**1**
	Background	1
	Methodology	2
Chapter 2	**Access and Equity in Malawi's Higher Education Sub-Sector**	**5**
	Introduction	5
	Access and Equity	5
	Factors Affecting Access and Equity	14
	Equity in Higher Education	22
	Enrollment Projections	28
	Alternative Options for Secondary School Leavers	29
	Conclusion	30
	Programmatic Policy Options	32
	Annexes for Chapter 2	33
	Notes	39
Chapter 3	**Quality and Relevance of Higher Education in Malawi**	**41**
	Introduction	41
	Quality Assurance Policies in Malawi	42
	Findings of the Study	42
	Relevance of Higher Education	62
	Conclusion	77
	Programmatic Policy Options	78
	Annexes for Chapter 3	80
	Notes	83

Chapter 4	The Financing of Higher Education	85
	Introduction	85
	Findings of the Study	85
	Resource Allocation	95
	Resource Utilization	98
	Costs Associated with the Projected Growth of Public Higher Education	112
	Conclusion	112
	Programmatic Policy Options	113
	Annexes for Chapter 4	116
	Notes	122
Chapter 5	Governance and Management in Malawi Universities	123
	Introduction	123
	Current Status of Higher Education Institutions in Malawi	123
	Challenges of Governance and Management in Higher Education	130
	Conclusion	140
	Programmatic Policy Options	141
	Annex for Chapter 5	143
	Notes	143
References		145

Boxes

3.1	Mining in Malawi	66
3.2	Agricultural Development in Malawi	68

Figures

ES.1	Enrollment in the Malawian Higher Education Institutions	xiv
ES.2	Enrollment in tertiary education per 100,000 inhabitants in selected sub-Saharan Africa countries	xvi
ES.3	Evolution of Enrollment by Provider and Gender—2008–11	xvii
ES.4	Distribution of Academic Staff by Grade—2011	xviii
ES.5	Higher Education Budget as a Share of the Total Education Budget	xxi
2.1	Absorption of MSCE Graduates into the Higher Education System—2008–11	6
2.2	Enrollment by Type of Institution and Gender—2008–11	7
2.3	Enrollment by Institution—2008–11	9
2.4	Number of Nonresidential Students by Institution—2008–11	10

2.5	Postgraduate Enrollment by Institution—2008–11	12
2.6	Percentage of Postgraduate Students by Institution—2008–11	12
2.7	Proportion of Females Enrolled in Graduate Studies by Institution	14
2.8	Enrollment in Tertiary Education by Socioeconomic Status	25
2.9	Enrollment by District at UNIMA for 2009 and 2010	28
3.1	Staffing Trends by Institution—2008–11	44
3.2	Student-Lecturer Ratios by Institution by Year—2008–11	44
3.3	Distribution of Staff by Qualification—2011	46
3.4	Staffing Levels by Designation by Institution—2011	47
3.5	Availability of Teaching and Learning Materials by Institution—2011	53
3.6	Availability of ICT Facilities by Institution—2011	55
3.7	Graduate Output by Institution—2008–11	57
3.8	Withdrawal Rates by Faculty and Type of Student—Chancellor College—2010	59
3.9	Withdrawal Rates by Type of Student, Faculty, and Gender: MZUNI—2010	60
3.10	Number of Withdrawals by Reason and Gender: Polytechnic—2010	60
3.11	Output of Master's Graduates by Gender and College—2010–11	63
4.1	Trends in Subventions to Public Universities—2008–11	86
4.2	Percentage Distribution of Sources of Income in Private Universities—2008–10	90
4.3	Direct Aid to Higher Education in Selected African Countries, Annual Average Commitments—2001–06	94
4.4	Funding Gaps in Subvention, and Internally Generated Income	96
4.5	Surplus/Deficit in Public Institutions—2008–10	101
4.6	Unit Costs by Institution—2008–10	103
4.7	Beneficiaries and Loans Disbursed—2006–10	110
4.8	Number of Nonresidential Students by Institution—2008–11	111

Tables

ES.1	Summary Policy Matrix: Main Reforms and Measures Suggested in the Study	xxvi
2.1	Enrollment (Total and per 100,000 Inhabitants) by Gender—2008–11	8
2.2	Cumulative Enrollment by Field of Study—2008–11	11
2.3	Composition of Staff by Qualification—2011	13

2.4	Comparison of Female Enrollment by Field of Study—2006 and 2011	24
2.5	Enrollment Projections by Institution	29
2.6	Policy Options	32
3.1	Student Lecturer Ratios by Institution and Faculty—2011	45
3.2	Distribution of 2011 Graduates by Field of Study	62
3.3	Policy Options	78
4.1	Sources of Income by Institution—2008–10	87
4.2	Comparison of Annual Tuition Fees for Universities in the SADC Region	91
4.3	Comparison of Tuition Fees for Universities in the SADC Region as a Percent of GDP per Capita	92
4.4	Methods of Allocating the Higher Education Budget in Select African Countries	97
4.5	Expenditure Trends for UNIMA—2008–10	98
4.6	Expenditure Trends at MZUNI—2008–10	99
4.7	Expenditure Trends at MAU—2009–10	99
4.8	Expenditure Trends at UNILIA—2008–10	100
4.9	Unit Cost Expenditure by Selected Expenditure Categories—UNIMA	104
4.10	Unit Cost Expenditure by Selected Expenditure Categories—MZUNI	105
4.11	Unit Cost Expenditure by Selected Expenditure Categories—MAU	105
4.12	Unit Cost Expenditure by Selected Expenditure Categories—UNILIA	105
4.13	Unit Cost by Faculty for UNIMA Colleges	108
4.14	Policy Options	114
5.1	Policy Options	142

Acknowledgments

The report was prepared by a team from the World Bank including: Michael M. Mambo (Consultant and lead author), Muna Salih Meky (Senior Education Specialist), Nobuyuki Tanaka (Economist), and Jamil Salmi (consultant) under the guidance of Sajitha Bashir (Practice Manager). The production of this report was made possible through a process of consultation with many stakeholders in the Malawian education sector. The team acknowledges the support and contributions of the Ministry of Education, Science and Technology (MoEST) in the conduct of study. Consultation with the Ministry was largely structured in the form of a working group with membership drawn from the respective directorates of, and institutions linked to, the MoEST. The team wishes also to acknowledge the contributions of the following institutions of higher learning: Mzuzu University (MZUNI); The University of Livingstonia (UNILIA), The Catholic University of Malawi (CUNIMA); The Malawi Adventist University (MAU); and The University of Malawi (UNIMA), inclusive of its five constituent colleges – Bunda College of Agriculture, Chancellor College (CHANCO), The College of Medicine (COM), The Kamuzu College of Nursing (KCN), the Polytechnic, and the central administration office for the five constituent colleges, The University Office. The following organizations assisted through the provision of data: the National Archives; the Center for Social Research; and the World Bank. The team wishes to thank all who contributed to the realization of this report, and encourage them to continue with their work in the same good spirit.

About the Authors

Michael Mambo is a consultant with the World Bank's Global Practice for Education. He also consults for other bilateral and multilateral organizations. He has over thirty years of experience in education and skills development in the Southern Africa Region, where he has conducted a series of studies in the education sector as whole specializing in Technical, Entrepreneurial, Vocational Education and Training and Higher Education. He served as a Senior Education Specialist in the World Bank before his retirement. He has a Master's degree in Education Leadership, a Specialist Degree in Policy and Planning and Comprehensive Vocational Education and a PhD in Policy and Planning in Comprehensive Vocational Education all acquired from Florida State University, where he received the Phi Kappa Phi National Society award for academic excellence. He is a former Permanent Secretary in the Ministry of Higher Education in Zimbabwe.

Muna Meky is a senior education specialist in the World Bank's global practice for education. She currently leads projects in India that focus on improving job opportunities for youth through providing relevant skills training and second chance education. Before joining the South Asia Region, Muna worked for 6 years in the Africa Region where she worked closely with education ministries and task teams to identify to design impact evaluations that tested the effectiveness of education interventions. Furthermore, she supported designing a results based programs in Malawi that focused on improving the market relevance of higher education institutions through financing programs in priority sectors and providing relevant skills training programs in rural areas. She holds a master's degree in economics from Brown University.

Nobuyuki Tanaka works as an economist in the World Bank's Global Practice for Education. Based in Washington DC, he is currently leading Malawi Skills Development Project. He is also a task team leader for the Partnership for Skills in Applied Sciences, Engineering and Technology (PASET) initiative. Prior to the current assignment, based in Dar es Salaam, Tanzania, he provided technical and operational support to the government for their implementation of the Science and Technology, Higher Education Project (STHEP). He has been engaged in several analytical studies on education and skills. He holds a Ph.D. from Kobe University, Japan.

Jamil Salmi is a global tertiary education expert providing policy advice and consulting services to governments, universities, professional associations, multilateral banks and bilateral cooperation agencies. Until January 2012, he was the World Bank's tertiary education coordinator. He wrote the first World Bank policy paper on higher education reform in 1994 and was the principal author of the Bank's 2002 Tertiary Education Strategy entitled "Constructing Knowledge Societies: New Challenges for Tertiary Education". In the past twenty-two years, Dr. Salmi has provided advice on tertiary education development, financing reforms and strategic planning to governments and university leaders in about 90 countries all over the world.

Executive Summary

Context and Objectives

As the Government of Malawi investigates options to expand access to higher education and improve the quality of higher education provision, the objective of this report is to contribute to an improved understanding of the challenges confronted by the higher education sub-sector in Malawi. The report summarizes the key findings of an in-depth study of factors affecting access and equity in the Malawian higher education sub-sector, the quality and relevance of educational outputs, the financing of the sector, and the frameworks structuring governance of the sector and its management. The study was initiated in response to a request from the Government of Malawi, to the World Bank, to support the Ministry of Education, Science and Technology (MoEST) in its pursuit of financially sustainable policy options to increase equitable access to higher education, and to improve the quality of higher education provision in alignment with the needs of the labor market.

The report is based on an analysis of data and information collected from public and private universities in the Malawian higher education sub-sector and information made available by the Government of Malawi relating to the financing of the sector. Data collection was undertaken through the use of questionnaires, semi-structured interviews, and site visits to institutions. Data analysis was complemented by a review of relevant literature in the key focus areas of the study, and draws on a number of secondary sources. The study was conducted in a consultative manner and is informed by the involvement of stakeholders in the Malawian higher education sub-sector. Consultation was structured through a series of workshops, and work was undertaken through contingent taskforces established by the MoEST. The membership of these taskforces included departmental staff from MoEST, academic staff and students of higher education institutions, the private sector, and civil society.

The report is divided into five chapters: chapter 1 provides background information relevant to the study and presents the report's methodology; chapter 2 presents the results of the study with regard to issues affecting access and equity in the Malawian higher education sub-sector; chapter 3 presents the findings of analysis on quality and relevance; chapter 4 presents the results of an analysis of the financing of higher education in Malawi; and chapter 5 presents the results of an analysis of systems of governance and management in Malawian higher education sub-sector. Chapters 2, 3, 4 and 5 include the presentation of policy options, and implementation strategies, towards improving the performance of the Malawian higher education system.

Introduction

The Malawi Growth Development Strategy (MGDS) recognizes the crucial role of higher education as a key driver of competitiveness and growth. At the request of MoEST, the World Bank supported MoEST in assessing the performance of the higher education system through this study.

The higher education sub-sector in Malawi is relatively under-developed. The sector is comprised of two public universities—the University of Malawi (UNIMA) and Mzuzu University (MZUNI); and five private universities—the Catholic University of Malawi (CUNIMA), Malawi Adventist University (MAU), the University of Livingstonia (UNILIA). Blantyre International University and Mangochi University. UNIMA, in turn, is comprised of five constituent colleges—Bunda College of Agriculture,[1] Chancellor College (CHANCO), the College of Medicine (COM), the Kamuzu College of Nursing (KCN) and the Polytechnic. Malawi's public universities were established by Acts of Parliament, and each private university was established through charters accredited by the state. Taken together, these seven institutions currently enroll approximately 12,000 students. Figure ES.1 shows the distribution of enrollment across the main institutions of higher education.

Overall, the performance of the Malawian higher education system is mixed. The supply of qualified graduates is inadequate both in terms of their

Figure ES.1 Enrollment in the Malawian Higher Education Institutions

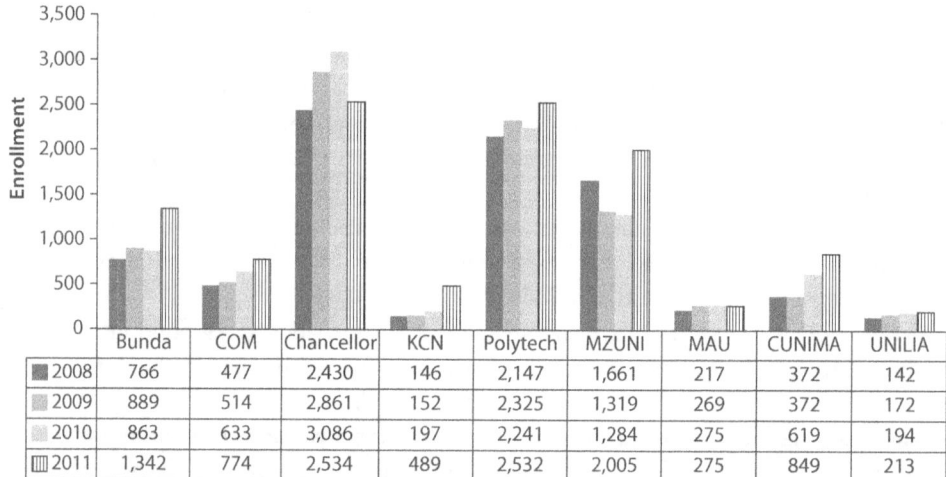

	Bunda	COM	Chancellor	KCN	Polytech	MZUNI	MAU	CUNIMA	UNILIA
2008	766	477	2,430	146	2,147	1,661	217	372	142
2009	889	514	2,861	152	2,325	1,319	269	372	172
2010	863	633	3,086	197	2,241	1,284	275	619	194
2011	1,342	774	2,534	489	2,532	2,005	275	849	213

Source: Higher Education Institutions.

quality and their absolute numbers. Malawi's tertiary gross enrollment rate is 0.4 percent, among the lowest in Africa.[2] In terms of the quality and relevance of programs offered by in the sector, available evidence suggests that the limited increase in enrollment is not aligned with the needs of the labor market, and that universities have weak linkages with the private sector with regard to program development and curriculum review. Moreover, the research output of the two public universities is small, and quality assurance systems remain under-developed. Governance of the sector needs to be reformed to improve the representation of non-government actors such as the private sector and civil society organizations. The current relationship between the MoEST and public universities does not appropriately balance the need for institutional autonomy and measures to ensure effective accountability. Despite the fact that the Government of Malawi spends a relatively high proportion of its education budget on higher education (28 percent in 2010), resource allocations are insufficient to sustain efforts to further expand enrollment and improve the quality of education delivered. Finally, from an equity perspective, students from higher income groups are disproportionately represented in higher education, accounting for 90 percent of current enrollment. In this regard, and in light of relatively low tuition fees and low rates of student loan repayment, public funding for higher education in Malawi is regressive.

Access and Equity

At less than one percent, Malawi's tertiary education enrollment rate is among the lowest in the world, and is well below the average for sub-Saharan Africa. With only 80 students enrolled in tertiary education per 100,000 inhabitants in 2011, Malawi compares unfavorably with other countries in the region (figure ES.2). Low sector-wide capacity results in only a small fraction of secondary school graduates holding the Malawi Secondary Certificate of Education (MSCE) being absorbed into tertiary education. The recent improvement in tertiary enrollment, largely a consequence of expanded private education provision, has eased some constraints to access, however private institutions still only account for approximately 12 percent of total enrollment.

The government recently introduced two initiatives aimed at expanding enrollment. Enrollment policies have shifted from one premised on bed space to one linked to classroom space. Secondly, the government has introduced a policy of "equitable access," with equal enrollment quotas for each region, designed to achieve an equitable distribution of students by district.

Enrollment data disaggregated by socioeconomic status demonstrates that 91.3 percent of students enrolled in higher education are drawn from the richest quintile (20 percent) of households, while the poorest quintile of households account for just 0.7 percent of higher education enrollment. Despite the intro-

Figure ES.2 Enrollment in tertiary education per 100,000 inhabitants in selected sub-Saharan Africa countries

Malawi	80
Tanzania	186
Madagascar	395
Kenya	428
Mozambique	454
Angola	651
Zimbabwe	654
Congo, Dem. Rep.	716
Swaziland	734
Ghana	1147
Botswana	1812
Mauritius	2865

Source: UNESCO Institute of Statistics.
Note: Year of data: 2009 for Kenya, 2010 for Tanzania, and 2011 for others

duction of affirmative action measures to encourage female education, and an increase in female enrollment in higher education from 2,838 in 2008 to 4,212 in 2011, enrollment data continue to demonstrate significant gender disparities. In 2011, the overall gender parity index (proportion of female to male students) for higher education in Malawi was 0.57, with female enrollment accounting for 46.2 percent of total enrollment in private institutions and 34.9 percent of enrollment in public universities (figure ES.3).

A dearth of data relating to the enrollment of students with disabilities suggests that very few disabled students are enrolled in higher education institutions. This is in spite of the fact that nearly 4,000 students with disabilities were enrolled in secondary school in 2011, 700 of whom were in Form 4. The majority of infrastructure in Malawian universities does not cater for the needs of people living with disabilities.

Persistently low levels of enrollment in higher education and unsatisfied demand on the part of the private sector for qualified graduates, has informed the decision on the part of the MoEST to prioritize improved access to, and equity in, higher education. Advancing these objectives will require interventions to, *inter alia*, improve and expand limited and suboptimal educational infrastructure, improve the use of information and communication technologies (ICT), enable alternative delivery methodologies, and expand current program offerings. In its attempts to attain its expansionary goals, the government must take decisions in a context defined by significant financial constraints, which are analyzed in the financing section of this report.

Figure ES.3 Evolution of Enrollment by Provider and Gender—2008–11

	2008	2009	2010	2011
■ Public, male	5,140	5,488	5,514	6,655
▨ Public, female	2,504	2,572	2,782	3,564
▦ Private, male	397	457	615	756
▥ Private, female	334	356	473	648
△ % of female, public	32.8%	31.9%	33.5%	34.9%
◇ % of female, private	45.7%	43.8%	43.5%	46.2%
● % of private	8.7%	9.2%	11.6%	12.1%

Source: Higher Education Institutions.

Quality and Relevance

It is difficult to objectively assess the quality of higher education programs in Malawi in the absence of a functional national accreditation system and adequately defined quality assurance procedures, including the assessment of academic staff. Anecdotal evidence suggests that higher education institutions have struggled to insulate the quality of education delivered from pressures associated with increased enrollment. Expanding enrollment has presented new challenges with regard to the provision of inputs, including academic staff, critical for the maintenance and enhancement of quality education. Due to a shortage of potential recruits with the requisite academic qualifications, the system has become increasingly reliant on assistant and associate lecturers who do not meet the requirements traditionally associated with teaching at the university level (figure ES.4). Moreover, in an effort to mitigate gaps associated with a shortage of qualified personnel, the system has become reliant on adjunct staff; a trend that is particularly acute in private institutions. The number of academic staff employed in the sector has not kept pace with expanded enrollment, resulting in rising in student-to-lecturer ratios. Significant variance in student-to-lecturer ratios is evident across institutions in the same fields of study, demonstrating divergence on the part of institutions in the efficient use of lecturers. In general, private universities have higher student-to-lecturer ratios than public institutions.

The majority of Malawian institutions of higher learning have abandoned, or restricted, the use external examiners to maintain standards, an established practice in most Commonwealth countries. Constrained funding has made it progressively more difficult to cover costs associated with bringing foreign academics to Malawian universities to serve on external examination committees, with negative effects for systems of quality assurance.

Figure ES.4 Distribution of Academic Staff by Grade—2011

	Bunda	COM	KCN	Polytechnic	MZUNI	MAU	CUNIMA	UNILIA
Associate Lecturer	19.6%	26.1%	20.3%	7.0%	22.8%	0.0%	10.9%	25.0%
Assistant Lecturer	0.0%	0.0%	0.0%	24.5%	0.0%	0.0%	0.0%	0.0%
Lecturer	50.6%	40.5%	54.2%	53.5%	59.6%	58.3%	63.0%	75.0%
Senior Lecturer	15.2%	18.9%	16.9%	14.0%	11.8%	25.0%	15.2%	0.0%
Associate Professor	8.2%	9.0%	8.5%	0.5%	4.4%	0.0%	6.5%	0.0%
Professor	6.3%	5.4%	0.0%	0.5%	1.5%	16.7%	4.3%	0.0%

Source: Higher Education Institutions.

Employers are concerned about the relevance of programs offered. The overall distribution of enrollment by field of study has generally not been aligned with areas critical for the economic development of Malawi. For example, enrollment is relatively low in engineering, business, ICT, and tourism—areas which are considered vital for Malawi's growth prospects. In addition, with the shift from the Board of Governors of the TEVET agency to the University of Malawi, technician programs in the core skills development areas have been neglected, or entirely abolished, leaving a considerable gap in the skills development edifice. Sector analyses demonstrate evidence of severe skills shortages in key growth areas of the economy, including mining, agriculture, tourism and the construction industry. In most instances these skills gaps are not addressed through programmatic study in universities or the TEVET sub-sector. There is need to conduct regular tracer studies and, with the active participation of the private sector, to institutionalize regular updates to curricula to ensure that programmatic offerings effectively address the needs of the economy.

Higher education institutions are yet to identify which programs contribute to institutional competitive advantage. The Malawian higher education sub-sector is characterized by duplication across institutions with regard to the introduction of new course offerings, and a general failure to diversify in response to the needs of growth sectors identified in the MGDS. In order for Malawi to realize its development objectives, it will be important to raise the status and quality of post-secondary vocational education, and to provide incentives for greater numbers of students to participate therein.

A good measure of the fitness of purpose of program offerings is the rate at which graduates of a system are absorbed into the labor market. The 2008 Tracer Study of TEVET and Higher Education Completers in Malawi (TSTHEM) found that 72.2 percent of graduates from higher education programs had full-time employment or had set up their own business (2.1 percent). A further 11 percent of graduates were engaged in part-time employment and 10 percent were still looking for employment. The study demonstrated that few graduates were willing or able to start their own business, with the report noting access to finance, regulatory policy uncertainty, and corruption as the primary constraints inhibiting self-employment. An additional countervailing feature of the Malawian higher education system, which may be contributing to low numbers of graduates pursuing entrepreneurial activities, is the relative absence of entrepreneurship and business skills development in current curricula. Universities should conduct regular tracer studies to ensure that that program offerings adequately address demand for skills in the economy.

Enrollment in university postgraduate education, as a proportion of total enrollment, is low, with the exception of the College of Medicine and Chancellor College. Low postgraduate enrollment is partly due to the fact that private universities do not yet offer postgraduate programs, as well as poor supply, throughout the system, of academic staff with senior degrees capable of teaching postgraduate courses. The College of Medicine and Chancellor College have the largest number of staff with postgraduate qualifications with the required capacity to teach and supervise research in postgraduate programs. The Polytechnic, in spite of its size, only offers two postgraduate degree programs neither of which is in engineering.

Research output in both public and private institutions is constrained by heavy teaching loads on the part of academic staff, and the poor supply of professors and staff with PhDs capable of supervising research. Research capacity has been further undermined by years of under-funding, a resulting legacy of inadequate infrastructure and facilities, and a relative scarcity of research grants.

In order to develop postgraduate studies, the Government of Malawi could consider the option of participating in regional initiatives aimed at establishing centers of excellence to combine advanced studies at the master and doctoral levels with high-quality research output. The Nelson Mandela Institutes of Technology and the Ouagadougou-based International Institute for Water and Environmental Management are two examples of successful regional institutions that offer advanced training and opportunities to advance research in alignment with internationally recognized standards. A complementary measure would be to facilitate strong partnerships with carefully selected universities in industrialized countries to help build capacity for postgraduate teaching and research in the universities of Malawi. The government could also explore opportunities for using capacity in existing centers of specialization and other institutions in the Southern African Development Community (SADC) region, as provided for in the SADC Protocol of Education and Training.

The establishment, in 2011, of the National Council for Higher Education (NCHE) to, *inter alia*, oversee quality assurance in higher education institutions, constitutes an important milestone in the development of the higher education system in Malawi. The NCHE is expected to monitor the quality and relevance of programs offered by higher education institutions and coordinate efforts to enhance quality. In order to improve the quality and effectiveness of Malawi's higher education system, a holistic approach with a focus on learning outcomes will be required. In consultation with national and regional employers, the NCHE should consider developing a broad compact with each public higher education institution that clarifies the institution's distinctive mission, the scope and focus of education provision, expectations for performance, and the needs of the labor market to which each institution's programmatic focus responds. To what extent the NCHE will have the human and financial resources to effectively carry out its mission remains to be seen, and the NCHE will require further support to realize its mandate.

Financing of Higher Education

Strategic Decisions Influencing Financing Needs

Expanding enrollment in Malawi's higher education sub-sector cannot rely exclusively on traditional modes of constructing and funding new public universities from governmental budgetary resources. Ensuring the achievement of government's enrollment targets on a financially sustainable basis will require the distribution of expanded enrollment across a variety of public and private tertiary education institutions with campus-based and distance education learning modalities. Balanced enrollment growth can be achieved through a three-pronged strategy: (i) the development of quality non-university tertiary institutions, (ii) the expansion of a dynamic private tertiary education sub-sector, and (iii) the development of distance education programs and institutions.

- **Development of the non-university sub-sector.** The Government of Malawi should actively promote the establishment of polytechnics and community colleges. In addition to protecting the resource base of the public universities by absorbing a significant proportion of secondary school graduates, non-university tertiary institutions can make a significant contribution to the development of the national skills base by offering training opportunities that respond in a flexible manner to labor market demand.
- **Development of the Private Sector.** Two sets of interventions should be weighed in advancing the goal of increased private institutional enrollment: Significant legal and administrative barriers inhibit the establishment of private higher education institutions and the expansion of private higher education in general. Introducing greater flexibility in the regulatory structure for private tertiary education with regard to the hiring of faculty, promotion practices, levels of remuneration and tuition fees, program and curriculum development, and procurement rules, would significantly improve the operational environment for private institutions. Concurrently, the Government of Malawi should establish appropriate licensing and mechanisms to ensure

effective quality assurance in the program offerings of private institutions. In the medium term, the government should consider the possibility of extending limited subsidies to private sector higher education institutions, to support teacher salaries and the development and delivery of programs catering to priority areas of skills development, such as engineering and the health sciences. The government could also explore mechanisms to enable the granting or leasing of land to private tertiary education institutions. Finally, poor students enrolled in quality private institutions should be eligible for financial aid (scholarships and student loans).
- **Establishing cost-effective distance education modalities**: A third pillar of Malawi's expansion strategy should consider the development of distance education programs, which in other parts of the world have been demonstrated to benefit large segments of the population; for example in India, South Africa and Thailand. Thailand's two open universities have contributed to a significant expansion in tertiary enrollment, particularly for students from rural areas and the poorest social strata. Today, about half of all students enrolled in tertiary education in Thailand are enrolled in these two open universities.

Resource Mobilization

Despite the relatively large share of the Malawian education budget allocated to higher education (between 20 percent and 28 percent over the past few years), this allocation remains inadequate to support the financial needs of the Malawian higher education system as it pursues efforts expand enrollment and improve the quality of education delivered (figure ES.5). As a consequence of the legacy of poor resource allocations in support of public higher education, several institutions have been running deficits in recent years.

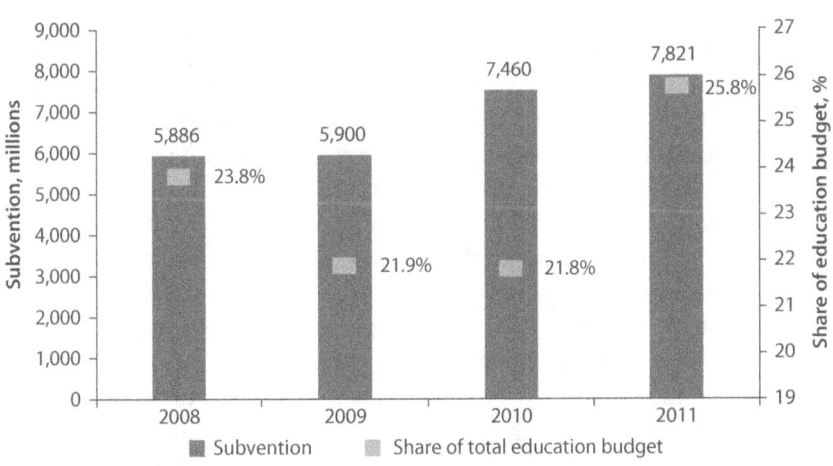

Figure ES.5 Higher Education Budget as a Share of the Total Education Budget

Source: Approved Estimates of Expenditure on Recurrent and Capital Accounts (Malawi).

Public universities in Malawi have three main sources of revenue: government subventions, tuition fees, and resources generated by the universities, primarily in the form of project and research grants. As is the case in most African countries, government contributions constitute the largest share of revenue for public institutions in Malawi, ranging from 75 to 85 percent of recurrent budgets. Tuition fees contribute between 4 and 14 percent of total income, with the balance accounted for by locally generated revenue. The share of generated revenues is lower than the share of revenues collected in the form of tuition fees in all public universities, with the exception of the College of Medicine. For private universities, tuition fees are their largest source of finance, contributing up to 80 percent of total revenue.

Tuition fees in Malawian higher education institutions are charged at a flat rate, regardless of the program of study, as opposed to the levying of differentiated fees that take into account variations in the cost of delivering courses of study in different fields. This practice is common in many countries; regional examples of universities implementing program specific fees include the University of Zambia and the University of Cape Town.

The public funding of universities is highly regressive with students from the highest quintile of household income accounting for 91 percent of university enrollment. Taking into account generally low tuition fees, and low rates of student loan repayment, the majority of costs associated with higher education in Malawi are subsidized by society at large.

Several resource mobilization measures should be explored to improve the financial sustainability of the Malawian higher education system. Steps must be taken to ensure greater equity in the higher education sub-sector through more effective cost sharing. The government should explore interventions in which matching grants are extended to universities and other higher education institutions that raise additional funds through contract work and fundraising from alumni and philanthropists. Promoting the further development of the private higher education sub-sector has the potential to form an important element of the overall financing strategy for the expansion of higher education. A particular advantage in this regard is that, with the right incentives, the private sector can complement the public higher education sub-sector in meeting the country's needs for quality graduates at no or little cost to government.

The current student loans system, and the uniform application of fees to all students regardless of family income, should be reassessed. Public institutions should be permitted to charge higher fees to students from well-off families who can afford to pay them. Moreover, the government must ensure that resources are available to support needy students. In this regard there is an urgent need to overhaul the student loan system to promote greater efficacy, especially with regard to loan recovery. Interventions intended to improve the collection of loan repayments should be informed by lessons learned from the experience of the student loan system being administered by the Public University Student Loan Trust, when levels of loan default were particularly high. The need for urgency in addressing outstanding deficiencies in the student loan system has been heightened by the withdrawal from the existing scheme of the Malawi Saving Bank, which had been expected to improve loan recovery. Student loans should be available to all eligible students including students enrolled in private institutions and non-residential students in public institutions, subject to these institutions and programs meeting satisfactory standards of quality. In order to improve the likelihood of students repaying their loans, the period in which students are required to repay their loans should be extended beyond the current time horizon of four years, and monthly repayments should be linked to income to protect unemployed graduates and those whose incomes are too low to service loan payments.

Resource Allocation

The Government of Malawi distributes the annual budget for higher education among public universities and institutions through a negotiated allocation system heavily informed by historical allocations, a practice that is common in many developing countries. In practice the Ministry of Finance uses the previous year's funding allocation as a benchmark for incremental change, taking into account anticipated government revenues and expected enrollment growth. In general, the current system does not link levels of public funding to measures of performance, such as quality or relevance, and no consideration is given to considerations with regard to an institutions efficiency or effectiveness in the management of resources. Many other countries premise public resource allocations on a combination of performance-based measurements in an attempt to incentivize higher education institutions to promote efficiency and innovation in the use of scarce resources.

To stimulate greater innovation and efficiency in the use of public resources, the government could introduce a combination of performance-based budget allocation mechanisms that provide financial incentives for improved institutional results in alignment with national policy goals. Four main types of innovative allocation mechanisms might be considered separately, or in combination, towards this end: output-based formulas, performance-based contracts, competitive funds, and vouchers.

Resource Utilization

Data provided by public universities indicates that the majority of expenditure is allocated to salaries and student services, with less than 10 percent of resource utilization expended on educational and research related expenditure. The distribution of expenditure is likely to negatively impact both the quality of education delivered, and the research output of universities. Unit costs associated with the provision of education per student are much higher in public universities than in private higher education institutions, ranging from 36 percent of per capita gross domestic product (GDP) in the most expensive programs to 8 percent in the least costly. While these differences reflect, to a large extent, the fact that more expensive programs (medicine, agriculture, engineering, and the basic sciences) are offered exclusively or primarily in public sector institutions, available data suggest that, in a context of greater resource scarcity, private institutions tend to use their resources more efficiently than their counterparts in the public sector. This view is buttressed by evidence of comparatively lower dropout rates in private institutions.

Implementation of the proposal to shift public resource allocation to a system informed by performance-based indicators should incentivize improved efficiency in resource utilization in public higher education institutions.

Governance and Management Systems

Malawian public higher education institutions fall under the jurisdiction of MoEST. The MoEST is responsible for developing the vision, mission and strategic direction of higher education in general and the Department of Higher Education in the Ministry liaises closely with universities on policy issues. However due to the fact that universities are statutory organizations, the Ministry does not have direct control them. Each individual institution is expected to elaborate its own strategic plan based on the Malawi Growth and Development Strategy and the National Education Sector Plan (NESP) 2009–17.

Public universities are governed by councils, which are responsible for the management and administration of institutions, including their property and revenues, and oversight of all university related activities. Councils establish, where needed, the colleges, and other academic divisions of each university, and oversee the assignment of faculties, schools or academic sections to specified colleges. Councils moreover determine the terms of service and conditions of employment for all staff in the institution, including salary scales and rates of payment, and fees charged to students. In the execution of its functions, the council receives recommendations from the senate and, in some instances, from the Vice Chancellor. Each private university is governed by a board of trustees, which fulfills the same functions as councils in public universities.

Malawian universities are relatively autonomous, with respect to organizational, academic and staffing concerns. However, financial autonomy is limited due to the fact that universities are not allowed to independently determine tuition fees. Tuition fees are in practice determined by government, and have remained static for a number of years.

Statutory considerations which require that the President of the country serve as the Chancellor of each public university, and the appointment of government officials as council members, further challenges the ostensive autonomy of public higher education institutions. While these appointments are intended to assist in aligning institutions with the government's general policy and development agenda, in practice they can contribute to tensions, and limit the autonomy of institutions as envisaged by their foundational Acts. It is anticipated that the

NCHE will help to mitigate tensions between the government and universities with regard to issues of autonomy and academic freedom.

Additional challenges arise as a consequence of the composition of university councils, which are currently limited to representatives drawn from the university and government. Councils would benefit from the participation of a wider pool of stakeholders, including the private sector and civil society, to expand the scope of professional experience and mix of skills represented in their membership.

Effective management of public universities is undermined by poor administrative capacity and an over-reliance on committees for decision-making. Information from institutions suggests that the functioning of various decision-making committees is inefficient, resulting in delays in the conduct of university business activities.

The findings of this study support the view that MoEST could provide more support to universities through appropriate leadership and management training to improve the efficiency and effectiveness of the system. The empowerment of senior management to more effectively run and provide leadership to their institutions requires support for the development of skills applicable to academic planning and financial management. Moreover, MoEST should assist institutions in the design and establishment of functioning management information systems to generate timely data and analysis with regard to enrollment, staffing and financial management.

Governance within the higher education system is further undermined by poor coordination between MoEST and authorities responsible for post-secondary vocational education, contributing to a tertiary education system characterized by fragmentation, insufficiently articulated mandates across different types of service providers, a lack of coherence across institutions with regard to curricula, and poor mobility on the part of students within the system. An example of a holistic approach to human capital development, from which Malawi can learn, is that of South Korea. Commencing in the early 2000s, South Korea transformed its Ministry of Education into the Ministry of Human Resources Development mandated with responsibility for the planning and oversight of education and training policies for all service providers in the country. Dubai's Knowledge and Human Development Authority, which assumes the responsibilities of Malawi's MoEST, the Ministry of Labor and the agency responsible for TEVET, offers another instructive example.

Conclusion

The Malawian higher education system's inability to supply sufficient numbers of well-qualified graduates in alignment with the needs of the economy is a major constraint inhibiting the development prospects of the country. In addition to quantitative bottlenecks, there is significant concern with regard to the quality and relevance of existing institutions and programs offered in the Malawian higher education sub-sector.

The MGDS forms the basis of a useful framework to inform the content of reforms for the higher education sub-sector. MoEST needs to take the lead in elaborating a comprehensive vision for the development of public and private higher education institutions, inclusive of appropriate quality assurance systems. Efforts to expand enrollment and improve the quality and relevance of higher education programs must pursued in line with a sustainable financing strategy characterized by measures to ensure, *inter alia*: the cost-effective institutional configuration of the higher education system as a whole, the adequate mobilization of public and private resources, cost-sharing with matching financial aid for needy students, and performance-based allocation mechanisms. In order to improve the management capacity of institutions, and to ensure effective implementation of proposed reforms, interventions will be required to improve governance at a systemic and institutional level. Table ES.1 presents the most important policy recommendations emanating from this study.

Table ES.1 Summary Policy Matrix: Main Reforms and Measures Suggested in the Study

Policy objectives	Issues to be addressed	Policy options
Increase access	Low enrollment rate Insufficient supply	• Expansion of non-university institutions • Further development of private sector • Emergence of distance education options
Improve equity	Under-representation of low-income students Gender imbalance in scientific disciplines	• Targeted scholarships and student loans for low-income students (in both public and private institutions) • Outreach programs to motivate girls in high schools to pursue STEM subjects
Enhance quality	Insufficiently qualified academics Insufficient pedagogical resources for teaching and learning Weak internal quality assurance mechanisms Under-developed national Quality Assurance system	• Government incentives for programs to train academics abroad and recruitment upon their return to Malawi • Ring-fencing of resources for pedagogical resources in institutional budgets • Strengthen broadband and ICT infrastructure • Development of internal Quality Assurance mechanisms, incl. performance evaluation of academics • External examination on a regular basis • Strengthening of national Quality Assurance Agency
Increase relevance	Lack of qualified graduates to meet the needs of an expanding economy Under-developed graduate programs	• Conduct regular tracer and employer surveys • Improve linkages between higher education institutions and productive sectors (incl. participation in curriculum design) • Include representatives of the private sector on university boards • Participation in regional centers of excellence projects • Strategic partnerships with foreign universities for capacity-building purposes

table continues next page

Table ES.1 Summary Policy Matrix: Main Reforms and Measures Suggested in the Study *(continued)*

Policy objectives	Issues to be addressed	Policy options
Allocate public subsidies on the basis of performance criteria	Current budgeting does not reward efficient and effective use of resources	• Design funding formula that takes unit costs and measures of effectiveness into consideration
Re-engineer the student loan scheme	Ineffective targeting and low repayment	• Redesign the student loan scheme; improve targeting; modernize its management; and strengthen repayment mechanisms
Strengthen institutional governance	Weak university boards	• Include representatives of the private sector and civil society, and revise TORs of university boards

Source: World Bank.

Notes

1. Bunda College of Agriculture has since withdrawn from UNIMA and combined with the Natural Resources College to form the Lilongwe University of Agriculture and Natural Resources (LUANAR).
2. The tertiary gross enrollment rate is defined as total enrollment in tertiary education, regardless of age, expressed as a percentage of the total population of the five-year age group following secondary school. UNESCO Institute for Statistics.

Abbreviations

AfDB	African Development Bank
AFSP	Agroforestry Food Security Program
AIDS	Acquired Immune Deficiency Syndrome
BOT	Build-Operate-Transfer
CAMS	Credit Accumulation and Modular Schemes
CARD	Center for Agricultural Research and Development
CERT	Center for Educational Research and Training
CHE	Council for Higher Education
CIDA	Canadian International Development Agency
COM	College of Medicine
CSR	Center for Social Research
CUNIMA	Catholic University of Malawi
CUTL	Committee on University Teaching and Learning
DelPHE	Development Partnerships in Higher Education
DfID	Department for International Development
DIAS	Directorate of Inspection and Advisory Services
ESSUP	Education Sector Support Program
EU	European Union
GDP	Gross domestic product
HE	Higher Education
HEST	Higher Education Science and Technology
HIV	Human Immunodeficiency Virus
HOD	Head of Department
HRD	Human Resources Development
ICT	Information and Communication Technology
IHS	Integrated Household Survey
JICA	Japan International Cooperation Agency
KCN	Kamuzu College of Nursing
LUANAR	Lilongwe University of Agriculture and Natural Resources

MANEB	Malawi National Examinations Board
MAU	Malawi Adventist University
MB	Megabytes
MBA	Master of Business Administration
MCA	Millennium Challenge Account
MERA	Malawi Energy and Regulatory Authority
MGDS	Malawi Growth and Development Strategy
MIRDC	Malawi Industrial Research and Development Center
MK	Malawi Kwacha
MoEST	Ministry of Education, Science and Technology
MOU	Memorandum of Understanding
MRA	Malawi Revenue Authority
MSB	Malawi Savings Bank
MSCE	Malawi School Certificate of Education
MTL	Malawi Telecommunication Limited
MZUNI	Mzuzu University
NBSAP	National Biodiversity Strategy
NCHE	National Council for Higher Education
NESP	National Education Sector Plan
NGOs	Nongovernmental Organizations
NORAD	Norwegian Agency for Development Cooperation
NUFU	Norwegian Council of Universities' Committee for Development Research and Education
ODL	Open and Distance Learning
PAYE	Pay as You Earn
PIEQM	Project to Improve Education Quality in Malawi
PPD	Public private dialogue
PPP	Public private partnership
PUSLT	Public University Student Loan Trust
RPC	Research and Publications Committees
SADC	Southern African Development Community
SLR	Student Lecturer Ratio
SSA	Sub Saharan Africa
Std	Standard
TEVET	Technical, Entrepreneurial and Vocational Education and Training
TEVETA	Technical, Entrepreneurial and Vocational Education and Training Authority

TP	Teaching Practice
TSTHEM	Tracer Study of TEVET and Higher Education Completers in Malawi
TVET	Technical and Vocational Education and Training
UCE	University Certificate of Education
UEE	University Entrance Examination
UMSU	University of Malawi Students Union
UNESCO	United Nations Education, Scientific and Cultural Organization
UNFPA	United Nations Population Fund
UNILIA	University of Livingstonia
UNIMA	University of Malawi
UO	University Office
URPC	University Research and Publications Committee
USAID	United States Agency for International Development
USD	United States Dollar
WASHTED	Water, Sanitation, Health, and Appropriate Technology Department
WB	World Bank
WHO	World Health Organization

CHAPTER 1

Introduction

Background

An efficiently functioning higher education sub-sector, producing quality educational outcomes, is recognized as a key driver of growth, and a critical precondition for improving competiveness in the global economy in the Malawi Growth Development Strategy (MGDS). In order for the Malawian higher education system to fulfill the role envisaged of it in the MGDS, the performance of the system will need to be optimized through policies and implementation strategies that address key supply- and demand-side constraints within a context characterized by significant resource constraints.

At the request of the Government of Malawi, the World Bank provided support to the Ministry of Education, Science and Technology (MoEST) in its efforts to explore financially sustainable policy options to promote equitable access to higher education, and to improve the quality of higher education provision in alignment with the needs of the labor market. Support was provided in the form of an in-depth review of the Malawian higher education sub-sector, the results of which are contained in this study.

The focus areas of this report were identified at a workshop which convened higher education practitioners and MoEST senior officials in October 2010. These were defined as: Access and Equity; Quality and Relevance; Financing; and Governance and Management. Based on the findings of the sector review, this report articulates recommendations intended to inform policy and strategy decisions to improve the alignment of the outcomes of the Malawian higher education sub sector with the economic and development needs of the country. The study specifically aims to contribute to the analysis of challenges confronting Malawian higher education in the four areas of focus; provide recommendations on viable and cost-effectiveness policy options that take into consideration the country's political economy; and to build the capacity of the MoEST, and higher education institutions, to enable further analysis of policy options and strategies for implementation.

Methodology

Task Force Members

Four task forces, corresponding with each focus area of the study, were created to facilitate the work of the study and to promote associated capacity-building objectives. Task force members were drawn from government, a cross section of public and private higher education institutions, and civil society, and included senior academic and administrative staff from public and private universities, senior students, officials from MoEST, the Malawi National Examinations Board (MANEB), and representatives of the private sector and civil society organizations.

The work of the task forces was structured through three workshops held in Lilongwe supported and facilitated by international and national consultants. The workshops focused the work of taskforce members on data analysis and report writing. Between workshops, members continued the work of their task forces from their respective locations. The collective work of the four task forces was supervised by a Technical Working Group on Higher Education (TWG) and MoEST. The output of the taskforces benefitted from the input of discussants from the university community appointed by MoEST who commented on draft reports prior to their finalization.

Data Collection

This report draws on primary and secondary sources of data. Data templates and questionnaires were distributed to higher education institutions to facilitate data collection. This was complemented by follow up visits to institutions in which members of the team interviewed staff including Vice Chancellors, principals of colleges, registrars and bursars, deans and heads of departments. In addition to primary data collected through surveys and interviews, the study drew on additional data and source material including, *inter alia*, household surveys, tracer studies, institutional strategic plans, and Acts of Parliament. To enhance the validity and reliability of the research findings and associated analysis, the research team deployed a triangulation method for the purposes of data validation. The study also draws on literature reviews aligned with the four primary areas of the study which were undertaken by the corresponding taskforces.

The data collected from institutions related to enrollment, staffing, income and expenditure, and graduate output. The analysis of this data, complemented by qualitative study, contributed to the report's analysis of governance and management structures, and practices; measures of teaching and research output; collaboration between institutions; access and equity; quality and relevance; liabilities and the outsourcing of non-core activities; delivery methodologies; curricula and curriculum review; equipment and infrastructure; the use of information technology and communication (ICT) networks; internal and external quality enhancement mechanisms; performance appraisals systems; research; public and private partnerships; academic freedom; and strategic planning.

Data Analysis

Where necessary, data was analyzed using Excel and SPSS, the output of which is presented in tables and graphs.

Limitations

Although a substantial amount of data was collected during the course of this study, some data that would have enriched the analysis was not readily available. Moreover, delays arose as a consequence of inconsistencies and errors on the part of institutions in capturing data.

It was intended that each task force would include, at a minimum, five people. However, this objective was not universally maintained and in some instances taskforces were constituted by only two people. Understaffed taskforces resulted in delays with regard to the finalization of reports, and this in turn constrained the time available for analysis. Limited and uneven representation from key stakeholders in the conduct of taskforce activities constrained the pool of expertise available to support activities, and, in some cases, this resulted in the need to verify information outside of the task force context. These factors contributed to further delays.

CHAPTER 2

Access and Equity in Malawi's Higher Education Sub-Sector

Introduction

This chapter articulates findings with regard to access and equity in Malawian higher education sub-sector. For the purposes of analysis, access is defined as opportunities for citizens to pursue higher education. Equity is defined as equality of opportunity in access to, and success in, higher education, regardless of place of birth, location, gender, ethnicity, religion, language, disability, and parental income.

Access and Equity

The Current Context

While Malawi has made progress in addressing challenges relating to access in higher education, the country continues to lag the performance of comparator countries.[1] Malawi's higher education system is small compared to those of the other countries in the Southern African Development Community (SADC) region, and total university enrollment rate is only 0.4 percent. As the country moves to accelerate access to education it faces significant challenges. Demand for university level education is increasing due to a rapid expansion of the secondary education system, and the capacity of the system to absorb aspirant applicants is insufficient across both the public and private sub-sectors of higher education (see figure 2.1).

Figure 2.1 illustrates the number of Malawi School Certificate of Education (MSCE) graduates who are eligible for university enrollment against the number of students who enroll in universities. The data demonstrates the limited capacity of Malawi's current university system, with fewer than 30 percent of MSCE graduates being admitted to higher education, with the exception of 2011 when 32.1 percent of eligible graduates secured university placement. In 2010 only 19.4 percent of students obtaining an MSCE pass were admitted to the system. However, the percentage of new MSCE graduates admitted into

Figure 2.1 Absorption of MSCE Graduates into the Higher Education System—2008–11

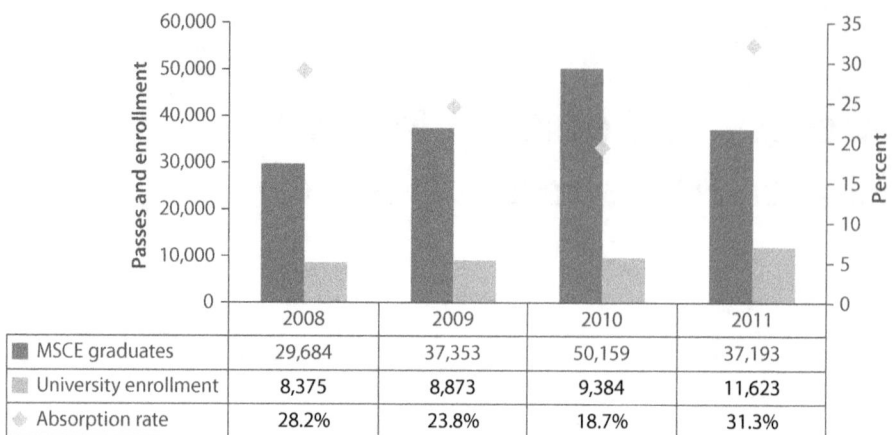

	2008	2009	2010	2011
MSCE graduates	29,684	37,353	50,159	37,193
University enrollment	8,375	8,873	9,384	11,623
Absorption rate	28.2%	23.8%	18.7%	31.3%

Source: MANEB and Higher Education Institutions.
Note: MSCE = Malawi School Certificate of Education.

higher education is likely to be even lower than what is presented due to the admission of students from previous MSCE cohorts who delayed entry to higher education. Moreover, universities also enroll students who have not completed the MSCE, and are admitted as mature students. Evidence of an improvement in 2011 is associated with policy changes discussed later in the report.

Net enrollment in public and private institutions rose from 8,375 to 11,623 between 2008 and 2011 which is equivalent to a 39 percent increase in enrollment. The expansion of enrollment through this period fell just short of the target for increasing undergraduate enrollment by 40 percent articulated in the Malawi Growth and Development Strategy (MGDS).[2] Female enrollment across the same period increased from 2,838 to 4,212, although this translates into only a marginal improvement of the share of female enrollment as a proportion of total enrollment which rose from 33.9 percent in 2008 to 36.2 percent in 2011. Figure 2.2 illustrates enrollments trends for the period 2008 to 2011 for both public and private institutions.

While the majority of students in the Malawian higher education sub-sector are enrolled in public universities, the two universities which currently comprise the public sub-sector will be incapable of accommodating projected enrollment alone. Private universities are playing an increasingly important role in improving access, and expanding the number of programs offered, in Malawian higher education. Enrollment in public universities increased from 7,644 to 10,219 between 2008 and 2011, equivalent to an increase of 33.7 percent, with a concurrent increase in private university enrollment from 731 to 1,404—or 88.4 percent—over the same period.

The largest increase in public university enrollment occurred between 2010 and 2011, when the year-on-year rate of increased admission rose from 5.4 to 23.2 percent. The acceleration of enrollments is attributed to the introduction of

Figure 2.2 Enrollment by Type of Institution and Gender—2008–11

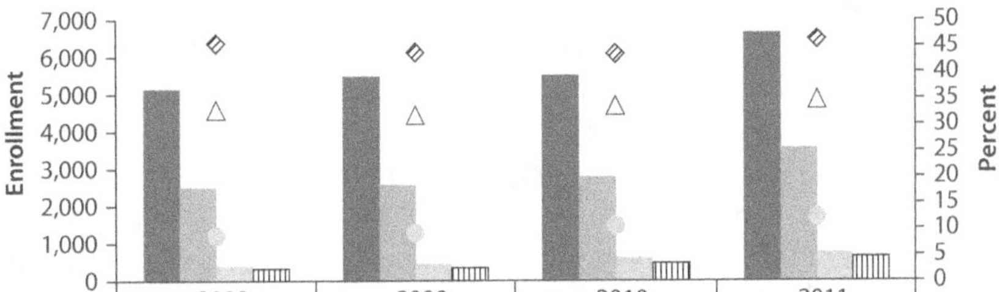

	2008	2009	2010	2011
■ Public, male	5,140	5,488	5,514	6,655
▨ Public, female	2,504	2,572	2,782	3,564
▤ Private, male	397	457	615	756
▥ Private, female	334	356	473	648
△ % of female, public	32.8%	31.9%	33.5%	34.9%
◇ % of female, private	45.7%	43.8%	43.5%	46.2%
● % of private	8.7%	9.2%	11.6%	12.1%

Source: Higher Education Institutions.

a new admissions policy premised on classroom space, and the move away from the previous policy which had been based on bed-space in residential facilities. At their inception, both of Malawi's public universities had been envisaged as residential institutions where all admitted students would be accommodated on campus, and as a result, enrollment was premised on the bed-space available at the institutions. Under this model of admissions, efforts to expand access to higher education were increasingly constrained by the limited expansion of college residential accommodation.

With the introduction of a new equitable access policy, government has extended support to what used to be called "parallel" students. Parallel students lived off campus, were required to pay fees above those levied on residential students did not receive any support from the government and were not eligible for government loans. These students are now called non-residential students and pay the same tuition fees levied on residential students. Previously parallel students paid of MK 125,000 at UNIMA and MK 155,000 at MZUNI, compared to the new universally applied fees of MK 25,000 at UNIMA and MK 55,000 at MZUNI.[3] Moreover, non-residential students are now eligible for government loans and a monthly subsistence allowance of MK 33,000 to defray expenses associated with off-campus accommodation, meals and transport. These interventions have led to an increase in the number of non-residential students admitted as illustrated in figure 2.4. Available data demonstrates that Bunda College has the lowest number of non-residential students in the public higher education sub-sector.[4]

Figure 2.2 illustrates increased enrollment in both private and public institutions, and improvements in female enrollment. The figure also demonstrates that the percentage of female enrollment as a proportion of total enrollment is on average approximately 11 percent higher in the private sub-sector than the public sub-sector, which may be in part a consequence of private institutions not offering programs, such as science and engineering, that have been historically been associated with low female enrollment. Combined female enrollment as a proportion of gross enrollment in higher education was 34.7 percent in 2010, approximately the same as the MGDS 2010 target of 35 percent. The data moreover demonstrates the relatively small component of total enrollment accounted for by private institutions, and that, despite an absolute increase in private sector enrollment in 2011, enrollment in this sub-sector as proportion of total enrollment fell in 2011 due to significantly expanded access in the public sub-sector. However, the data demonstrates consistently higher rates of enrollment growth in private institutions relative to their public counterparts: Private enrollment increased by 29.0 percent between 2010 and 2011 (up from 11.2 percent between 2008 and 2009) compared to an increase of 23.2 percent between 2010 and 2011 in the public sub-sector (up from 5.4 percent between 2008 and 2009).

While enrollment in private higher education is escalating off a low base relative to the public sub-sector, the consistent expansion of enrollment in private universities is associated with expanded academic programmatic offerings at the Malawi Adventist University (MAU) and the Catholic University of Malawi (CUNIMA). Total enrollment at the University of Livingstonia (UNILIA) increased from 142 in 2008 to 213 in 2011, and CUNIMA's total enrollment increased from 372 in 2009 to 849 in 2011.

Enrollment per 100,000 Inhabitants

Table 2.1 illustrates an improvement in the incidence of higher education enrollment per 100,000 inhabitants. The table shows that the number of Malawian males per 100,000 male inhabitants enrolled in higher education increased by 17 points from 83 males enrolled per 100,000 men in 2008 to 100 in 2011. The equivalent measure for females improved at a lesser magnitude, from 41 females enrolled per 100,000 Malawian women in 2008 to 55 in 2011. All measures illustrated in table 2.1 represent significant progress. In 2003, the overall incidence of higher education enrollment per 100,000 inhabitants was 37, with corresponding measures of 53 and 22 for males and females respectively (World Bank 2010).

Table 2.1 Enrollment (Total and per 100,000 Inhabitants) by Gender—2008–11

	Enrollment			Enrollment per 100,000 inhabitants		
	Male	Female	Total	Male	Female	Total
2008	5,537	2,838	8,375	83	41	61
2009	5,945	2,928	8,873	86	41	63
2010	6,129	3,255	9,384	85	44	64
2011	7,411	4,212	11,623	100	55	77

Source: Higher Education Institutions and National Statistical Office.

Enrollment by Institution

Figure 2.3 captures changes in enrollment by institution, with the data illustrating rising enrollment across all institutions, albeit at difference rates. Chancellor College and the Polytechnic account for the highest proportion of enrollment in absolute terms, while UNILIA accounts for the fewest enrollments in the period under review. The largest increase in enrollment in public institutions occurred between 2010 and 2011, except at Chancellor College which shows a reduction in enrollment in 2011. The decline in enrollment at the Polytechnic between 2009 and 2010 was in part a consequence of a reduction in the number of non-residential students. Large increases are evident at Bunda College, the Kamuzu College of Nursing (KCN), MZUNI and CUNIMA.

Figure 2.4 shows that until 2010 the Polytechnic had the highest percentage of non-residential students followed by the Chancellor College, while Bunda College had the lowest percentage of non-residential in the period under review. There was a significant reduction in the percentage of non-residential students at Bunda College from 33 percent in 2010 to 17.6 percent in 2011, as well as at the Polytechnic where non-residential students accounted for 36.6 percent of enrollment in 2011 down from 43.9 percent in the previous year. Non-residential enrollment as a percentage of total enrollment increased at Chancellor College from 33.8 percent in 2010 to 40.7 percent in 2011 (annex 2A.2). The relatively low number of non-residential students at Bunda College may be associated with its comparatively rural location, which impacts the ability of students to find accommodation close to campus. Chancellor College and the Polytechnic are located in urban centers, making it much easier for students to find off-campus accommodation. The effectiveness of the equitable access policy and the

Figure 2.3 Enrollment by Institution—2008–11

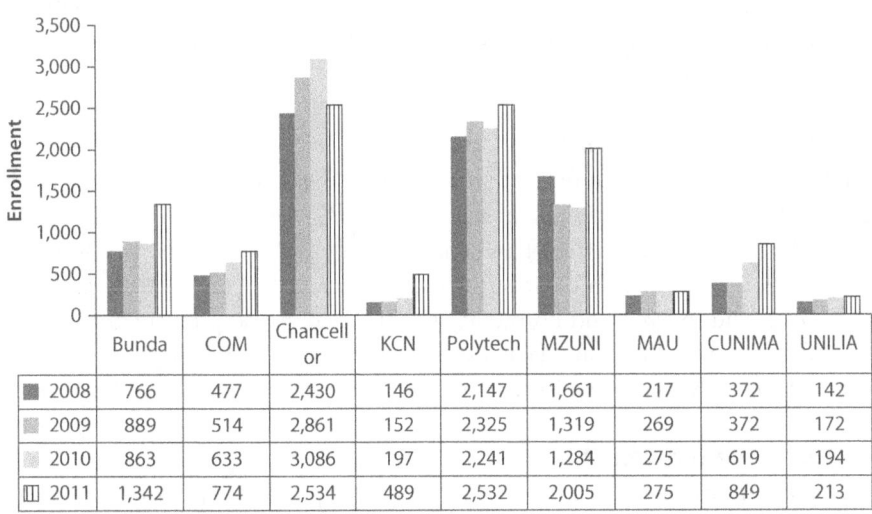

	Bunda	COM	Chancellor	KCN	Polytech	MZUNI	MAU	CUNIMA	UNILIA
2008	766	477	2,430	146	2,147	1,661	217	372	142
2009	889	514	2,861	152	2,325	1,319	269	372	172
2010	863	633	3,086	197	2,241	1,284	275	619	194
2011	1,342	774	2,534	489	2,532	2,005	275	849	213

Source: Higher Education Institutions.

Figure 2.4 Number of Nonresidential Students by Institution—2008–11

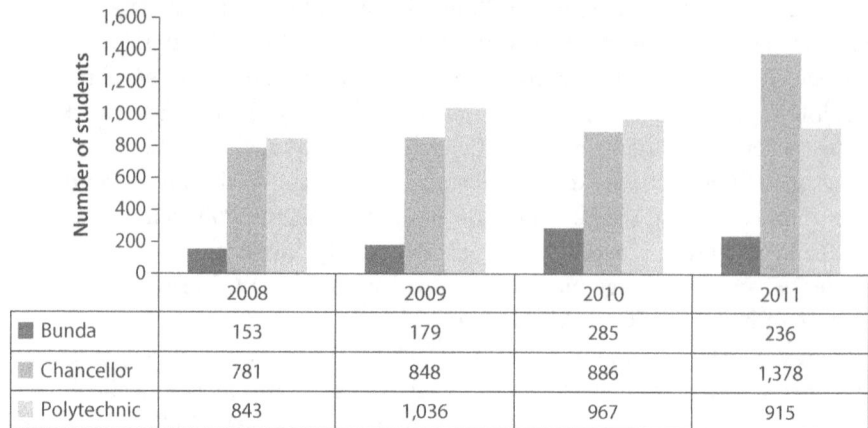

	2008	2009	2010	2011
Bunda	153	179	285	236
Chancellor	781	848	886	1,378
Polytechnic	843	1,036	967	915

Source: Higher Education Institutions.

non-residential model for expanding enrollment, is likely to be constrained going forward due to limited accommodation options.

The shift from an admissions policy based on bed-space to one premised on classroom space was informed by an assumption that there was underutilized classroom space in the system. In some cases the application of new policy has led to the overcrowding of classrooms and a deterioration of the learning environment. Some students now have to sit on the floor due to an insufficient number of desks and chairs within classrooms, while other students sit in adjacent corridors due to the lack of classroom space. This has resulted in the coining of the phrase "learning by rumor" to describe the practice of students sitting in corridors, and asking their colleagues in the classroom what the lecturer is saying because they are unable to hear the content of lectures. Due to expanded enrollment, Chancellor College has been forced to hold some classes in the Great Hall, which was not built for this purpose, and Bunda College resorted to erecting a marquee as a teaching facility.

Enrollment by Field of Study

Table 2.2 illustrates cumulative enrollment by field of study for the period 2008–11: The highest number of students (9,285) enrolled in education, followed by social science (4,193) and commerce (4,102). The data demonstrates low rates of enrollment in engineering (1,557), science (1,488), business (696), ICT (712) and tourism and hospitality (322) programs, despite the importance accorded to these fields in Malawi's chosen trajectory for economic development. Annex 2A.4 contains further statistics for enrollment.

Postgraduate Enrollment

Postgraduate studies contribute to national development through research, and the creation of new information and knowledge. Theme 3 of the MGDS

Table 2.2 Cumulative Enrollment by Field of Study—2008–11

Field	Male	Female	Total	Percent of total enrollment	Percent female enrollment
Education	5,939	3,346	9,285	23.4	36.0
Social Science	2,443	1,660	4,103	10.4	40.5
Commerce	2,588	1,514	4,102	10.4	36.9
Humanities	1,860	1,157	3,017	7.6	38.3
Environmental Studies/Science	1,708	725	2,433	6.1	29.8
Applied Sciences	1,547	820	2,367	6.0	34.6
Medicine	1,473	788	2,261	5.7	34.9
Nursing	397	1,487	1,884	4.8	78.9
Agriculture	1,112	619	1,731	4.4	35.8
Engineering	1,317	240	1,557	3.9	15.4
Science	1,017	471	1,488	3.8	31.7
Built Environment	942	298	1,240	3.1	24.0
Development Studies	839	389	1,228	3.1	31.7
Information and Communication	498	214	712	1.8	30.1
Business	393	303	696	1.8	43.5
Health Sciences	354	213	567	1.4	37.6
Law	316	160	476	1.2	33.6
Tourism & Hospitality	193	129	322	0.8	40.1
Theology	99	30	129	0.3	23.3
TOTAL	**25,035**	**14,563**	**39,598**	**100.0**	**36.8**

Source: Higher Education Institutions.

articulates the need to "Increase [the] postgraduate enrollment ratio to 10% of the undergraduate student population". At present, enrollment in postgraduate programs is low, accounting for only 4 percent of total enrollment at public institutions. None of Malawi's private universities currently offer programs for postgraduate education, with programmatic offerings limited to the two public universities of UNIMA and MZUNI. Figure 2.5 demonstrates that Chancellor College accounts for the largest cohort of postgraduate students within the system.[5] Not all colleges within the public higher education system offer programs for postgraduate study, and in some institutions the number of programs for postgraduate study is very limited. Further interventions will be required to sustain the upward trend in postgraduate enrollment, and to increase access to postgraduate studies.

Figure 2.6 shows the percentage of postgraduate students as a proportion of total enrollment by institution.[6] In the years for which data is available, Chancellor College maintained a ratio above 10 percent, reaching a peak of 14.9 percent in 2010. This is despite the fact that Chancellor College only offers three postgraduate programs, with the Master of Business Administration (MBA) accounting for a large share of its postgraduate cohort.

Figure 2.5 Postgraduate Enrollment by Institution—2008–11

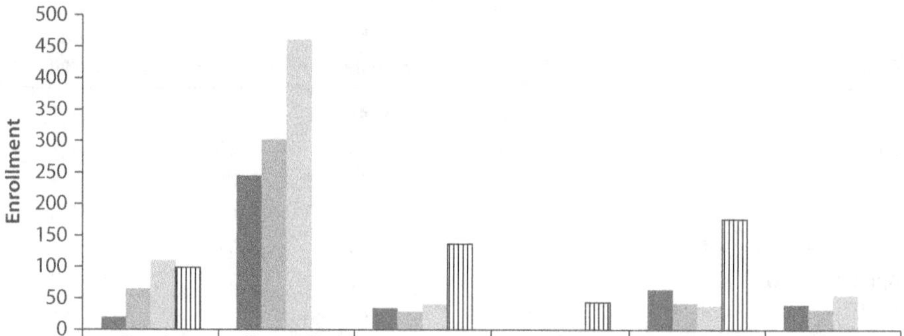

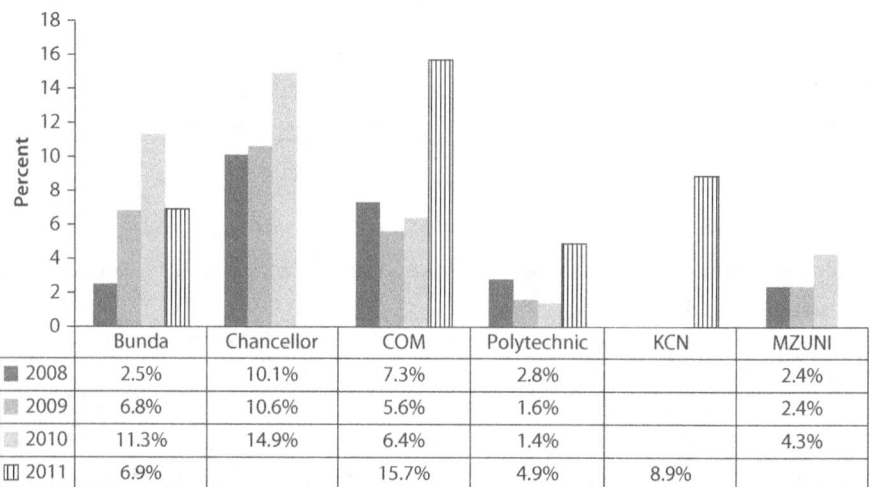

	Bunda	Chancellor	COM	KCN	Polytechnic	MZUNI
■ 2008	20	245	35	0	64	40
■ 2009	65	302	29	0	42	32
■ 2010	110	461	41	0	38	55
Ⅲ 2011	99		137	44	176	

Source: Higher Education Institutions.

Figure 2.6 Percentage of Postgraduate Students by Institution—2008–11

	Bunda	Chancellor	COM	Polytechnic	KCN	MZUNI
■ 2008	2.5%	10.1%	7.3%	2.8%		2.4%
■ 2009	6.8%	10.6%	5.6%	1.6%		2.4%
■ 2010	11.3%	14.9%	6.4%	1.4%		4.3%
Ⅲ 2011	6.9%		15.7%	4.9%	8.9%	

Source: Higher Education Institutions.

The percentage of postgraduate enrollment as a proportion of total enrollment at Bunda College's rose from 2.5 percent in 2008, to a peak of 11.3 percent in 2010, but dropped thereafter to 6.9 percent in 2011. COM's ratio of postgraduate enrollment as a share of total enrollment increased substantially in the period under review, jumping from 5.6 percent in 2009 to 15.7 percent in 2011. Postgraduate enrollment at the Polytechnic has been consistently low as a share of total enrollment, with a peak of 4.9 percent of total enrollment in 2011. The ratio of postgraduate enrollment as a share of total enrollment is similarly low at

MZUNI, with a peak of 4.3 percent in 2010. The data underscores a perception of limited access to postgraduate studies in public universities compared to undergraduate study.

Generally poor enrollment in postgraduate study can be attributed to the low number of staff with senior degrees relative to the student population. Table 2.3 illustrates the number of staff holding PhDs, a prerequisite for the teaching and supervision of postgraduate studies. In 2011 Chancellor College had the largest number staff holding PhDs (66) as well as the largest number of postgraduate students (461). The COM had the second largest cohort of staff holding PhDs (40) and total enrollment of 137 students in postgraduate study; the Polytechnic had 19 staff holding PhDs and 176 postgraduate students; and Bunda College had 23 staff holding PhDs and postgraduate enrollment of 99. Significant variance is evident with regard to the number of students per PhD holder across institutions: at Bunda College, the ratio of postgraduate students to members of staff holding PhDs is 4:1 while at COM it is 3:1. Poorer ratios are evident at KCN (8:1), Chancellor College (7:1) and at the Polytechnic (9:1). Interventions will be required to improve the ratio of PhD holders to postgraduate students in conjunction with interventions to increase the number of postgraduate students more generally.

While female enrollment in higher education in general is much lower that of males, in the postgraduate sub-sector the representation of female students in some instances is significantly better than the undergraduate level. Figure 2.7 shows the percentage of females enrolled by institution, demonstrating an increase in female postgraduate enrollment from 17.1 percent in 2008 to 31.3 percent in 2010 at Bunda College; a rise from 40 percent in 2008 to 61 percent in 2011 at COM; 15.6 percent in 2008 to 25 percent in 2011 at the Polytechnic; and a significant increase at MZUNI where the percentage female enrollment rose from 15.6 percent in 2010 to 38.2 percent in 2011. While this trend is encouraging, female enrollment as a percentage of total postgraduate enrollment declined from 27.3 percent in 2008 to 18.4 percent in 2010 at Chancellor College, the institution with the largest cohort of postgraduate students in the country.

Table 2.3 Composition of Staff by Qualification—2011

Institution	Undergraduate	Master	PhD	Total
Bunda	31	104	23	158
Chancellor	27	165	66	258
COM	29	42	40	111
KCN	12	42	5	59
Polytechnic	63	118	19	200
MZUNI	30	86	20	136
MAU	3	10	3	16
CUNIMA	11	31	4	46
UNILIA	5	15	0	20

Source: Higher Education Institutions.

Figure 2.7 Proportion of Females Enrolled in Graduate Studies by Institution

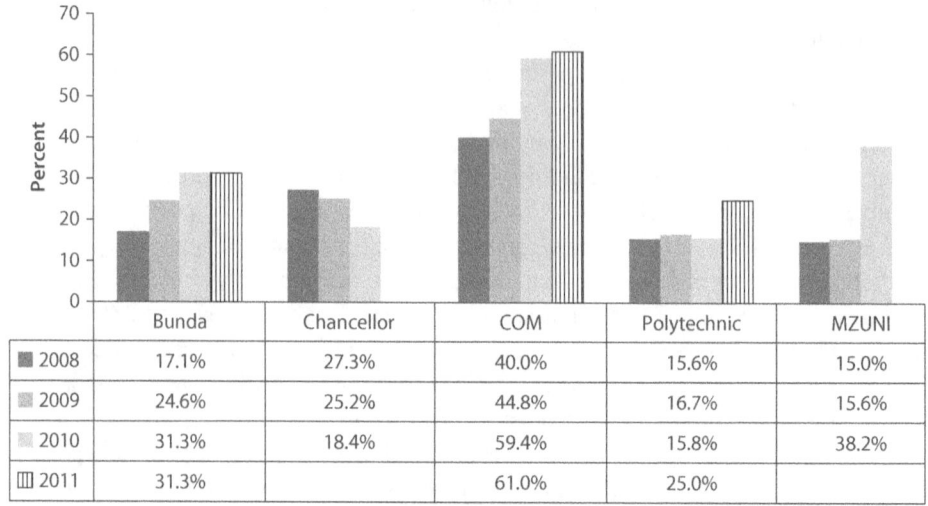

	Bunda	Chancellor	COM	Polytechnic	MZUNI
■ 2008	17.1%	27.3%	40.0%	15.6%	15.0%
■ 2009	24.6%	25.2%	44.8%	16.7%	15.6%
2010	31.3%	18.4%	59.4%	15.8%	38.2%
ⅢⅢ 2011	31.3%		61.0%	25.0%	

Source: Higher Education Institutions.

Annex 2A.5 lists the postgraduate program offerings in the period under review. In many instances enrollment in existing programs is low, and in some cases no students are currently enrolled in programs offered by institutions. Moreover, few students graduate from programs at the postgraduate level. The total number of graduates from postgraduate programs in 2011 was 154 compared to 4,289 graduates at the undergraduate level. In the same year only 4 percent of total graduate output was accounted for by the postgraduate subsector, well below MDGS target of 10 percent.

Factors Affecting Access and Equity

A number of factors affect access to, and equity in, higher education in Malawi, including: enrollment policies and entry requirements; government and household financing; institutional infrastructure; modes of delivery; and levels of staffing at institutions.

Enrollment Policies and Entry Requirements

Enrollment policies play an important role in with respect to improving access and addressing issues relating to equity. The decision to move away from an enrollment policy premised on bed-space to one based on classroom space has increased enrollment in the Malawian higher education sub-sector. Moreover, from an equity perspective, affirmative action policies have been instrumental in increasing female enrollment in public institutions.

The continued requirement that universities may only admit students at the beginning of the academic year contributes to the underutilization of facilities.

Universities are unable to enroll students at the commencement of each semester to, for example, take the place of a student who may have dropped out, and institutions must wait for the next school year to correct for any underutilized capacity. The adoption of an "open entry open exit" system would enable greater flexibility for both institutions and students.

The ongoing use of entry examinations, such as the University Entry Examination (UEE) administered by UNIMA, as a prerequisite for admission works to undermine efforts to improve access for students from poorer families. Students from disadvantaged backgrounds tend to perform more poorly on these tests, with negative implications for equity. Inadequate remedial programs within institutions disadvantage graduates from poorly funded Community Day Secondary Schools (CDSSs) who account for more than 70 percent of total secondary enrollment. Due to poor performance in university entrance examinations on the part of pupils from CDSS schools, graduates from these schools are under-represented in higher education, and students from the poorest quintile of households only account for 0.7 percent of total higher education enrollment.

Financing

Poor financing on the part of government and limited institutional finance represent significant constraints to expanding access in both public and private higher education institutions. An analysis of the sources of income for public institutions demonstrates that government allocations account for approximately 80 percent of total income, and that tuition fees only account for approximately 10 percent of total expenditure. The total funding envelope for public institutions is inadequate to support operational costs and the developmental expenditure required to expand and service infrastructure. The existing stock of higher education infrastructure—with respect to both its supply and quality—has become a significant constraint to increasing enrollment. Infrastructure related challenges have become more acute following the adoption of an enrollment policy premised on classroom space.

Since 2009, government subventions to public higher education have progressively increased. However, it is likely that the government will continue to operate in a context characterized by limited fiscal space, and if the decision to establish five new universities is realized, current subventions to support public universities will not be sufficient to maintain quality. In the absence of measures that enable institutions to increase tuition fees and substantively improve their own revenue generation in alignment with real costs, institutions are likely to face increasing financial constraints that will reduce their capacity to expand and service facilities in response to growing demand and address challenges related to maintaining and enhancing the quality of education delivered.

The government has introduced a new system of student financing to promote access for students from financially disadvantaged backgrounds. The impact of the system is yet to be evaluated, and the extent to which it has been effective in improving access is not known. The pattern of enrollments in public institutions shows that the majority of students come from comparatively well-to-do well families that can afford to pay fees. Fewer than 10 percent of enrolled students are drawn from households outside of the richest quintile. A sub-set of these students may be benefitting from the new loan scheme, with the remainder benefitting from other government subsidies.

Private universities enroll an even lower percentage of students from the poorest quintile of households. This is primarily related the greater dependence of private universities on tuition fees, and that fees charged in private institutions are significantly higher fees than those levied in public universities. The admission of poorer students to private higher education institutions is further prejudiced by the fact that students enrolled in private colleges are not eligible for government loans and must privately fund all costs associated with their study. Malawi should explore examples from other countries where students enrolled in private institutions can access loans equal in value to those extended to students in public colleges.

Until recently, parallel—or non-residential—students were not eligible for government financed students loans through the Public University Student Loan Trust. In order to increase access and improve equity, non-residential students are now eligible for loans and a monthly government subsistence allowance of MK 33,000. While the new scheme has increased the overall number of non-residential students in public institutions, in two of the three UNIMA colleges for which data was available, the number of non-residential students dropped, buttressing the view that access to finance is not the only constraint limiting the enrollment of non-residential students.[7] The delayed payment of student allowances has resulted in student demonstrations which have been disruptive to teaching and learning.

Infrastructure

Limited infrastructure constitutes the largest constraint to expanding enrollment in both public and private higher education. An admissions policy premised on classroom space will only be effective in expanding access to higher education if there is adequate classroom space. The stock of existing infrastructure at public institutions was designed to cater for small classes enrolled in programs with limited infrastructural needs. It has proven difficult to adapt the use of this infrastructure to a context of higher enrollment and a greater diversity of program offerings.

Poor funding allocations in support of infrastructural maintenance has resulted in a steady decline in the quality of many facilities which, in some cases, are no longer conducive to learning. Rising enrollment has increased the pressure on limited student accommodation as well as classroom, laboratory, and library space. Libraries are poorly resourced and the use of ICT is limited due to its cost. These factors, in conjunction with inadequate and in some cases obsolete teaching and learning materials, has limited the expansion of the Malawian public higher education sub-sector, and to some extent has negatively affected the quality of education delivered.

Surveys of universities demonstrate the strain placed on current infrastructure as a consequence of rising enrollment and poor maintenance:[8] MZUNI reported infrastructure usage at around 95 percent, due to high enrollment and the failure to bring on-line additional buildings that have been under construction for a number of years. MZUNI experienced a crisis in 2010/11 when the admission of an additional 300 students resulted in a situation wherein the university did not have inadequate classroom space to accommodate all students and the college failed to reopen in May 2011.

Bunda College reported the use of infrastructure and facilities at between 80 percent and 90 percent. Bunda's current infrastructure includes between 13 and 15 classrooms, 10 laboratories, three lecture theatres, and one hall, and much of this infrastructure requires rehabilitation. In order to cater for increased enrollment, Bunda was forced to pitch a marquee which is used as a mass classroom.

At Chancellor College the over-use of facilities has resulted in scheduling challenges, and the overcrowding of classrooms and laboratories results in some students having to stand outside during lessons. Chancellor College's current stock of infrastructure which caters for of 3,387 enrolled students is comprised of two lecture theatres each intended for 100 students; the Great Hall which can seat 400 students; four classrooms intended for 100 students; 15 tutorials rooms; and 20 laboratories.

There is variance in the intensity with which facilities at the Polytechnic are used; with some classrooms reportedly being used up to 100 percent of their capacity due to their use in delivering evening classes, while other facilities are used less intensively. Following the finalization of an initiative to modularize curricula, the Polytechnic plans to provide degree programs during vacation periods. This will increase enrollment but further strain the capacity of existing infrastructure.

At KCN classrooms are underutilized during the periods when students move to hospitals for clinical study.[9] KCN estimates that it could optimize the use of this space if it was able to recruit an additional thirty clinical instructors to train an expanded cohort of students. However, practitioners with the requisite training are in short supply, and the institution has battled to recruit qualified staff. KCN currently does not offer evening classes which could be used to improve the utilization of infrastructure and increase enrollment.

The use of infrastructure at private universities is limited due to absence of afternoon and evening classes, and due to their relatively isolated locations which limit the ability of students to commute to institutions. At CUNIMA, usage of facilities was estimated at 60 percent. While the university's library stays open until 22:30, the two computer laboratories are open only until 17:30 and there is a case to be made for the extension of these hours. At UNILIA, the usage of facilities was reported at around 95 percent. UNILIA uses the May vacation to provide additional classes for levels 1 and 3 of their programs, which has resulted in increased usage of facilities and expanded enrollment.

The continued expansion of enrollment in public institutions will be dependent on the availability of more classroom space, lecturer theatres, seminar rooms and laboratories. Institutions can also work to improve the utilization of existing infrastructure by offering evening and vacation programs.

The expansion of the non-residential enrollment is limited by the availability of decent low-cost accommodation close to institutions, as well as escalating costs associated with transport. Despite the move away from an admissions policy premised on bed space, limited student accommodation, as opposed to classroom space, has the potential to negatively impact the ability of universities to continue to increase enrollment.

Public private partnerships (PPPs) have the potential to attract additional investment to the higher education sub-sector, and could help to address infrastructure constraints especially with regard to student accommodation. Interviews with institutions in support of this study indicate that there is generally little engagement with the private sector in this regard. UNIMA has developed a Build-Operate-Transfer (BOT) Framework Agreement for the Construction of Building Units on University of Malawi Campuses, which spells out the obligations and undertakings of parties engaged under the auspices of the BOT, but the framework is yet to be implemented. The government has subsequently passed the PPP Act which should to facilitate implementation of BOT framework agreements.

The development and expansion of lifelong programs and tailored on-demand courses have the potential to contribute to increased enrollment and the optimized use of infrastructure. However, not all institutions offer lifelong learning programs, and those that do, like Chancellor College, have limited program offerings on weekends (Diploma in Law and Administrative Studies). The Pan-African e-Network Project, offered through an agreement with an Indian institution, presents an opportunity to amend the terms of the program to provide lifelong education programs once the agreement comes to an end. The Management Development Center and the Continuing Education Center at the Polytechnic enroll up to 930 students annually in a large number of programs in Human Resources, Journalism, Community Development, Business Management, Marketing, Accounting, Secretarial, Administration, Media studies, and Graphic Design which are delivered through block learning during semester breaks and evening classes. The Polytechnic also offers postgraduate programs in the evenings. These interventions have resulted in the improved use of infrastructure and facilities, have increased enrollment, and have introduced a new stream of revenue for the institution.

Private universities are evaluating the introduction of lifelong learning programs on a part-time basis, but their comparatively rural location will limit their market. MAU is planning to introduce block release programs during vacation periods in theology, education and business (accounting and auditing), and plans to establish a satellite campus in Blantyre to facilitate access. CUNIMA and UNILIA plan to offer demand-driven short-courses during vacation periods when student accommodation will be available for participants. These envisaged interventions will generate additional income for these institutions, will help to optimize the use of current facilities, and will expand opportunities for those seeking lifelong learning programs. The National Qualifications Framework, which is being finalized, should promote lifelong learning through recognition of prior learning.

Introduction of Alternate Modalities for Delivery

Open and distance learning (ODL) have been used effectively by many countries to increase access to tertiary education. All of Malawi's public institutions plan to establish capacity for ODL. The constituent colleges of UNIMA are in the process of introducing ODL to facilitate access for more students, with varying progress. A case in point is the collaboration between the Polytechnic and MZUNI, which has already established a Center for Open and Distance Learning. With assistance from the University of Strathclyde, which will provide a Video-Conference facility for teaching and learning, the Polytechnic and MZUNI are working together to introduce ODL programming. Bunda College currently offers diploma courses using ODL in combination with on-site weekend instruction. These diploma courses demonstrate a model for the use of ODL in delivering other programs offered by the college.

The use of e-learning in Malawi is still relatively undeveloped, and is currently only used to improve the quality of instruction, as opposed to increasing access. Additional investment is required to expand and operationalize e-learning systems in support of increased access to higher education.

Traditional face-to-face lectures, supported by tutorials, remain the dominant method of delivery in both private and public higher education institutions. Given constraints on classroom space, the effectiveness of this mode of delivery in supporting the objectives of increasing enrollment and improving the quality of education delivered, is increasingly limited. E-learning has been introduced at COM, Chancellor College, KCN, the Polytechnic and MZUNI to improve the quality of learning and is at different stages of development in each institution. E-learning enables staff to upload lecture notes and other education materials for students to access through the intranet and Internet. Expanding the use of ICT will require infrastructural improvements which in turn depend on resources which are currently not available.

Chancellor College is currently participating in the Pan-African e-Network which aims to provide tele-education services to enable 10,000 African students to pursue postgraduate and undergraduate degree and diploma programs, and skill enabling certification courses in subjects such as Business Administration, Information Technology, International Business, Tourism and Finance. The institution hopes to use the capacity developed through this initiative to offer ODL programs when the terms of its existing partnership expire. In order to effectively scale up this capacity Chancellor College will need to invest in more computers and the recruitment and training of staff to develop ODL materials.

At MZUNI, an e-learning system has been established to complement traditional learning activities. Over 105 courses have been uploaded to the system for access via the Internet and intranet. An advantage of this system is that is runs on free open source software. Challenges with regard to the optimization of the current system include the need to train staff in the use of computers, the production of online course materials, poor bandwidth and insufficient numbers of computers to facilitate access to the system.

The Polytechnic has commenced an e-learning program using a knowledge-based web system, and has trained students in the use of associated software. Three labs containing 20 computers each will be provided at the Malawi College of Accountancy, with an additional two labs with 20 computers each to be located at sites in Blantyre. KCN also intends to establish capacity for e-learning to be complemented by a computer lab in Lilongwe housing 50 computers and a lab in Blantyre accommodating 30 terminals.

Major constraints to the expansion of ODL capacity include a lack of facilities and equipment; costs associated with the development of programming and the procurement of equipment; and poor ODL expertise on the part of staff to initiate programs. In a context wherein these challenges constitute prohibitive barriers for many institutions, Malawi should weigh the merits of establishing an Open University to facilitate ODL. Successful interventions in this regard include the Open University of Tanzania, which currently enrolls over 10,000 students, and Zimbabwe's Open University, with enrollment of 18,000 students (Bloom, Canning, and Chan 2006). Scaling up the nascent collaboration between Chancellor College, the Polytechnic and MZUNI would help to avoid duplication and minimize expenses in a context of limited resource availability.

Advantages associated with the Credit Hour System

The rigidity of curricula currently offered in public institutions, and the requirement that students stay in college for four years towards the fulfillment of their qualification, limits enrollment. Curricula premised on a credit hour system would introduce greater flexibility for students to optimize their time in support of their studies. A credit hour system would also mitigate the opportunity costs associated with four years of full time study, and give students greater flexibility in balancing study and work commitments (World Bank 2010b).

Public institutions are at various stages of adopting the credit hour system. Chancellor College has already implemented a modularized curriculum, in conjunction with the introduction of Graduate Point Average (GPA) system to monitor student performance. The Polytechnic has modularized curricula for programs in Engineering and the Applied Sciences, and curricula in all other departments will be modularized in due course. Bunda College is in the process of converting courses to the modular format and the subsequent introduction of a credit hour system will enable students to access study through multiple-entry and multiple-exit. KCN and MZUNI are still in the process of planning the modularization of curricula. CUNIMA and MAU currently use the credit hour system, and UNILIA is in the process of exploring a transition to this system. The UNIMA Council has approved the implementation of a multiple-entry and multiple-exit system but implementation at the institutional level will take some time due to ongoing efforts on the part of colleges to modularize courses and the need, in some cases, for technical assistance to achieve this.

The credit hour system allows students to finish their studies more quickly than the traditional system allowed, with some students completing a full degree in three years instead of four. The potential for students to move more quickly through the system would free up space and resources for the enrollment of additional students. However, the government's school calendar, which requires that all new students enter the system at the beginning of the school calendar year and prohibits multiple-entry and exit from the system on a semester basis, will limit the expansionary potential of the credit hour system. A rigid school calendar is appropriate for systems of school education, but is less applicable in a context of higher education. Enabling universities to use flexible approaches to enrollment will positively impact gross enrollment in university education.

Staffing

It is not clear to what extent staffing has affected enrollment in higher education in Malawi, particularly at the undergraduate level. Universities have tended to address staffing shortages through the recruitment of associate and assistant lecturers and, in some cases, adjunct staff. However, the use of lecturers who do not have the qualifications to teach university level courses could negatively impact quality.

There is evidence of low student-to-lecturer ratios (SLRs) in some university departments and faculties, which suggests poor optimization of the use of staff time. Addressing incidences of low student-lecturer ratios would result in higher enrollment. In instances where universities or faculties lack staff, infrastructure tends to be under-utilized, as evidenced by idle infrastructure during the evening, on weekends and during college breaks.

The relative shortage of staff with PhDs capable of supervising and teaching postgraduate study contributes to very low postgraduate enrollment and limits course offerings, particularly at the Polytechnic. The chronic nature of this problem is demonstrated by national postgraduate output of only 76 in 2009 and 159 in 2010. Access to postgraduate programs may also be constrained by relatively high student fees which range between MK 200,000 and MK 300,000. The prohibitive nature of costs associated with postgraduate study is exacerbated by the fact that students enrolled in postgraduate programs are ineligible for government student loans. Increased postgraduate enrollment could be supported by interventions to, *inter alia*, extend scholarships to students enrolled in priority programs; the introduction of teaching assistantship programs in colleges wherein postgraduate students teach undergraduate programs while pursuing their postgraduate studies in return for reduced fees or a tuition waiver; the introduction of postgraduate student allowances that can be used to defray costs associated with tuition; the further subsidization of postgraduate tuition fees; and allowing postgraduate students to access loans.

Equity in Higher Education

As the Government of Malawi intensifies its efforts to improve access to higher education a number of equity related challenges will need to be addressed. Specific interventions will be required to address evidence of inequity associated with gender, socioeconomic status, spatial location, and disability.

Gender

The Malawian education system demonstrates significant gendered disparities with regard to access to education. Annex 2A.6 demonstrates how the Gender Parity Index (GPI) progressively deteriorates from Standard 7 onwards: the ratio of female to male enrollment drops from 1.017 in Standard 6 to 0.889 in Standard 8, and further deteriorates to 0.868 in Form 1. Comparatively poor female enrollment in Form 1 reduces the pool of female candidates who can sit the MSCE examination for entry to university. Moreover, the MSCE pass rate for female students is lower than that associated with male students: in 2010, 51.4 percent of females sitting the exam passed compared to a male pass rate of 59.9 percent; and female students comprised only 37.6 percent of those who passed the MSCE exam.

Poor female student performance and comparatively high dropout rates are, in part, a consequence of cultural biases. The government has initiated programs to reframe the dominant perception of women in society as the stewards of their husband's household and child minders. The majority of Malawi's population lives in rural areas where girls have limited exposure to professional female role models with the potential to reshape girls' aspirations. The school system plays a role in reinforcing some female stereotypes in the assignment of chores to female pupils. Implementation of the Primary Curriculum and Assessment Review (PCAR) aims to addresses some of the shortcomings associated with the perpetuation of gender bias in the primary education system.

The adoption of affirmative action policies which lowered admissions requirements for female applicants to public higher education has positively impacted female enrollment at UNIMA. For example the proportion of female students in medicine rose from 31 percent in 2008 to approximately 40 percent today. At the college of nursing, KCN, female enrollment accounts for a majority of enrollment. In alignment with the principle that all professions benefit from the participation of men and women, men's hostels have been constructed in an effort to boost male enrollment which currently constitutes only 25 percent of KCN's student body.

Bunda College's administration has targeted equal representation of male and female enrollment, but progress has been constrained by the lack of suitable accommodation. In 1998, the institution's facilities adequately met the needs of the 7 percent of students who were female, but in the intervening period female enrollment has increased to 40 percent without a concurrent expansion of infrastructure catering to female students. At Chancellor College, female enrollment currently accounts for 41 percent of the student body. The institution is in the process of renovating old staff houses, which have already increased female accommodation by sixty beds, to create additional capacity for female enrollment. In the longer term, Chancellor College plans to establish satellite campuses in areas where enrollment will less limited by accommodation space. The Polytechnic has targeted a student population of 5,000 with equal numbers of male and female students by 2016. The share of female enrollment at MZUNI has increased to approximately 30 percent as a result of affirmative action policies. In the private sub-sector, MAU has stated its intention to increase total enrollment to 700 by 2016, off a current base of 324, and in so doing achieve a gender ratio of 1:1. UNILIA has performed consistently well with regard to the admission of female students, demonstrating average female enrollment of 49.2 percent over the course of the past four years, with a low of 44.1 percent in 2011.

Figure 2.2 illustrates how the share of female students as a proportion of total enrollment in public and private institutions has averaged 35.9 percent for the period under review, with an improvement in the GPI from 0.54 in 2008 to 0.60 in 2011 against the government's target of 0.61 for 2010.[10] While it is encouraging that the GPI is increasing and that the 2010 target, for all practical purposes, has been met, stark gender disparities are evident at the program level particularly in the fields of science and engineering. Performance with regard to the number of females admitted to higher education per 100,000 inhabitants[11] and with regard to poor female representation in postgraduate study[12] buttresses a view that much work remains to be done to address entrenched challenges undermining the enrollment of female students in higher education.

Improved enrollment of females in public institutions can be attributed to the implementation of affirmative action policies supporting the admission of female candidates. Private universities tend to have higher female enrollment than public institutions as a consequence of the nature of the programs they offer, and, to date, private universities do not apply affirmative action policies to female admissions.

CUNIMA is the only private institution that currently offers an equity measure promoting access for female students in the form of a six-week bridging course for students who did not meet the stated entry requirements. Bridging programs could be offered at other institutions, and a number of institutions have plans to introduce a preliminary year of remedial education targeting students who do initially meet entry requirements. Public institutions have indicated their interest in introducing remedial programs if government funding is made available to support institutions and students. These programs could be used to target women who want to enter the male dominated fields of science and engineering and to cater to the needs disabled persons who are poorly represented in higher education. Bunda College provides academically weak students with remedial education in the form of additional tutorials, following their entry to the university in line with existing enrollment criteria.

Table 2.2 illustrates the share of female enrollment by academic program. (cumulative, 2008 – 11)[13] The share of female enrollment as a proportion of total program enrollment is highest in Nursing (78.9 percent) followed by Business (43.5 percent), and Social Science (40.5 percent). Fifteen programs demonstrate female enrollment below 40 percent of total enrollment, with female participation dipping to below 30 percent in Environmental Studies (29.8 percent), Theology (23.3 percent), the Built Environment (24 percent) and Engineering (15.4 percent). Since 2006 a number of programs demonstrate significantly improved gender equity (see comparison in table 2.4), with notable improvement evident in the historically male dominated fields of the Applied Sciences, where female enrollment increased from 19.6 percent of total enrollment in 2008 to 34.6 percent in 2011, and in Science, where female representation rose from 24.4 percent to 31.7 percent. Deterioration in the representation of female students as a share of total enrollment is evident in Agriculture (from 36.7 in 2008 to 35.8 percent in 2011); Environment Science (33.9 to 29.8 percent) and the Health Sciences (56.3 to 37.6 percent).

Further interventions will be required to increase female enrollment, especially in fields historically dominated by men. Females are severely under-represented in the management structures of universities, evidenced by the fact that not one Vice Chancellor or pro-Vice Chancellor in any Malawian higher education institution is female. Fewer than 20 percent of deans within the system as a whole are female, and the Polytechnic accounts for the only female registrar.

Table 2.4 Comparison of Female Enrollment by Field of Study—2006 and 2011

Field	Percentage female 2006	Percentage female 2011	Change
Tourism	24.1	40.1	16.0
Applied Science	19.6	34.6	15.0
Science	24.4	31.7	7.3
Commerce	30.8	37.2	6.4
Law	28.2	33.6	5.4
ICT	26.1	30.1	4.0
Engineering	12.2	15.4	3.2
Medicine	32.3	34.9	2.6
Built Environment	21.5	24.0	2.5
Social Science	39.0	40.6	1.6
Nursing	78.2	78.9	0.7
Education	35.4	36.1	0.7
Humanities	38.0	38.3	0.3
Agriculture	36.7	35.8	−0.9
Development Studies	32.7	31.7	−1.0
Environmental Science	33.9	29.8	−4.1
Health Science	56.3	37.6	−18.7

Source: Higher Education Institutions.

Socioeconomic Status

The vast majority of university students in Malawi come from the wealthiest strata of the country's population. In 2006, 91.3 percent of students in higher education were from the fifth—or richest—quintile of households compared to just 0.7 percent drawn from the first quintile. The 2012 Integrated Household Survey (IHS 3, 2012) demonstrated a marginal improvement in the distribution of university enrollment, with the fifth quintile of households accounting for 81.9 percent of higher educational enrollment and 1.5 percent from the first quintile of households (figure 2.8). The concentration of relatively well-off students in the university population is a reflection of the disparities that manifest themselves in the education system starting at secondary level.

While children from across the socioeconomic spectrum access primary education in relatively equal numbers, the performance of children from the fifth quintile diverges significantly at the primary level, with subsequent implications for access to secondary education. Sixty-seven percent of children from the richest households (quintile 5) complete a full course of primary education compared to only 23 percent of children from the poorest 20 percent of households. As a result, less than 10 percent of children from poor families enter the lower and upper secondary education. Children from the poorest quintile of households moreover demonstrate low completion rates of 8 percent and 2 percent for lower and upper secondary education respectively, with further negative effects for the likelihood of their accessing higher education. Relative inequity impacting the likelihood of a child's educational survival is also reflected in the share of household expenditures allocated to education: households from the first quintile spend on average 0.31 percent on education related expenses, compared to

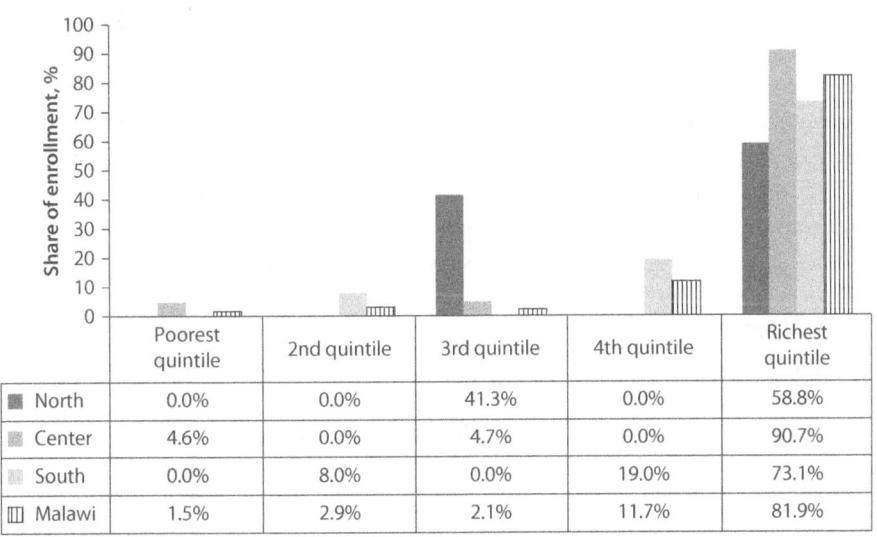

Figure 2.8 Enrollment in Tertiary Education by Socioeconomic Status

	Poorest quintile	2nd quintile	3rd quintile	4th quintile	Richest quintile
North	0.0%	0.0%	41.3%	0.0%	58.8%
Center	4.6%	0.0%	4.7%	0.0%	90.7%
South	0.0%	8.0%	0.0%	19.0%	73.1%
Malawi	1.5%	2.9%	2.1%	11.7%	81.9%

Source: Data from the IHS3.

0.9 percent in the fourth quintile and 2.84 percent in the fifth quintile. The socioeconomic profile of current university enrollment means that the wealthiest members of society disproportionately benefit from the government's subsidy to higher education in the form of budget allocations and student loans.

Disability

A person with a disability is defined as a person with a physical or mental condition that limits their movement, senses or activities. In Malawi persons living with disabilities are entitled to all human rights, however in practice they are often denied these rights. According to Section 44 (g) of the Constitution of Malawi, every person has an equal right to education at the primary, secondary and tertiary levels. In order to practically achieve the Constitutional imperative for equality of access to education, measures will need to be taken to facilitate improved access to higher education for persons living with disabilities.

The 2008 census counted 498,122 Malawians living with disabilities disaggregated by physical impairment related to sight (133,273), hearing, (82,180), speech (30,198), mobility (108,870) and other (143,601). Children with special needs constitute 1.5 percent of primary school enrollment compared to the 3.8 percent of Malawians with disabilities in the general population (MoEST 2011). In secondary education, the enrollment of persons with disabilities constitutes approximately 1.5 percent of total enrollment, equivalent to 3,600 students. If one applies the average MSCE pass rate of 56.4 percent to the population of disabled students in the secondary sub-sector, approximately 500[14] students with disabilities graduate with an MSCE certificate and are eligible for entry into university. There is little data on the enrollment of persons with disabilities in the university system. In the course of this study, Chancellor College was the only institution that indicated it has retained the services of a Special Needs lecturer to assist the 15 students with disabilities currently enrolled at the institution. MZUNI indicated it that it currently has one disabled student in its student body. Available information suggests that the majority of school leavers with disabilities who qualify for admission to university are not being absorbed into higher education. In general the system is characterized by an absence of infrastructure, learning and teaching materials, and equipment tailored to the needs of disabled students.

The provision of infrastructure, and associated programmatic support, will be required to address this shortfall, and enable qualified Malawians living with disabilities to access higher education, as required by the Constitution.

Spatial Inequity

The data suggests significant spatial disparities in enrollment, with a minority of regions accounting for the majority of university enrollment. Moreover, some districts benefit more from higher education and associated government subsidies than others.[15] Urban districts account for a higher share of enrollment compared to rural districts, in part due to the concentration of poverty in rural Malawi.

In an effort to address spatial disparities, the government has implemented an Equitable Access Policy which requires that public institutions enroll a minimum of 10 merit-based students from each district. If districts are unable to supply ten students, spare places are distributed between districts according to their population. The policy applies to government supported students only, and is not considered in the enrollment of mature and parallel students.

Analysis of the incidence of UNIMA enrollment per 100,000 residents in each district for 2009, the first year in which the Equitable Access Policy was implemented, demonstrates significant variation between districts in enrollment.[16] The districts of Neno, Ntcheu, Mwanza and Rumphi benefitted the most with 14 students per 100,000 residents drawn from each, while only 6 students were admitted from Lilongwe and Mzimba. Analysis of enrollment data for 2010 demonstrates an improvement in the allocation of enrollment by district per 100,000 inhabitants, with the mean for admission from each district rising from 10 to 17 per 100,000. A Paired Means Test was used to determine the equality of independent means, and found that the observed differences were statistically significant. This suggests the equitable access policy is positively impacting the equitable distribution of enrollment across districts. There is need to continue to monitor implementation and outcomes associated with this policy to ensure its ongoing contribution towards improved equitable access.

Gender disparities are evident in enrollment per district, to the disadvantage of females. The average admission per 100,000 residents for each district in 2009 was 7 for females and 12 for males, rising to 15 for females and 18 for males in 2010. The minimum and maximum number of students drawn from districts increased from 6 and 14, to 10 and 25 respectively, demonstrating increased enrollments in the districts. The biggest increase in the number of students between 2009 and 2010 was in Lilongwe (84) followed by Mzimba (67) and Mangochi (58). The districts with the smallest change in enrollment were Mwanza and Rumphi both of which demonstrated an increase of 11 students.

Figure 2.9 illustrates a scatterplot of data points representing the number of students enrolled per 100,000 inhabitants in each district for 2009 and 2010. An R value of 0.591 demonstrates a weak correlation between the two years, which implies that increased district level enrollment was not systematic. However the Equitable Access Policy has the potential to continue to improve equity if it is implemented rigorously. While the implementation of the policy can improve enrollment by district, it will not address poverty related disparities between the rural poor and the rich that are associated with high rates of repetition and drop out among poorer, predominantly rural, students in the secondary sub-sector. A long term strategy to improve access for comparatively poor and rural students will require interventions to improve the quality of education provided in CDSS schools, which cater predominantly to the poor. The government should also consider the introduction of affirmative action policies to promote access for poor students, and the introduction of targeted bridging programs to improve access for poor and CDSS students.

Figure 2.9 Enrollment by District at UNIMA for 2009 and 2010

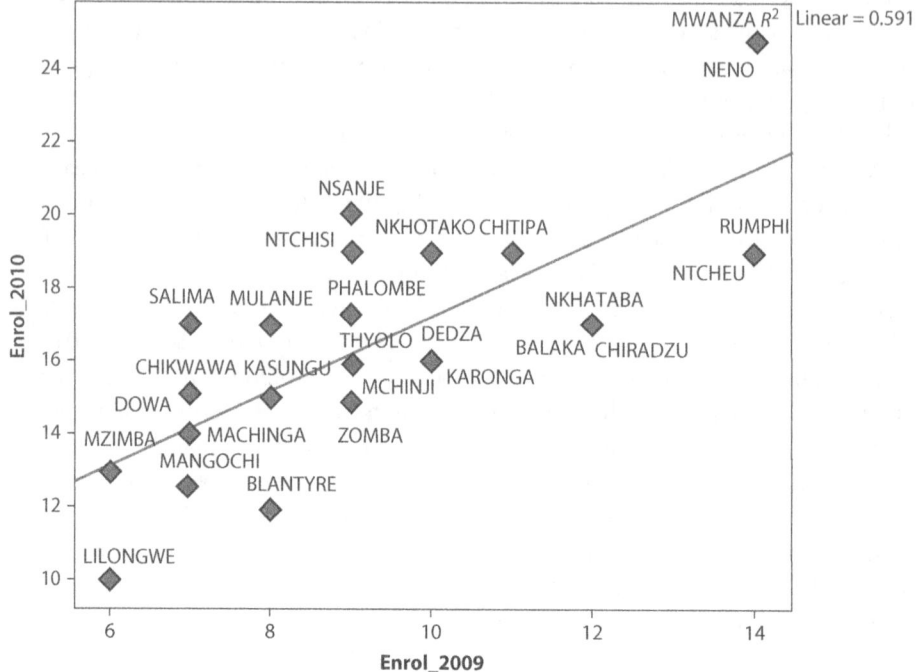

Source: Annex 2A.3.

Enrollment Projections

All institutions, with the exception of UNILIA, plan to increase enrollment in the short to medium term. The constituent colleges of the UNIMA plan to increase cumulative enrollment to 17,500 by 2017[17]; MZUNI plans to increase enrollment to 4,000 by 2015 off a current base of 2000, and increase graduate output to 3,500 over the same time period; MAU plans to increase enrollment to 700 students by 2016; and CUNIMA plans to increase enrollment from 849 (2011) to 1,500 by 2015, in part through the development of satellite campuses at Chiradzulu and Lilongwe. Table 2.5 illustrates projected enrollment for institutions for which the project team had data.

Projected increases in enrollment will compromise the quality of higher education provision in the absence of measures to construct additional classroom infrastructure, laboratories, improve and expand ICT infrastructure, recruit additional teaching staff and improve library facilities. Annex 2A.8 captures information relating to the quality of the existing stock of infrastructure and the intensity of its use. Careful and deliberate planning will be required to mobilize resources for the financing of infrastructure expansion in a resource constrained environment, and to ensure that additional enrollment does not compromise the quality of learning for all students. Universities need to plan staff recruitment drives, and ensure that newly recruited staff enhance

Access and Equity in Malawi's Higher Education Sub-Sector

Table 2.5 Enrollment Projections by Institution

Institutions	Enrollment in 2011	Projected enrollment
UNIMA Colleges	8,700	17,500 by 2017
MZUNI	1,960	4,000 by 2015
MAU	315	700 by 2015
CUNIMA	849	1,200 by 2015

Source: Higher Education Institutions.

the quality of teaching instead of diluting it. There is also need to improve the utilization of current staff, through *inter alia* increasing student-to-lecturer ratios (see annex 2A.7).

In order alleviate the potential burden increased enrollment will place on existing staff and infrastructure universities should pursue the introduction of delivery methods in addition to traditional face-to-face teaching. ICT and ODL are methods which are currently underutilized in Malawi with demonstrated utility in expanding access and improving quality. Collaboration with the Commonwealth of Learning will assist in moving this agenda forward.

The government plans to increase the number of universities in support of its efforts to increase access and to improve the alignment of higher education programming with the economic development needs of the country. The following new institutions have been proposed: The University of Science and Technology, which is already financial support from the Chinese government; a University of Marine Biology; the Lilongwe University of Agriculture and Natural Resources, to be comprised by a merger of the Bunda College of Agriculture, a Naturals Resources College, AURET and Chitedze Research Station in line with a bill already passed by Parliament; the University of Nkhotakota; and the University of Mombera.

Alternative Options for Secondary School Leavers

Post-Secondary Programs

The Government of Malawi needs to develop additional post-secondary programs to cater to the skills development needs of the large number of secondary school graduates who are not absorbed into university education. Expanding the provision of Technical, Entrepreneurial and Vocational Education and Training (TEVET) will help to absorb some students who pass the MSCE but are not accepted into universities, and alleviate demand for university education.

TEVET in Malawi is currently an underutilized sub-sector of tertiary education, as demonstrated by relatively low levels of enrollment. The discontinuation of technician programs at the Polytechnic created a shortage at this level of training. While TEVET has demonstrated a significant expansion in enrollment since 2008, in 2011 total TEVET enrollment was the lowest of any sub-sector in post-secondary education accounting for just 6,105 students, compared to 10,993 enrolled in teacher education and 12,203 in universities. Despite the public subsidization TEVET programs, the proportion of students publically funded by the Technical, Entrepreneurial and Vocational Education and Training Authority (TEVETA) has fallen and the percentage of privately funded students increased from 27.8 percent in 2007 to 70.4 percent in 2009. In addition to creating opportunities for further education, expanding the TEVET sub-sector will help to address the critical shortage of artisans and technicians in all sectors of the economy. Studies demonstrate that the work of each engineer needs to be supported by five technicians, who in turn require support from five artisans. Current enrollment will not support these work place ratios without the expansion of the TEVET sub-sector. In 2011, the recurrent unit costs associated with a university education were seven times higher those associated with technical education, demonstrating the relative cost effectiveness of technical education as a means for increasing access to post-secondary education. Serious consideration should be given to reintroducing the technician, diploma and supervisor programs that were phased out at the Polytechnic following the dissolution of the Board of Governors. The discontinuation of these programs exacerbated critical skills shortages in the labor market.

Regional Cooperation

Intensifying the use of opportunities available through the SADC Protocol on Education and Training can improve access to higher education for Malawian students, without placing additional strain on Malawian facilities and systems. The Protocol enables students from SADC member countries to enroll at institutions in other member countries while paying the equivalent of local fees. The Protocol aims to improve economies of scale in higher education through the establishment of Centers of Excellence and Centers of Specialization in different member states to cater to the needs of the community as a whole, in turn reducing institutions of specialization across member states. While there is evidence of increasing collaboration between member states the efficient implementation of the Protocol continues to be undermined by attempts to set up state specific institutions as opposed to strengthening existing capacity in the region as a whole. Malawi should pursue the opportunities available under the SACD protocol in support of its objectives to increase access and improve skills development.

Conclusion

Enrollment in public and private higher education increased throughout the period under review. Improved enrollment in public institutions is largely a result of the shift in admissions policy, from the one based on bed-space to the one based on classroom space, and the extension of government support to non-residential students. Not only has enrollment improved in absolute terms, but the number of students enrolled per 100,000 inhabitants has increased. However, the proportion of Malawi's population engaged in higher education remains small compared to other countries in the region and abroad.

Unintended consequences associated with the introduction of the new admissions policy have led to the over-crowding of learning facilities and a deterioration of student-lecturer ratios, with concurrent and negative effects for the quality of learning provided. Poor and over-burdened infrastructure will limit the potential for enrollment growth in most public institutions.

The number of students enrolled at private higher education institutions has increased throughout the period under review, but this has been off a relatively low base and remains low relative to enrollment in public institutions of higher learning. Private institutions increasingly face infrastructure challenges similar to those prevalent in the public sub-sector, and their ability to expand is mitigated by their financial dependence on tuition fees.

Undergraduate and postgraduate enrollment in fields with the potential to catalyze national development—specifically in the sciences, engineering and ICT—remains low despite articulated government targets to increase graduate output in line with the MGDS.

Enrollment in postgraduate education is inadequate to address the needs of the economy, and while enrollment in postgraduate education has improved, it has not kept pace with the expansion of undergraduate enrollment. The further expansion of postgraduate enrollment faces additional challenges relating the comparatively high cost to students and insufficient and poorly qualified staff incapable of teaching and supervising postgraduate study.

In the absence of measures to address bottlenecks and constraints, efforts to continue the expansion of university enrollment will be undermined by: constrained and degraded infrastructure; inadequate support for capital and recurrent expenditure; insufficient numbers of suitably qualified staff, especially at the postgraduate level; a rigid undergraduate curriculum that requires four continuous years of enrollment; the limited use of diversified delivery methods; and relatively high costs associated with postgraduate education. Public and private institutions are working to overcome these challenges, and some progress is evident with regard to the adoption and expansion of ICT and ODL initiatives. Support for these interventions will need to be sustained for tangible results to materialize.

Despite some improvement, the Malawian higher education sub-sector continues to demonstrate significant inequity with regard to access to higher education. Interventions to boost female enrollment will need to be sustained and intensified, in conjunction with specific actions to boost female enrollment in fields that continue to be dominated by men. The introduction of the Equitable Access Policy has improved equity with regard to the representation of students from all districts of the country, but socioeconomic disparities in enrollment patterns continue to be very pronounced resulting in a regressive public subsidy for higher education. Interventions throughout the system of education will be required to improve access for students from poor and rural households. The number of students with disabilities in higher education is low relative to their representation in society at large, and evidence of initiatives to address obstacles to their enrollment is scarce. Further study to inform a holistic policy focusing on the reasons for the low enrollment of persons with disabilities is required.

The Malawian TEVET sector is underdeveloped relative to regional and international comparator countries, and there is evidence of significant unfulfilled demand within the labor market for technical skills. The government should consider the expansion of TEVET diploma education and programming to address demand for critical skills and to reduce demand for university education on the part of MSCE graduates.

Programmatic Policy Options

Based on the findings of this study, policy options intended to address challenges undermining access to, and equity of, higher education in Malawi are laid out in table 2.6. The government and its partners will need to weigh the relative cost-effectiveness of interventions to inform a sustainable program of reform.

Table 2.6 Policy Options

Policy objective	Issue	Programmatic options to address supply/demand constraints	Expected impact
Improved access	High demand for higher education coupled with low enrollment due to supply side constraints.	Increased use of ICT-based delivery methods to reach more students, including e-learning and open and distance learning.	Increased access to higher education without physical infrastructure constraints
		Update fields of study to cater to needs of economy and attract students.	Improve the responsiveness of the system to the education and training needs of students and the country.
		Create a Qualifications Framework for higher education that enables multiple entry points and facilitates the movement of students from one institution to another, and opportunities to transfer to higher levels of study.	Flexible entry to and exit from the system. Improve the responsiveness of the system to the needs of students, with positive implications for retention.
		Address legal constraints to student loan recovery and extend the government's loan scheme to Malawian students at private universities.[a]	An equitable student financing system. Increased private financing to higher education leading to increased access to, equity and relevance in higher education institutions.
		Use of centers of specialization and other institutions in the SADC region as provided for in the SADC Protocol of Education and Training, particularly for the postgraduate study.	Improve access to finance to support postgraduate study, leading to an increase in postgraduate enrollment. Improved access to specialized education and training not available in Malawi

table continues next page

Access and Equity in Malawi's Higher Education Sub-Sector 33

Table 2.6 Policy Options *(continued)*

Policy objective	Issue	Programmatic options to address supply/demand constraints	Expected impact
Improved equity	Gender imbalance in enrollments and graduation patterns, low enrollment of students from disadvantaged socioeconomic backgrounds and those living with disabilities	Provide remedial programs and special tuition programs to boost female enrollment in male dominated programs. Adopt a policy that requires institutions to provide facilities for those with living with disabilities, including specialized teaching and learning materials and aids. Provide special grants for students from disadvantaged socioeconomic households and those living with disabilities; explore the possibility of private sector involvement in such a scheme.	Increased female enrollment and retention in programs Increased enrollment and retention of students living with disability

a. Current tuition of MK 55, 000 is aligned to the loan for which students in public institutions qualify. Students also qualify for an additional support of MK 30,000 to cover the cost of learning materials. The loan scheme would require an additional MK 76 million to support tuition fees and 42 million for the book allowance to finance the 1,377 students in private universities. Tuition fees for UNMA and MZUNI have now been rationalized at MK 55,000.

Annexes for Chapter 2

Annex 2A.1 Comparison of Enrollment per 100,000 Inhabitants—2009

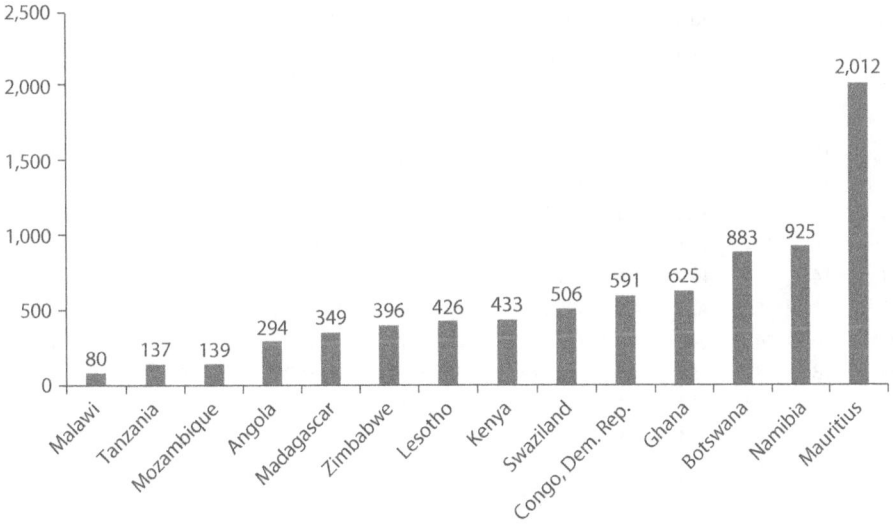

Source: UNESCO Institute for Statistics.

Annex 2A.2 Percentage of Non-Residential Students by Institution—2008–11

	Bunda	Chancellor	Polytechnic
2008	20.0%	35.7%	40.5%
2009	20.1%	33.1%	45.4%
2010	33.0%	33.8%	43.9%
2011	17.6%	40.7%	36.6%

Source: Higher Education Institutions.

Annex 2A.3 Enrollment at UNIMA per 100,000 Inhabitants by District

District	Enrollment					Population			Enrollment per 100,000 (2009)	Enrollment per 100,000 (2010)
	Male	Female	Total	% of female	% of total	Male	Female	Total		
Balaka	25	14	39	35.9	3.4	157,514	170,629	328,143	12	17
Blantyre	44	35	79	44.3	6.9	519,995	520,715	1,040,710	8	12
Chikwawa	23	10	33	30.3	2.9	222,794	225,862	448,656	7	15
Chiradzulu	20	15	35	42.9	3.1	137,958	155,513	293,471	12	17
Chitipa	13	8	21	38.1	1.8	88,964	95,438	184,402	11	19
Dedza	35	28	63	44.4	5.5	306,184	334,872	641,056	10	16
Dowa	25	16	41	39.0	3.6	288,237	298,193	586,430	7	15
Karonga	16	11	27	40.7	2.4	135,397	144,023	279,420	10	16
Kasungu	28	25	53	47.2	4.6	326,670	328,060	654,730	8	15
Lilongwe	78	44	122	36.1	10.7	984,777	1,000,692	1,985,469	6	10
Machinga	21	14	35	40.0	3.1	241,564	265,409	506,973	7	14
Mangochi	33	22	55	40.0	4.8	395,130	431,888	827,018	7	13
Mchinji	25	20	45	44.4	3.9	237,303	239,472	476,775	9	15
Mulanje	23	18	41	43.9	3.6	248,074	281,850	529,924	8	17
Mwanza	9	4	13	30.8	1.1	45,594	49,204	94,798	14	25
Mzimba	34	24	58	41.4	5.1	435,576	460,812	896,388	6	13
Neno	10	6	16	37.5	1.4	54,313	58,625	112,938	14	25
Nkhatabay	17	10	27	37.0	2.4	108,707	114,066	222,773	12	17
Nkhotakota	21	10	31	32.3	2.7	156,322	158,100	314,422	10	19
Nsanje	14	8	22	36.4	1.9	118,185	126,283	244,468	9	20

table continues next page

Annex 2A.3 Enrollment at UNIMA per 100,000 Inhabitants by District *(continued)*

District	Enrollment					Population			Enrollment per 100,000 (2009)	Enrollment per 100,000 (2010)
	Male	Female	Total	% of female	% of total	Male	Female	Total		
Ntcheu	38	30	68	44.1	6.0	232,235	254,058	486,293	14	19
Ntchisi	14	8	22	36.4	1.9	114,330	119,151	233,481	9	19
Phalombe	16	12	28	42.9	2.5	152,846	169,121	321,967	9	17
Rumphi	16	8	24	33.3	2.1	87,297	89,934	177,231	14	19
Salima	17	6	23	26.1	2.0	170,985	178,662	349,647	7	17
Thyolo	31	23	54	42.6	4.7	282,923	302,262	585,185	9	16
Zomba	38	27	65	41.5	5.7	330,977	355,915	686,892	9	15

Source: Higher Education Institutions.

Annex 2A.4 Male and Female Enrollment by Program—2008–11

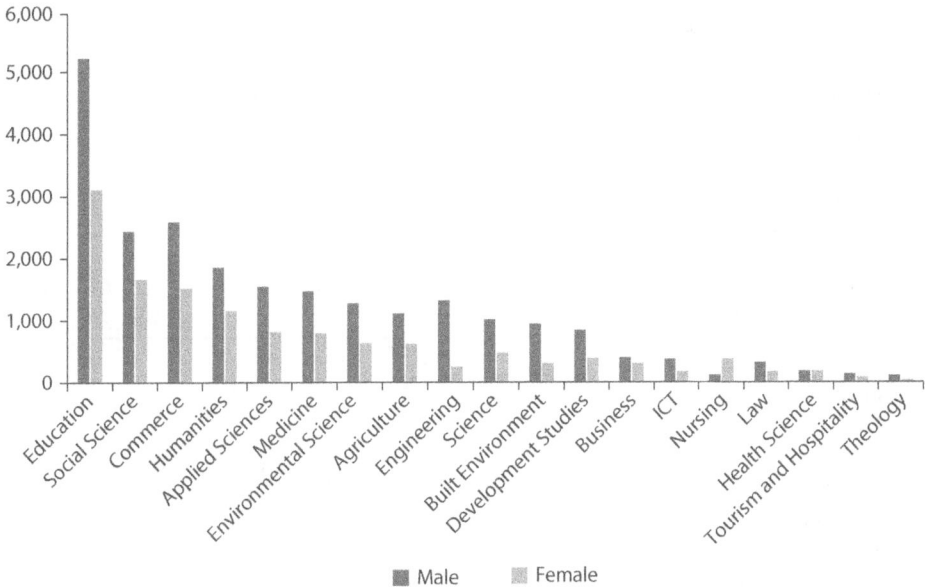

Source: Higher Education Institutions.

Annex 2A.5 Postgraduate Programs Offered in Institutions by Faculty

Bunda

Agriculture
Masters Plant Breeding
Masters Agronomy
Masters Nutrition
Masters Crop Protection
Masters Soil Science
Masters Animal Science
Masters Entomology
Masters Food Science & Human Nut
PhD Animal Science

Development Studies
Masters Agribusiness Management
Masters Agricultural Economics
Masters Agricultural Extension
PhD Agriculture & Resource Economics
PhD Agricultural Extension

Environmental Studies
Masters Fisheries
Masters Agro Forestry
Masters Horticulture
Masters Social Forestry
Masters Aquaculture & Fisheries
PhD Aquaculture & Fisheries

College of Medicine

Medicine
MPH
Mmed Internal Medicine
Mmed Pediatrics
Mmed Surgery
Mmed Psychiatry
Mmed Anesthesia

Kamuzu College of Nursing (KCN)

Nursing
Masters of Science Child Health Nursing Year I
Masters of Science Child Health Nursing Year II
Masters of Science Midwifery I
Masters of Science Midwifery II
Masters of Science Reproductive Health Year I
Masters of Science Reproductive Health Year II

table continues next page

Table 2A.5 Postgraduate Programs Offered in Institutions by Faculty *(continued)*

Malawi Polytechnic

Postgraduate Diploma Management Studies (DMS)
Masters Business Administration (MBA)
Masters of Science Infrastructure Development and Management (MScIDM)

MZUNI

Faculty of Education
MA Theology & Religious Studies
PhD Theology
MA Education
MSc (ITCC)

Faculty of Information & Communication
MA Information Theory Coding & Cryptography
Postgraduate Diploma (Instructional Technology)

Source: Higher Education Institutions.

Annex 2A.6 Gender Parity Index by Standard (Primary and Secondary Education)—2010

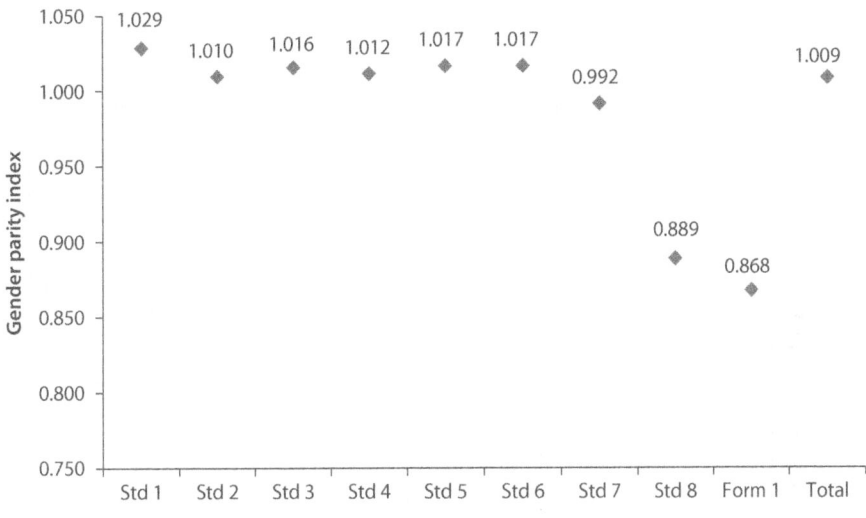

Source: 2011 EMIS Data.

Annex 2A.7 Student/Lecturer Ratios by Institution and Faculty—2011

Institution	Education	Business	Theology	Social Science	Commerce	Agriculture	Development Studies	Environment Studies	Health Science	Tourism	ICT	Applied Science	Built Environment	Engineering	Medicine	Law	Humanities
Bunda						10	12	8									
Chancellor																	
COM															7		
KCN									9								
Polytechnic	12				16												
MZUNI	12							25	12	20	16						
MAU	14	35										10	17	9			
CUNIMA	4			38	34												
UNILIA	11																

Source: Higher Education Institutions.

Annex 2A.8 Summary of Usage of Infrastructure in Institutions

Institution	Efficiency percentage	Infrastructure
Malawi Adventist University	There is a 95 percent usage of the facilities. Facilities are used from 7 am to 9 pm.	Seven classrooms, one lecture room, two computer labs and one multipurpose hall.
Bunda College of Agriculture	Usage of the infrastructure and facilities was estimated at between 80 percent and 90 percent.	Between 13 and 15 classrooms; 10 laboratories; 3 lecture theatres; and one Hall.
Chancellor College	The infrastructure in the institution is overused and poses timetabling challenges. The institution was established a long time ago for a small number of students and as a result the classes are far too small for the current class sizes resulting in crowding.	Infrastructure comprises of two lecture theatres for 100 students; great hall which can sit 400; four classrooms for 100 each; 15 tutorials rooms; 20 laboratories
Catholic University	Usage of facilities is estimated at 60 percent	Two computer labs with 40 and 60 computers which are open until 17:30.
Kamuzu College of Nursing		Classrooms are under-utilized when students take up clinical placements. More students could be enrolled if more clinical instructors could be engaged. About 30 would be needed.
University of Livingstonia	Usage of facilities is around 95 percent.	The institution used the May vacation to provide additional classes for levels 1 and 3. This resulted in increased usage of the facilities.
Mzuzu University	Due to high current enrollment and incomplete buildings, usage of infrastructure is approximately 95 percent.	

Source: Higher Education Institutions.

Notes

1. See annex 2A.1.
2. This figure does not include enrollment at the private universities of Blantyre International University and the Baptist University of Mangochi.
3. Exchange Rate USD 1 = MK 165 (2011).
4. The College of Medicine and Kamuzu College of Nursing do not enroll non-residential students because of the nature of the programs they offer. Data on non-residential students was not provided by MZUNI.
5. 2011 data for Chancellor College was not available.
6. Data for Chancellor College and MZUNI are missing.
7. See figure 2.3.
8. See annex 2A.8 for summary of usage of infrastructure.
9. Students spend time at the hospitals during clinical period leaving the classrooms empty.
10. This is the target that has been set in the Monitoring and Evaluation Framework for the MoEST.

11. See table 2.1.
12. See figure 2.7.
13. See annex 2A.4.
14. This figure is obtained by assuming that the students in Form 4 are a quarter of the total secondary enrollment.
15. It was not possible to verify enrollments by districts prior to the introduction of the Equitable Access Policy as universities did not record this information routinely.
16. See annex 2A.3 for details.
17. Both the UNIMA and MZUNI projects do not provide annual growth rates but the total growth over the plan periods. This poses problems of monitoring progress in enrollments over the plan period.

CHAPTER 3

Quality and Relevance of Higher Education in Malawi

Introduction

This chapter reports on the findings of the study with regard to the quality and relevance of programs offered in the Malawian higher education sub-sector. In general, quality in higher education is difficult to define, due to the absence of universally applied and internationally recognized academic standards. While standards frame the level of achievement a student must demonstrate in order to be granted an academic award, academic quality relates to the learning opportunities available to a student in the achievement of their award. Quality is product of the appropriateness and effectiveness teaching, support for students, assessment, and learning opportunities provided to them through their course of study.

Traditionally, quality has been measured in relation to the characteristics of inputs to institutions and programs, *inter alia*: admission requirements; the qualifications of faculty; class sizes and student-lecturer ratios; the availability of appropriate infrastructure and physical facilities; assessment procedures; and, in some cases, the tuition fees. In recent years, however, there has been a shift from inputs towards a focus on outputs, as the latter is considered a more useful measure of value-for-money and the relevance of programs. An assessment of outputs may include: the number of graduates; the appropriateness of degrees offered to a country or region's development needs; the number of graduates who find employment in their field of study, or who are accepted into advanced degree programs; and the quantity and appropriateness of the research output and community outreach activities. Materu (2007) defines quality as "fitness for purpose"; meeting or conforming to generally accepted standards as defined by an institution, quality assurance bodies and appropriate academic and professional communities. In the diverse arena of higher education, fitness for purpose varies significantly by field and program.

Ensuring quality is also associated with accountability in a number of ways. States require accountability with regard to optimizing the use of public resources allocated to higher education, and the alignment of output with national economic need. Moreover, accountability serves to protect the interests of consumers, ensures value in return for the investments students make in higher education programs, and in ensuring that programs meet the expectations of both students and employers. Accountability also ensures the attainment and preservation of appropriate standards for professional programs (such as medicine, law and accounting) that directly impact the public.

Quality Assurance Policies in Malawi

To ensure the maintenance and protection of standards, many countries establish quality assurance bodies. Towards this end, the Parliament of Malawi passed a National Council for Higher Education Act in 2011. Materu (2007) notes that quality assurance systems are a relatively recent development in Africa, but that the concept is gaining momentum as a result of the growing importance of private tertiary institutions whose activities need to be regulated.

The NCHE is tasked with promoting and coordinating higher education; harmonizing admissions standards across all public universities; the determination, maintenance and regulation of standards for teaching, examinations, academic qualifications, and academic facilities; the development of a national qualifications framework compatible with regional and international standards; and the design and implementation of institutional quality assurance systems for higher education. The NCHE will register and deregister higher education institutions using established criteria and procedures. The NCHE commenced operations in 2013, however there is a need to speed up the implementation of complementary legislation to strengthen the regulation of universities and institutions of higher learning. Some functions currently overseen by university councils with regard to quality could be superseded by the activities of the NCHE, enabling councils to concentrate on their administrative and management functions.

Findings of the Study

Quality of Higher Education in Malawi

This report measures quality through an analysis of inputs in terms of levels of staffing, staff qualifications, infrastructure supporting the learning environment, ICT facilities, the quality and relevance of curricula and learning and teaching materials, and the financing of higher education. The report also presents an analysis of processes to assess of staff and lecturers, and the assessment methods used to validate standards for degree programs. The quality of graduates is assessed using the results of a tracer study administered in 2006 which provided information on the satisfaction of employers with regard to the relevance and quality of the university graduates.[1]

Impact of Increased Enrollment on Quality

As noted in chapter 2, net enrollment in public and private higher education increased from 8,375 in 2008 to 11,623 in 2011. Expanded enrollment has generated increased systemic pressures and has presented challenges to the sector with regard to the maintenance of quality.

Staffing Levels

A critical input for the delivery of quality education in any institution is the presence of suitably qualified academic and administrative staff in the appropriate numbers. Due to the gaps in data, and suboptimal data provided by institutions with regard to their "establishments", it was difficult to assess the adequacy of staffing or evaluate the prevalence of vacancies in the Malawian higher education system through this study.[2] As a consequence this report does not make a determination as to whether current staffing levels are appropriate in the context of current enrollment of student. Most public institutions indicated that their establishments were set a long time ago and were no longer realistic in terms of current staffing needs, suggesting that there has not been a review of establishments despite increasing enrollments. Some institutions like MZUNI were in the process of initiating a functional review to update their establishments in line with enrollment trends. UNILIA does not have establishments and staff are recruited on the basis of need in an effort to reduce institutional dependence on adjunct staff, a common practice in private institutions faced with staff shortages. CUNIMA indicated that its establishment is fully subscribed.

Institutions indicated that a lack of funding was the biggest constraint to the expansion of establishments. Evidence suggests that public institutions have frozen posts as a cost saving measure, leading to a greater reliance on adjunct staff. However, the use of adjuncts in response to increasing enrollments tends to erode short-term savings associated with the freezing of posts. One institution was able to provide information on cost-savings arising from the freezing of establishments, but these were not substantive.

Figure 3.1 illustrates staffing trends for the period under review. The data demonstrates that at Bunda, COM and MZUNI the number of academic staff has remained relatively constant despite a steady increase in student enrollment. The Polytechnic experienced a downward trend in staffing levels, while KCN, CUNIMA, MAU and UNILIA modestly increased their cohort of academic staff. Progressive increases in enrollment resulted in a system-wide increase in Student Lecturer Ratios (SLR) from an average of 6:1 (2003–08) to 12:1 by 2011.

Figure 3.2 illustrates trends in SLRs for institutions for the period under review (2008–11). The figure shows variation in SLRs both within and between institutions, with SLRs ranging from 4:1 to 27:1 in 2008, and 7:1 to 19:1 in 2011. MAU had the highest SLR in 2008 (27:1), and while it managed to improve this to 19:1 by 2011, MAUs SLR remains the highest of surveyed institutions.

With the exception of MAU, KCN and MZUNI, the SLRs for all institutions demonstrate an upward trend suggesting (if well managed) improved and more

Figure 3.1 Staffing Trends by Institution—2008–11

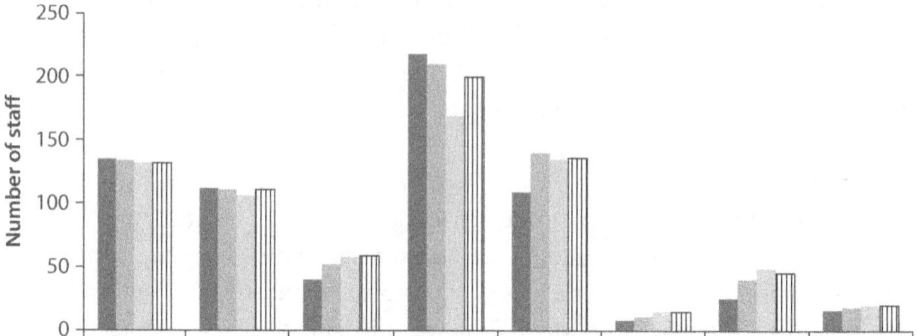

	Bunda	COM	KCN	Polytech	MZUNI	MAU	CUNIMA	UNILIA
2008	135	112	40	218	109	8	25	16
2009	134	111	52	210	140	11	40	18
2010	132	106	58	169	135	15	49	20
2011	132	111	59	200	136	15	46	20

Source: Higher Education Institutions.

Figure 3.2 Student–Lecturer Ratios by Institution by Year—2008–11

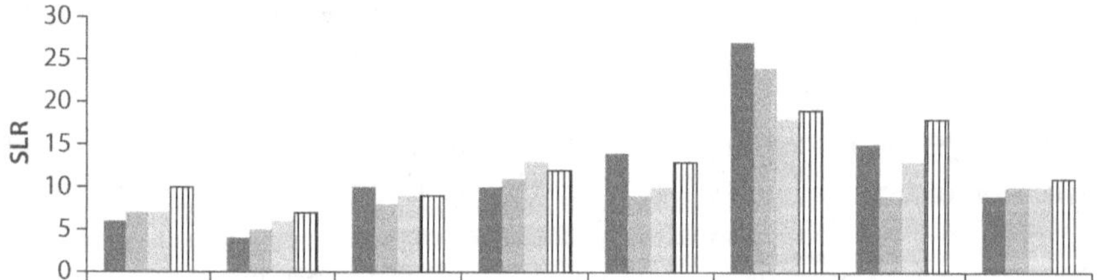

	Bunda	COM	KCN	Polytech	MZUNI	MAU	CUNIMA	UNILIA
2008	6	4	10	10	14	27	15	9
2009	7	5	8	11	9	24	9	10
2010	7	6	9	13	10	18	13	10
2011	10	7	9	12	13	19	18	11

Source: Higher Education Institutions.
Note: SLR = Student Lecturer Ratios.

efficient use of staff in the institutions. This suggests that there is room for increasing enrollment without necessarily increasing the number of lecturing staff.

Table 3.1 illustrates SLRs by faculty for universities that were able to provide data. The table demonstrates significant variance in SLR across faculties within institutions, as well as large differences between SLRs for the same faculties across institutions. For example the SLR for Education was 4:1 at CUNIMA, 12:1 at MZUNI and the Polytechnic, and 14:1 at MAU, and the SLR for Commerce was 16:1 at the Polytechnic and 34:1 at CUNIMA. These differences may be associated with differences in the ways in which staff are used in

Table 3.1 Student Lecturer Ratios by Institution and Faculty—2011

Institution	Education	Business	Theology	Social Science	Commerce	Agriculture	Development Studies	Environment Studies	Health Science	Tourism	ICT	Applied Science	Built Environment	Engineering	Medicine	Law	Humanities
Bunda						10	12	8									
Chancellor																	
COM															7		
KCN									9								
Polytechnic	12				16												
MZUNI	12							25	12	20	16	10	17	9			
MAU	14	35															
CUNIMA	4			38	34												
UNILIA	11																

Source: Higher Education Institutions.

institutions. Moreover, differences in SLRs for similar programs offered in different institutions, raises questions with regard to the quality of the degrees offered by different institutions. This study was not able to make a determination with regard to the impact of SLRs on quality.

It is also not clear to what extent changes in SLRs have impacted the quality of graduates from universities from the point of view of employers. This study is limited by its reliance on one tracer study administered in 2006, before changes in admissions policies and equity provisions began to impact enrollment. The 2006 study found that the majority of graduates—irrespective of their gender, year of graduation and occupational status—believed that their qualifications enabled them to fulfill their professional obligations, that graduates perceived that they were in a position to apply the knowledge accrued through university study in their work, and that graduates were generally satisfied with their professional situation. The study found that employers were somewhat satisfied with the level of knowledge and skills of graduates, noting that the performance of approximately 15 percent to 20 percent of graduates did not meet their expectations. Satisfaction on the part of employers varied greatly with regard to their assessment of graduates from different institutions.[3]

Staff Qualifications

The qualifications of staff are important determinants of quality in higher education. University lecturers in Malawi are required to hold, at a minimum, a master's degree in the field in which they are teaching and conducting research. However studies show that in practice a large number of lecturers employed as associate lecturers at Malawian universities hold only undergraduate qualifications (World Bank 2010b). Annex 3A.1 summarizes statistics on the number of staff in each institution and their qualification, while

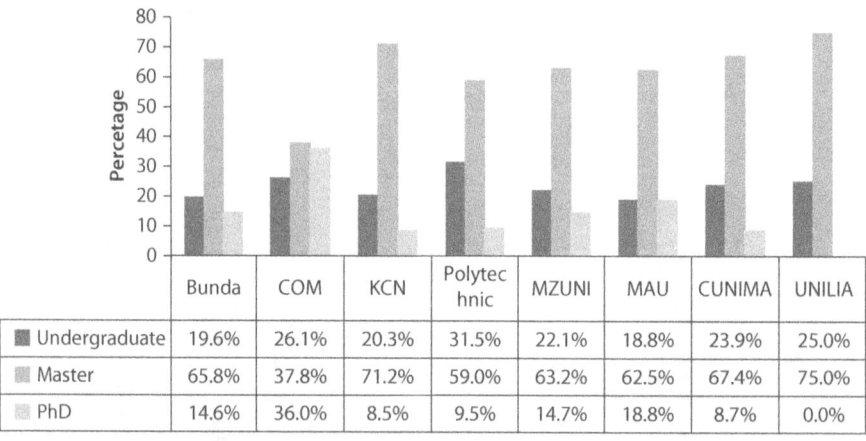

Figure 3.3 Distribution of Staff by Qualification—2011

	Bunda	COM	KCN	Polytechnic	MZUNI	MAU	CUNIMA	UNILIA
■ Undergraduate	19.6%	26.1%	20.3%	31.5%	22.1%	18.8%	23.9%	25.0%
■ Master	65.8%	37.8%	71.2%	59.0%	63.2%	62.5%	67.4%	75.0%
■ PhD	14.6%	36.0%	8.5%	9.5%	14.7%	18.8%	8.7%	0.0%

Source: Higher Education Institutions.

figure 3.3 illustrates the distribution of staff by qualification in each institution in 2011. The data demonstrates that with the exception of COM, where a plurality of lecturing staff hold a masters qualification, lecturers with masters qualifications constitute a majority of lecturers at all institutions. The proportion of lecturers with master's degrees ranges from 37.8 percent at COM to 75 percent at UNILIA. The proportion of lecturers holding undergraduate degrees only ranges from 18.8 percent at MAU to 31.5 percent at the Polytechnic.[4] Of concern is the fact that, with the exception of COM and MAU, a larger percentage of lecturers holds undergraduate degrees than PhD qualifications.

Figure 3.4 illustrates staffing levels by professional designation within institutions, with the highest percentage of staff retained at lecturer grade, ranging from 40.5 percent at COM to 75 percent at UNILIA.

With the exception of MAU and CUNIMA, institutions have higher percentages of associate lecturers than senior lecturers. The percentage of senior lecturers ranges from 11.8 percent at MZUNI to 18.9 percent at COM, and UNILIA does not have any staff at grades higher than lecturer grade. The percentage of associate professors and professors (generally associated with a PhD qualification) is very small for all institutions, with the highest percentage evident at MAU (16.7 percent), followed by Bunda College (14.5 percent). Annex 3A.2 shows the number and distribution of lecturers by designation.

The trend over the period 2008–11, although erratic, shows that the percentage of the lecturers with master's and PhD qualifications has increased. Annexes 3A.3 to 3A.6 show trends in staffing by qualification for the institutions surveyed. The annexes demonstrate a general increase in the number of staff holding master's degrees, with the exception of COM where a decrease in the

Figure 3.4 Staffing Levels by Designation by Institution—2011

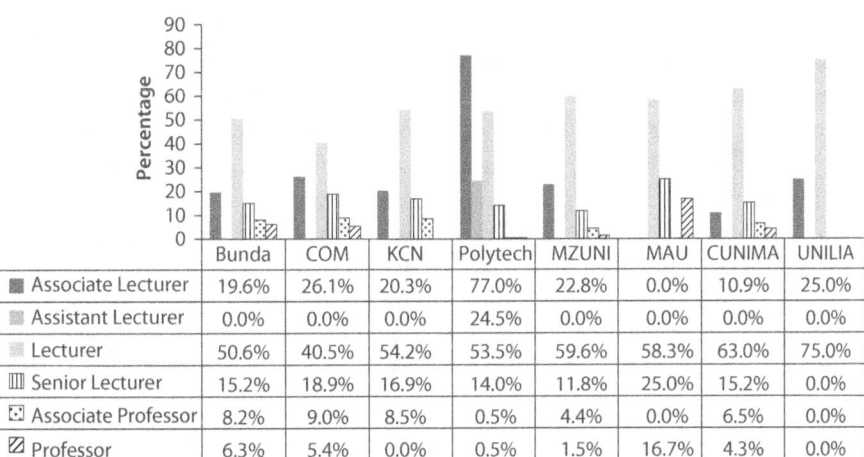

	Bunda	COM	KCN	Polytech	MZUNI	MAU	CUNIMA	UNILIA
■ Associate Lecturer	19.6%	26.1%	20.3%	77.0%	22.8%	0.0%	10.9%	25.0%
▒ Assistant Lecturer	0.0%	0.0%	0.0%	24.5%	0.0%	0.0%	0.0%	0.0%
░ Lecturer	50.6%	40.5%	54.2%	53.5%	59.6%	58.3%	63.0%	75.0%
▥ Senior Lecturer	15.2%	18.9%	16.9%	14.0%	11.8%	25.0%	15.2%	0.0%
⋮ Associate Professor	8.2%	9.0%	8.5%	0.5%	4.4%	0.0%	6.5%	0.0%
▨ Professor	6.3%	5.4%	0.0%	0.5%	1.5%	16.7%	4.3%	0.0%

Source: Higher Education Institutions.

number of staff holding masters degrees is offset by an increase in the number of staff holding PhDs. The number of staff with PhDs has remained consistently low across the system, with only COM demonstrating a healthy increase in this cohort of staff. The number of staff with undergraduate degree qualifications demonstrates an upward trend in private institutions and a downward trend in public institutions. This trend is likely a consequence of staff development initiatives in public institutions, in which faculty members are given support to pursue advanced degrees.

Staff Development Programs

The need to improve the qualifications of lecturers is recognized as an important component of overall strategies to improve the quality of instruction in the higher education sub-sector. As a consequence, institutions have initiated staff development and training programs to improve the qualifications of lecturers. Annex 3A.7 shows the number of academic staff in both private and public universities pursuing programs to upgrade their qualifications. The majority of staff being supported through these initiatives are pursuing PhDs and master's degrees. Chancellor College has the largest number of staff studying at PhD level (33) followed by the Polytechnic (12) and KCN (10). MZUNI has the largest number of staff studying at master's level (15) followed by the Polytechnic (12) and Chancellor College (9). Information from the institutions indicates that the majority of staff supported through these programs are pursuing their degrees through institutions in the United Kingdom and the United States, as well as institutions in the SADC region. A minority of supported staff are studying in China, while some staff from private institutions are studying at the colleges of UNIMA and MZUNI.

Staff development and training programs in public institutions are financed primarily by the government, with some support from development partners. For example the World Bank-supported Education Sector Support Project (ESSUP) supported the training of staff from the education faculties of Chancellor College and Polytechnic at the master's and PhD. Staff studying in China receives support from the Chinese government. A number of those enrolled at Chancellor College and the Polytechnic are supported through externally-funded projects with staff development components. Staff pursuing higher degrees at the three private institutions surveyed, support the cost of these studies independently as the institutions do not have the resources to support staff development. In spite of the support afforded by public institutions to employees enrolled in development programs, some staff support themselves (as is the case of three lecturers at the Polytechnic). Other sources of funding for upgrading staff include Commonwealth Scholarships, The Fulbright Program, Beit and Rhodes Scholarships, the Norwegian Agency for Development Cooperation (NORAD) and Collins for Southern Africa for Postgraduate Programs.

Information on the cost of staff development is poor, but it is estimated that the total budget for the program at MZUNI was approximately MK 73 million. The ESSUP project provided MK 5 million for staff development at the

Polytechnic and Chancellor College. Government supported staff development programs in the public universities have been aligned with the priority of the MDGS to improve the quality of higher education through the provision of PhD level training to existing staff and the training of new staff.

Staff development should ensure practical teaching skills relating to the structure of courses, planning for lectures, effective teaching methodologies, the management of classrooms, and the assessment of students. It is unclear to what extent these areas of development have been incorporated into existing programs.

Institutions have adopted different strategies aimed at upgrading teaching methodologies and the quality of teaching. Each UNIMA college has established a Committee on University Teaching and Learning (CUTL) which inducts new staff on how to teach and assess students. Each CUTL is expected to organize in each semester workshops to update lecturers' teaching and assessment methods. In practice, CUTLs have not been very active, and attendance at workshops is reportedly poor. As a result, there are plans to introduce a postgraduate diploma in university teaching to incentivize improvement and regularize programs across UNIMA colleges and MZUNI. However it is not yet clear how participation will be incentivized or if it will be compulsory.

MZUNI has introduced a program on teaching methodologies, at the end of which staff will receive a University Certificate of Education (UCE). However this program has not been customized to the needs of different faculties. Workshops on the delivery of lessons have been run occasionally, but participation, especially on the part of senior staff, has reportedly been poor.

CUNIMA organizes workshops on teaching supervision, testing and measurement, and student evaluation, as well as orientation courses for new lecturers. MAU organizes seminars and training sessions on teaching methods, provides lecturers with notes on grade assessment at the beginning of each year, and has developed a manual for the induction of new lecturers. UNILIA has also developed manuals for use by lecturers but does not have a formal program for staff in this regard.

Information provided by universities demonstrates a commitment on the part of institutions to training and staff development. These efforts will need to be sustained and intensified to ensure their effectiveness. Programs should be monitored and evaluated to ensure efficiency, and that the content of schemes is relevant to the needs of lecturers and students. To date, there have been no attempts to measure the quality and relevance of these programs. The situation is made more difficult by the absence of system wide standards, but it is expected that the NCHE will address once it is fully operational.

Internal Academic Staff Assessment Methods, Performance Incentives and Promotion Criteria Used in Institutions

Staff Assessment

One means of incentivizing improved quality in the delivery of teaching, research and community outreach, is to conduct regular performance assessments of staff and align the output thereof with clearly delineated promotion criteria to motivate staff. Currently, institutions in Malawi do not have internal quality assurance mechanisms, and information provided by institutions shows that there are no formal assessments of staff performance with regard to teaching, research and community outreach. In general, staff performance is only assessed when, at their own initiative, they apply for promotion. In the absence of any records of previous performance, it is not clear how these assessments are undertaken.

UNIMA recently implemented a system of student assessment of staff in which, at the end of each semester, students use a form designed to evaluate the performance of the lecturer and the usefulness of the course. The exercise is coordinated by the registrar of the university with analysis of outcomes performed by the University Office (UO). While the introduction of some form of assessment is welcomed, the results of the assessment have not been made available, and as a consequence it is not known how useful and effective this method will be in assessing the performance of the staff and the relative worth of programs offered. As can be expected, there has been some resistance to the assessment on the part of lecturers and it is not known to what end the data is being collected. Staff concerns cannot be dealt with until the assessment results are published. At the time of data collection, a Job Evaluation and Performance Appraisal consultancy was being prepared to inform a performance appraisal system for the UNIMA colleges.

There is no regular form of staff evaluation at MZUNI, and staff appraisal is only done in cases of career advancement and promotion. At the time of data collection, student evaluations of lecturers and courses had been introduced in one department and it was expected that it would be applied to other faculties in due course.

Staff assessment takes a slightly different form in the private colleges. At CUNIMA and MAU, staff is evaluated by heads of departments (HODs). CUNIMA is yet to define the assessment format it will use, while MAU has a more formalized system wherein staff evaluations are initiated by the HODs and forwarded to the Dean of Academic Affairs for review. Part of staff evaluation at MAU takes the form of lesson observation by HODs who evaluate classroom instruction against pre-formatted criteria. CUNIMA also uses student evaluations to evaluate lecturers and courses at the end of each semester. UNILIA currently does not use student evaluations to assess staff and courses, but the university maintains that there are avenues for students to pursue concerns and complaints, and that these are adequately addressed.

The absence of appraisal arrangements is not unique to the Malawian higher education system, and has been identified as a weakness in the management of higher education institutions in general (Scribbin and Walton 1987). However, other systems have introduced forms of staff appraisal as part of a wider system of performance management linked to institutional strategic goals (Morris, Stanton, and Young 2007). Malawi has lagged other countries in establishing these types of systems. Staff appraisal was defined by Edward (1984) as an opportunity to review and discuss with each individual, his/her past performance and based on the conclusions reached, agree on a plan of action/priorities for the future (Edward 1984). In this context, staff appraisal is intended to improve staff performance, contribute to staff development, and should constitute an important component of broader strategies to improve the quality of higher education provision. Staff appraisal is also essential for ensuring academic accountability with respect to the use of resources allocated to higher education institutions. However, staff appraisal can be misused and there have controversies with the way in which it has been implemented, leading to resistance on the part of lecturers to participate in assessment activities. Consequently it is vital to develop a fair and transparent system of staff appraisal aimed at enhancing staff productivity and improving the quality of teaching and research activities.

Performance Incentives
Incentives are used to encourage workers to pursue excellence and maintain good performance (Baldwin and Krotseng 1985), and are also useful in promoting workforce stability, and to stimulate productivity (Eventual 1976). Smith (2005) highlights the fact that there are no perfect incentives that appeal to all workers, and that achieving sustained excellence in higher education depends on the alignment incentives with personal and institutional values. While much of the literature focusses on extrinsic incentives, intrinsic incentives aligned with self-actualization are often ignored. Examples of extrinsic incentives that have been used in higher education institutions include: money, allowances, awards, praise, promotion and other task-related incentives, which may be monetary or non-monetary.

Aside from promotion, there are no performance incentives evident in either of the public institutions and two of the private universities.[5] MAU is the only institution that has a comprehensive package of allowances and incentives for its staff, including a "yard allowance" (towards the maintenance of yards at their houses); additional pay for lecturers who take on heavy workloads; a thirteenth paycheck for all staff; tax assistance; education and health assistance; air time for cell phones; and book and equipment allowances. Of these the allowances and incentives offered to staff at MAU, only the measure to provide additional pay for comparatively heavy workloads is performance related. However, in the absence of defined criteria and standards for measuring quality, it is difficult to determine the impact of the incentives on the performance of the lecturers and on the quality of education delivered at MAU.

Promotion Criteria
Public institutions have clearly articulated criteria which staff must fulfill in order to be promoted from the grade of lecturer to professor related to the publication of research in peer reviewed journals. Promotion from lecturer to senior lecturer requires the publication of a minimum of two articles in refereed journals; promotion from senior lecturer to associate professor requires a minimum

of an additional five new articles published in peer reviewed journals; and thereafter promotion from the grade of associate professor to full professor requires the publication of an additional seven new articles in peer reviewed journals. However, information on the number of articles published by Malawian academic staff was not readily available. The authoring of book chapters, and the production of music compositions, plays and art exhibitions are also taken into consideration in the promotion of academic staff at public institutions. Feedback from universities, however, highlighted the insufficient number of mentors in the colleges to assist junior staff in publishing and research, due to a brain drain of PhD holders and professors (except in COM, as already noted above).

External Examiners

The use of external examiners to enhance and maintain the quality of degrees awarded by institutions is a fairly standard practice in systems of higher education in Commonwealth countries. External examiners are considered to be more objective in their assessment of education programs than professors and other staff whose livelihoods are dependent on the system in question. The role of external examiners is critical for the assessment and award of qualifications at the discipline level; processes of validation and review; verification and maintenance of standards and their comparability; and for institutional development (Assuring Quality and Standards in Higher Education: The Quality Assurance Agency for Higher Education 2010).

The system of utilizing external examiners in Malawi public higher education institutions is not as prevalent as it used to be due to the cost of bringing external examiners to the country. The system varies from institution to institution, and from faculty to faculty, especially in undergraduate programs. Those that do use external examiners, generally use examiners from the region rather than bringing in examiners from overseas. In instances where external examiners are not used for quality assurance, examination scripts are assessed at departmental level, and then at the college level, before approval by the Senate.

The departments select their own external examiners. To defray costs, external examiners are sometimes brought in every two years rather than every year. In some cases, interaction with external examiners is conducted by mail, wherein courses and examination scripts are sent to the examiners by post for review. These practices have cumulatively reduced the rigor of the external examiner system.

Information made available for the purposes of this study indicates that all public universities use external examiners to assist with quality assurance in the provision of postgraduate degree programs. This is important, especially in light of the low number of PhD holders in Malawian institutions. In order to address challenges with regard to the retention of external examiners, MZUNI created a Department of Quality Assurance, comprised of three senior academic staff tasked with ensuring quality in the university by identifying and addressing weaknesses and the monitor of teaching. It was not possible to rigorously assess the use of external examiners in Malawian institutions, due to poor and inconsistent record keeping, and due to the fact that the intensity of their use changes from year to year.

Private universities utilize local examiners, generally from the public higher education sub-sector, to perform the duties of external examiners in an effort to reduce associated costs. UNILIA use examiners from MZUNI and UNIMA, while CUNIMA utilizes examiners from Chancellor College, the Polytechnic and MZUNI. MAU is affiliated with Baraton University in Kenya, which provides external examiners. External examiners in the private sub-sector are used to moderate examinations and review course outlines prior to their finalization and implementation.

The piecemeal and haphazard use of external examiners, representing the erosion of a previously entrenched system which contributed to quality assurance, is cause for concern. While it is costly to retain external examiners, more significant real and social costs are incurred if the quality of higher education is compromised.

Availability of Teaching and Learning Materials

Teaching and learning materials are recognized as important inputs associated with quality. Figure 3.5 visualizes feedback from universities rating the availability of library books, journals and publications. Institutions were asked to assess the availability of these resources on a scale of 1 to 5 (1-Very Poor, 2-Poor, 3-Satisfactory, 4-Good, and 5-Very Good).

Universities generally reported the availability of library books as Satisfactory, with MAU and KCN rating their availability as "Good". Similarly, the availability of journals and publications was rated as "Satisfactory", except at CHANCO and

Figure 3.5 Availability of Teaching and Learning Materials by Institution—2011

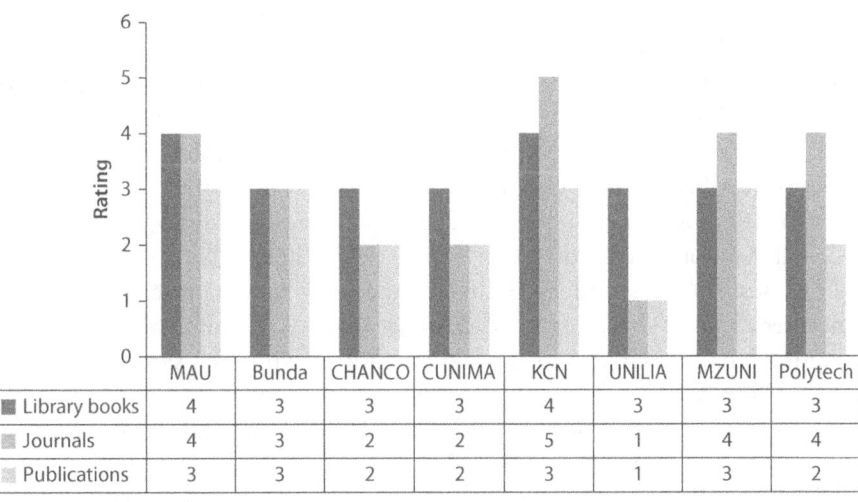

	MAU	Bunda	CHANCO	CUNIMA	KCN	UNILIA	MZUNI	Polytech
Library books	4	3	3	3	4	3	3	3
Journals	4	3	2	2	5	1	4	4
Publications	3	3	2	2	3	1	3	2

Source: Higher Education Institutions.

CUNIMA which rated access to journals and publication as "Poor", and UNILIA which rated it "Very Poor". The universities indicated that funding for learning and teaching materials is generally provided by government and donors, with few private contributions in this regard.

Government resources to fund the procurement of library books and journals in public universities are ring-fenced to ensure the availability of these important teaching and learning materials. The improved availability of journals and publications is due to that fact that the majority of institutions now subscribe to e-journals through the Internet at comparatively favorable rates, making access to journals more cost-effective. Feedback from universities noted that there was some resistance on the part of older lecturers with regard to accepting e-journals as quotable sources in assignments. While the general trend towards increased access to journals is positive, it is difficult to accurately assess availability due to the complexities of online access and multiple routes of entry. As a result, both students and staff may be unaware of the range of resources available on the Web (Hale 2010). Hale (2010) reports in a case study of four African universities, that awareness of the extent of online resources was lowest at Chancellor College, generally satisfactory at the University of Dar es Salaam, good at the National University of Rwanda, and highest at the University of Nairobi.

Information and Communication Technology (ICT) Facilities

ICT is recognized as an important quality input in that facilitates student access to, and the use of, reading materials on a flexible basis. ICT can also be used to increase access to higher education resources and reduce reliance on traditional face-to-face instruction. In an effort to increase access and the quality of education, most institutions are in the process of introducing e-learning in the form of uploaded course materials that students can access via institutional intranets or the Internet. The successful introduction and use of e-learning will be dependent on the availability of computers for both students and lecturers, and the quality of associated bandwidth.

Figure 3.6 visualizes feedback from institutions with regard to the availability of ICT facilities. UNILIA rated the availability of both computers and Internet connectivity as "Poor", while KCN and Bunda rated the availability of computers as "Satisfactory" and "Good" respectively. The majority of institutions allocated an unfavorable rating to the availability of computers. Connectivity was rated "Poor" by five institutions and "Satisfactory" by the Polytechnic.

Feedback from institutions buttresses the view that there are insufficient computer facilities to meet the needs of students. MAU, for example, has two computer labs containing a total of 48 computers, with each student allocated just one hour of access per day. Moreover, connectivity at MAU is reportedly poor due to the location of the institution. CUNIMA does not have an institutional intranet, and Internet bandwidth is limited to 512kbs. Institutional bandwidth at CUNIMA is very poor considering the number of potential users and

Figure 3.6 Availability of ICT Facilities by Institution—2011

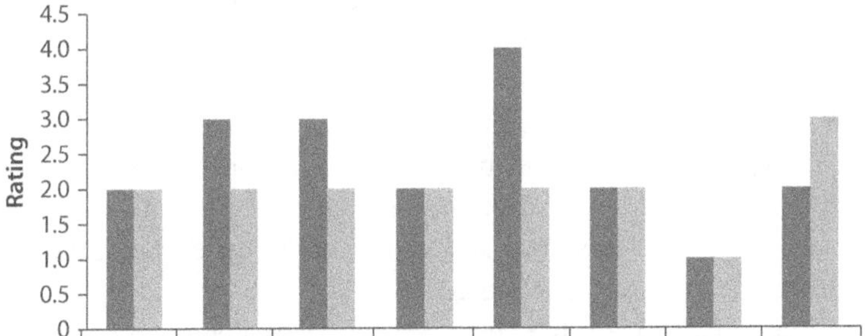

	MAU	Bunda	CHANCO	CUNIMA	KCN	UNILIA	MZUNI	Polytech
Computers	2	3	3	2	4	2	1	2
Internet connectivity	2	2	2	2	2	2	1	3

Source: Higher Education Institutions (1-Very poor, 2-Poor, 3-Satisfactory, 4-Good, and 5-Very Good).

as a result Internet access is severely restricted. UNILIA has a current bandwidth of 1 MB per second which is functions well if access is limited to 20 users at a time.

At MZUNI, access to ICT is limited by the availability of computers. The institution has 60 computers spread across three computer labs catering to the needs of over 2,000 students. As a consequence bandwidth of approximately 1 MB per second is significantly strained. These factors limit the effectiveness of the e-learning program that the institution has introduced. However feedback from the university indicates that almost 50 percent of students now have their own laptops, facilitating greater access to e-learning materials.

At the Polytechnic and Bunda, limited numbers of computers result in an average student-to-computer ratio of 20:1. Chancellor College has joined the Pan-African project supported by the Indian Government which has helped to develop a relatively good network at the institution. The fees paid by the students to access this program have enabled the Chancellor College to increase the number of computers available at the institution.

At UNIMA, a committee has been established to introduce a system-wide ICT system. The institution's financial system has already been digitized and is in the process of being put online. The introduction of an online management information system is in the process of being formulated, and UNIMA plans to upload modules to the Web to facilitate online enrollment. At COM, students are now able to access their examination results on the Internet, and it is expected that this model will be extended to the other colleges of the UNIMA and MZUNI in due course.

Feedback from institutions visualized in figure 3.6 paints a picture of poor Internet connectivity across almost all colleges and universities. With the exception of the Polytechnic, which rated connectivity as "Satisfactory", all institutions rated internet connectivity as "Poor", with MZUNI providing a rating of "Very

Poor". Even if computers were widely available, poor connectivity undermines the ability of students and staff to access information, and stunts the utility of ICT resources. Moreover, due to the fact that institutions do not regularly upgrade their antivirus software—a consequence of poor management and a lack of resources—viruses and spam undermine the use of networks. At Chancellor College, the absence of a campus-wide policy for maintaining filtering and blocking software, and few restrictions on what can be downloaded from the Internet, exacerbates this problem, and significantly undermines the use of available facilities and resources (Hale 2010).

The installation of three high-speed undersea fiber-optic cables in 2009–10 has helped to improve internet connectivity in Africa (Hale 2010). Malawi needs to be more proactive in harnessing improved connectivity to the benefit of the higher education sub-sector. Comprehensive use and management policies are critical to optimize the usability and success of ICT in higher education institutions.

Time Allocated to Teaching, Research and Community Outreach

It was difficult to clearly establish the distribution of institutional time dedicated to three focus areas of university activity: teaching, research and community outreach. However, information reported by institutions indicated that the largest block of time was dedicated to teaching, followed by research and then community outreach. Notwithstanding this general pattern, times allocations varied among institutions and, in some cases, there was no evidence of deliberate efforts to allocate specific portions of time to each of the three activities.

The data indicates that, for both public and private universities in Malawi, the number of teaching hours varies from 9 to 16 hours per week. With the exception of MAU, where three hours per week are allocated to research, no other university indicated prescribed hours in support of research and outreach activities, which tend to be managed independently by staff.

UNIMA has established a committee to evaluate the teaching load of lecturers with the objective of moving towards the achievement of an SLR of 25:1.[6] In support of this objective, it is expected that teaching loads for each lecturer will be between 12 and 16 hours per week. To address variance in contact time by faculty and by institution, the committee is also addressing the distribution of teaching hours with respect to subject areas. For example, fulfillment of a degree program in any faculty at MZUNI requires 120 contact hours per year, accruing to a total of 480 hours for the degree. With the information available, it was not possible to ascertain the number of hours students spend studying.

Graduate Output

The quality and productivity of an institution is in part determined by an assessment of the graduates it produces both in terms of their numbers and in terms the relevance of their knowledge and skills to the needs of society and the economy. An important attribute related to quality is the percent of passes an institution achieves in the delivery of programs across faculties. Analysis of institutional graduate output for this report was constrained by the fact that not all institutions provided complete information for the years under review.[7]

Figure 3.7 illustrates the graduate output of Malawian institutions based on data provided by institutions for graduates enrolled in institutions between 2004 and 2007. Data from World Bank (2010b) demonstrates that university enrollment in Malawi increased from 5,583 in 2004 to 8,474 in 2007, corresponding to a total increase in enrollment of 2,891 and an annual average increase of approximately 950 students. One would generally associate increasing enrollment with an increase in graduate output. In the absence of uniform information from all institutions for the years under review, it was not possible to track the national incidence of graduate output. However as illustrated in figure 3.7, graduate output has followed different trajectories at each institution, with available data indicating an overall upward trend in graduate output. For example, graduate output at Bunda increased between 2008 and 2009, but steadily declined thereafter despite increased enrollment in the period spanning 2004–07. Similarly graduate output at the Polytechnic fell between 2008 and 2009 but has since increased steadily in line with the general trend observed in other institutions.

The data demonstrates that the largest cohorts of graduates are produced by Chancellor College and the Polytechnic, and that the number of graduates from private institutions is low in comparison to public institutions. Despite the limitations of the data provided, figure 3.7 illustrates an increase in total graduate output from 877 in 2008 to 1,994 in 2011. Data for 2010 and 2011 demonstrates that Chancellor accounted for 30.5 and 31 percent of total graduate output respectively, while graduates from the Polytechnic accounted for 26.4 and 24.6 percent of graduates over the same period. UNILIA contributed the lowest

Figure 3.7 Graduate Output by Institution—2008–11

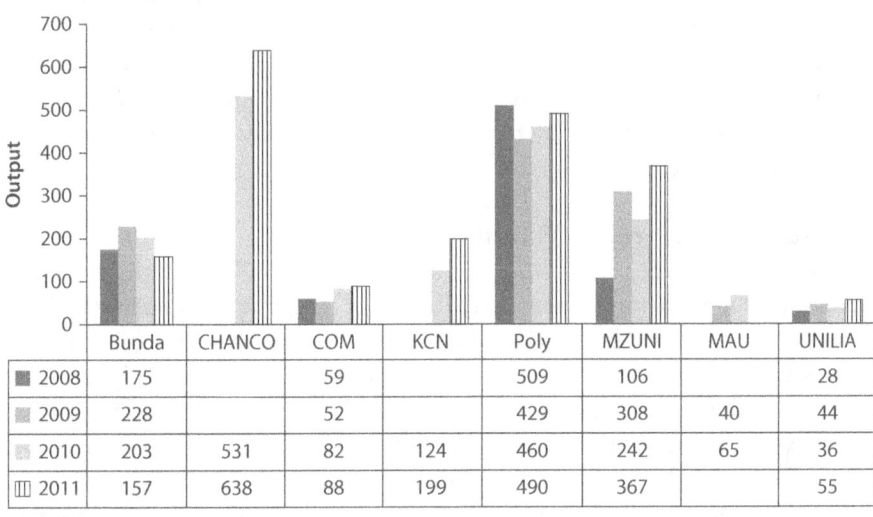

	Bunda	CHANCO	COM	KCN	Poly	MZUNI	MAU	UNILIA
2008	175		59		509	106		28
2009	228		52		429	308	40	44
2010	203	531	82	124	460	242	65	36
2011	157	638	88	199	490	367		55

Source: Higher Education Institutions.

number of graduates to total graduate output, representing 2.1 and 2.8 percent of total output in 2010 and 2011 respectively.

As discussed in the analysis of staffing, the percentage of cohorts demonstrating a pass in their program of study has steadily declined since 2005. While the percentage of passes should not be considered an absolute measure of quality, it is an important proxy for the quality of instruction at the institution. A drop in pass rates could also be associated with other factors such as the overcrowding of classrooms at institutions, or the quality of the MSCE graduates. As enrollments increase, the potential for enrolling a larger number of weaker students also increases.

Available data suggest that a very large portion of the current cohort successfully graduates, with approximately 90 percent of students enrolled in public institutions graduating in the period under review (this rate may be lower in engineering and the sciences where comparatively high dropout rates have been noted).[8] In private institutions the percentage of students who pass is close to 98 percent. Each institution establish a rigorous monitoring system to provide reliable and timely data on dropout and pass rates, and to more accurately assess graduation rates and the length time students take to complete a full course of study. This information is critical to inform an accurate assessment of the internal efficiency of, and the quality of programs offered in, institutions. Universities should also consider the introduction of remedial programs to assist students who struggle with the rigor of higher education and reduce the incidence of dropouts.

Annex 3A.8 shows that, with the exception of KCN where approximately 70 percent of graduate output is female and the private sub-sector, the proportion of female graduates as a share of institutional graduate output has been consistently low despite the introduction of policies to develop more female graduates. In the private sub-sector the percentage of female graduates as a share of total graduate output increased from 22.7 percent in 2009 to 37.3 percent in 2010, and then decreased to 34.9 percent in 2011.

Table 3.2 shows that female graduate output is particularly low in Medicine (23.9 percent), Development Studies (22.9 percent), Law (18.8 percent), Health Science (14.3 percent), and Engineering (10.9 percent). Specific interventions will be required to improve female graduate output in these male dominated programs, through *inter alia*, increasing female enrollment and the provision of remedial programs.

Withdrawal Rates in Higher Education

For the period under review, the rate at which students withdraw from programs without graduating was reportedly low in both public and private higher education institutions. Rates of repetition, and of students switching to programs other than that in which they were originally enrolled, were higher than rates of withdrawal, although rates of withdrawal vary by faculty and institution. Withdrawals in public institutions are mainly related to the performance of students supported by government, and the withdrawal of this support due to poor performance. For self-funded students in public institutions and students enrolled in private institutions, withdrawal is more likely to be related to an inability on the part of these students to sustain the payment of fees. Private institutions try to accommodate students experiencing financial hardship to reduce withdrawal rates and losses incurred through sunk costs associated on the part of students and the institution.

The withdrawal rate as a proportion of total enrollment at Bunda was reported as 3.2 percent in 2010, with the majority of withdrawals concentrated in the science programs. At Bunda the proportion of students repeating a year, inclusive of students who changed their programs without withdrawing from the institution, was reported at 24.2 percent. KCN also reported low withdrawal rates of around one percent of total enrollment, which the institution aligned with rigorous admission methods.

Data from Chancellor College indicates a higher percentage of withdrawals in the fourth year compared to the other years, with the highest number of withdrawals concentrated in Science (21.3 percent) followed by Education (18.5 percent), Social Science (14.4 percent) and the Humanities (2.6 percent) as illustrated in figure 3.8. At Chancellor College non-residential students have higher rates of withdrawal than residential students. In Science the withdrawal rate for non-residential students was 38.7 percent compared to 15 percent for residential students. The pattern associated with comparatively higher rates of withdrawal among non-residential students is observed across other faculties. Female withdrawal rates are also slightly higher than the rates of withdrawal demonstrated by male students.

Data from MZUNI, presented in figure 3.9, shows that in 2010, 26 students withdrew, equivalent to 2.1 percent of total enrollment. Withdrawal percentages are higher for non-residential students in the faculties of Environmental Science, Education and ICT, and higher for residential students in the faculty of Tourism

Figure 3.8 Withdrawal Rates by Faculty and Type of Student—Chancellor College—2010

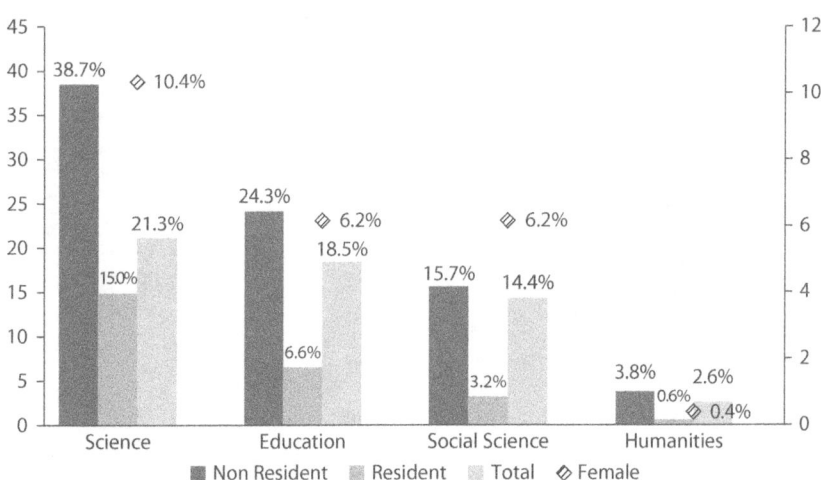

Source: Higher Education Institutions.

and Hospitality. At MZUNI there is no discernible gender trend in withdrawal patterns. The percentage of females who withdrew in Environmental Science was 29.4 percent, 66.7 percent in Tourism and Hospitality, 100 percent in ICT and none in education. There was also a 100 percent withdrawal of non-residential students in ICT.

Data provided by the Polytechnic indicated withdrawal rates below five percent with no gender bias. Fields associated with higher numbers of withdrawals include Engineering, reportedly due to its complexity, and Commerce, because of the large number of students enrolled in the program. Figure 3.10 shows the

Figure 3.9 Withdrawal Rates by Type of Student, Faculty, and Gender: MZUNI—2010

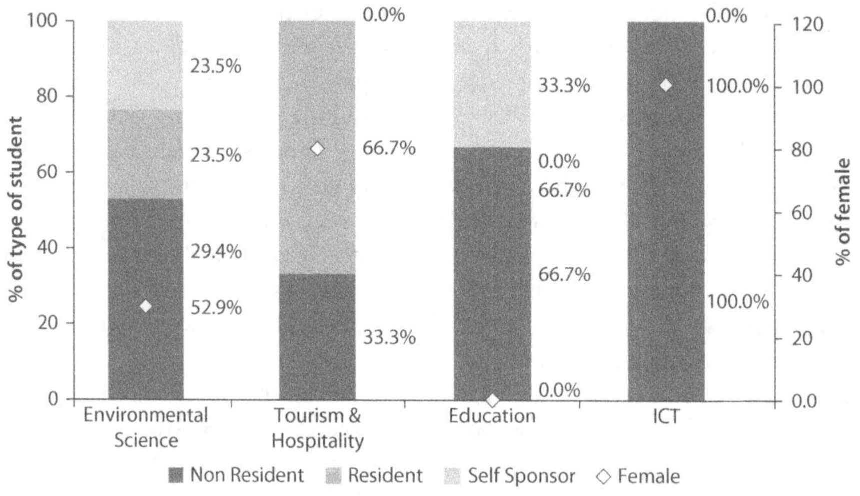

Source: Higher Education Institutions.

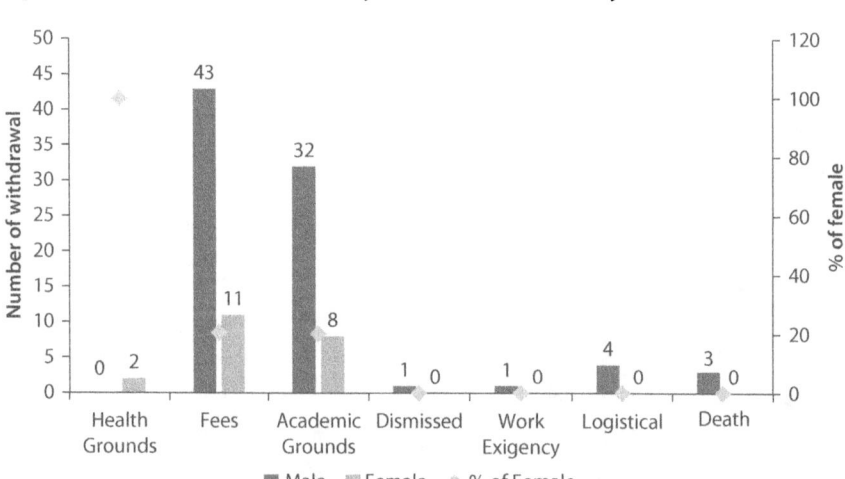

Figure 3.10 Number of Withdrawals by Reason and Gender: Polytechnic—2010

Source: Malawi Polytechnic.

http://dx.doi.org/10.1596/978-1-4648-0798-5

reasons for the withdrawal of 105 students (4.7 percent of total enrollment) in 2010. Fees were cited by 51.4 percent of students as the reason for their withdrawal, followed by 38.1 percent of students who withdrew due to poor academic performance. Health and death accounted for 1.9 and 2.9 percent of withdrawals respectively. The percentage of women who withdrew was lower than that for males.

The relatively high number of students who withdraw due to their inability to service tuition fees implies that the student loan scheme may not be adequately addressing the needs of the high risk groups it was intended to support. The waste of human potential and financial resources associated with withdrawals premised on financial need and poor academic performance, particularly in the fourth year is significant, representing a loss for both the institution and society at large. Academic withdrawals can be reduced through the introduction of remedial programs to support weaker students. Moreover, institutions could do more to identify week students earlier in the program to mitigate dropouts in the final year, by which time many students will have already accrued loans.

The comparatively high rate of withdrawal demonstrated by non-residential students will require further study, especially in light of the intention to expand non-residential enrollment under UNIMA's 3-Phase Plan. In light of the fact that the government provides each non-residential student with a monthly allowance of MK 33,000, the withdrawal of supported students represents a significant financial loss.

MZUNI stopped the practice of administering entrance examinations following the results of a study demonstrating no correlation between performance in the entrance examination and subsequent performance in the degree program. Comparatively low rates of withdrawal at MZUNI seem to confirm that the suspension of entrance examinations has not compromised performance. However MZUNI selects its students before UNIMA, and some students who initially accept places at MZUNI withdraw after receiving offers from UNIMA. The spaces left open by departing students are then difficult to fill.

The introduction of the policy to facilitate equitable access has generated problems at MZUNI and UNIMA, due to the fact that to meet quota requirements, in some cases, both institutions admit the same students. It is anticipated that the NCHE will address these and other selection problems, and help to harmonize the admissions processes across all public institutions.

As previously indicated, withdrawals at private institutions are comparatively low relative to the public sub-sector. MAU reported no dropouts, although some students were excluded on the basis of their inability to pay fees during their final two years of study. Only five students withdrew from CUNIMA in 2010, representing 0.8 percent of total enrollment and withdrawals demonstrated no gendered characteristics. At UNILIA, withdrawal is similarly negligible, and is associated with an inability to service fees rather than academic performance.

Relevance of Higher Education

Universities play a critical role in developing human resources and promoting technological innovation in support of socioeconomic development. Universities should be cognizant of the need to generate knowledge and human capacity in alignment with shifting demand in the economy, and the concurrent need to keep pace with technological and environmental developments. Due to the subsidy afforded to it on the part of taxpayers, from an accountability perspective, there is added impetus for universities in the public sector to effectively generate research and quality learning in support of national development.

Graduate Output by Field of Study

Table 3.2 shows the distribution of graduate output in 2011 by undergraduate program in public and private institutions (the most current data available).[9] The data shows, consistent with the distribution of enrollment, that the largest number of graduates is concentrated in Education (24.6 percent), followed by Business/Commerce (11.9 percent), Science/Applied Science (10.1 percent). Agriculture constitutes 2.2 percent of the graduate output, down from 3.0 percent in World Bank (2010b), despite the continued importance of agriculture for Malawi's economic development.[10] Given the importance supportive role ICT plays in the development process, as well as the stated MGDS goals to develop and enhance the Malawian ICT industry, and achieve ICT literacy, the increase to 1.6 percent in the share of ICT graduates as a proportion of total graduate output

Table 3.2 Distribution of 2011 Graduates by Field of Study

Field of study	Male	Female	Total	% of female	% of total
Education	326	173	499	34.7	24.6
Business Admin/Commerce	181	68	241	28.2	11.9
Science/Applied Science	157	49	206	23.8	10.1
Nursing	45	154	199	77.4	9.8
Humanities	126	69	195	35.4	9.6
Social Science	117	74	191	38.7	9.4
Environmental Studies/Science	71	34	105	32.4	5.2
Medicine	67	21	88	23.9	4.3
Development Studies	54	16	70	22.9	3.4
Engineering	57	7	64	10.9	3.1
Agriculture	28	17	45	37.8	2.2
Information and Communication	23	10	33	30.3	1.6
Law	26	6	32	18.8	1.6
Built Environment	18	11	29	37.9	1.4
Tourism & Hospitality	19	9	28	32.1	1.4
Health Science	6	1	7	14.3	0.3
Total	**1,321**	**719**	**2,032**	**35.4**	**100.0**

Source: Higher Education Institutions.

Quality and Relevance of Higher Education in Malawi

in 2011 off a base of 0.7 percent (World Bank 2010b) is good news. The lowest concentration of graduates in 2011 was in the Health Sciences (0.3 percent).

Other key growth areas of the economy include Tourism and Hospitality, Construction (part of Built Environment), and Mining. Current graduation patterns indicate that graduate output in these key areas is limited. Only 28 students graduated with qualifications in tourism and hospitality in 2011, just 1.4 percent of total graduate output. At present Malawian students cannot pursue programs in mining and a review of programs offered in engineering at the Polytechnic indicates that no courses directly related to mining, like metallurgy, are on offer. Chancellor College offers courses in geology in the Department of Geography and Earth Sciences, but this is only tangentially related to mining.

Low numbers of graduates in some programs raises questions with regard to their viability and whether or not they should continue to be offered. To improve efficiency and the cost effectiveness of the system, a minimum class size should be considered before a course can be offered. To this end, CUNIMA has set a minimum class size of 12 at the undergraduate level.

Postgraduate Output

Figure 3.11 illustrates master's level graduate output for UNIMA colleges and the number of graduates for each institution for each year. Data for MZUNI was not provided and none of the private colleges currently offer postgraduate programs. The cumulative total for 2010 and 2011 was 235 master's graduates. Chancellor College has the largest graduate output, contributing 58.3 percent of total master's output, followed by COM with 14.9 percent.

Figure 3.11 Output of Master's Graduates by Gender and College—2010–11

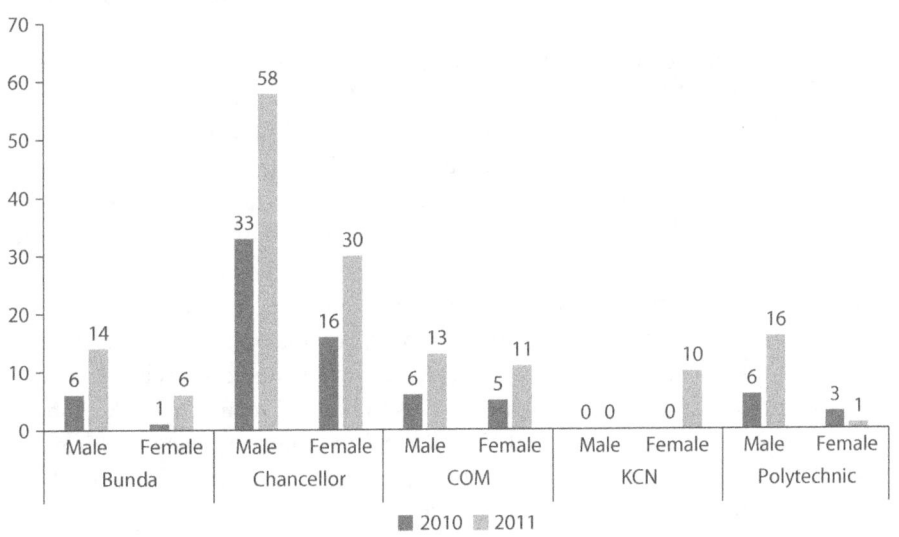

Source: Higher Education Institutions.

The Polytechnic, in spite of its large undergraduate enrollment and graduate output, only contributed 11.1 percent to the cumulative total of master's level graduates in 2010 and 2011. This is in part a consequence of the Polytechnic only offering two master's programs: a master's in Business Administration and a master's in Science in Infrastructure Development and Management. KCN graduated its first master's students in Midwifery in 2011, contributing 4.3 percent to cumulative masters graduate output. It is encouraging that the cumulative number of female master's graduates increased between 2010 and 2011, despite a decrease in female graduates from the Polytechnic.

The fields with the highest output at the master's level are the Social Sciences (29.4 percent), Medicine (14.9 percent), Science (12.3 percent), Education (7.7 percent), the Humanities (5.1 percent), Nursing (4.1 percent) and Development Studies (3 percent). Given Malawi's developmental trajectory, current graduate output does not generate sufficient knowledge and skills in science and technology. Master's programs should be reviewed to more effectively align their output with the needs of growth sectors identified in the MGDS.[11]

The Malawian higher education system produced no Doctoral graduates in 2010 or 2011. This is a significant concern, and must be addressed to improve development-oriented research. The MGDS II emphasizes the need for collaborative research programs spanning the public and private sub-sectors, and the need to undertake research and development and innovation surveys. The supply of high level skills associated with doctoral study to the sector will be required to achieve these ends.

Employment after Graduation

A priority of the government's higher education policy is to address the mismatch between the demand for skills and knowledge in the economy and its supply, and to improve the alignment of human capital formation with the needs of the labor market.

The report of the Tracer Study of TEVET and Higher Education Completers in Malawi (TSTHEM) of 2008 found that 72.2 percent of graduates had full-time employment or had set up their own business (2.1 percent). Eleven percent of surveyed graduates were employed part-time, while 10 percent were still looking for employment. Of concern is the low number of graduates willing or able to start their own business. This may be a consequence of university programs that do not adequately prepare students for self-employment, or it may be related to a general mind-set favoring absorption into the labor force. To promote entrepreneurial activity, programs that prepare, and encourage students, to pursue self-employment will need to be introduced at the universities level. A 2006 Investment Climate study highlighted access to finance, regulatory policy uncertainty, and corruption as constraints inhibiting investment in Malawi. Challenges relating to access to finance, especially access to start-up capital, are likely to negatively affect graduates who want to start their own businesses.

The TSTHEM found that it took an average of 5.5 months for graduates to secure employment, and that after six months, 75 percent of employment seekers had found a job.[12] Further tracer studies are needed to ensure that higher education programs are addressing the demand for skills in the labor market. The study found that all Law graduates were engaged in full-time employment. Other fields for which the study found evidence of healthy levels of full-time employment included Engineering (79.5 percent); Economic and Business (78.2 percent); and the Humanities (72.5 percent). Fields with the lowest percentage of graduates engaged in full time employment were: Science (65.5 percent); ICT (63.3 percent) and other (60.0 percent). However, there was some variation in the time taken by graduates to secure employment after graduation. An analysis of the length of time it took to get employed showed that the following fields had the shortest periods: Law (2.75 months); Humanities (4.75 months); Engineering (5.12 months); Economics/Business (5.16 months). The fields that had the longest periods for seeking employment were: Agriculture (6.64 months); Science (6.57 months) and ICT (5.45 months). The data implies that students graduating from fields like Law, Engineering, Economics and Business are in demand. This view is further buttressed by average salaries: Law had the highest monthly gross income of MK 113,333, followed by Engineering with a monthly gross income of MK 94,419 and Pure Science, which had a gross income of MK 88,455. The field with the lowest gross income was ICT with MK 69,125.

All institutions reported some level of engagement with the private sector. Private sector companies participate in curriculum design and offer feedback on its quality and relevance. However, while students are able to visit private sector companies, there were no examples of visiting lecturers recruited from the private sector or the extension of internships to students. Collaborative research programs engaging private sector companies are operational at the Polytechnic and Chancellor College. Bunda College has signed Memorandum of Understanding (MOU) with non-governmental organizations (NGOs) such as CRISAT International and World Vision and government entities such as the Ministry of Agriculture, and the Ministry of Forestry and Natural resources, which provide feedback on the quality and relevance of their programs. The Polytechnic has established Industry Link Boards that are chaired by representatives from industry. These boards are engaged by the university for the purposes of curricula review and to mobilize resources for faculties. The Polytechnic has signed an MOU with Malawi Telecommunications Limited for research and capacity building and for some outreach activities. KCN engages the Ministry of Health, CHARM, the Nurses Council, UNFPA, and the WHO in the review of its curricula.

Boxes 3.1 and 3.2 present some examples of collaboration between higher education institutions and private sector.

Box 3.1 Mining in Malawi

The mining industry in Malawi is not well-developed, but demonstrates significant growth potential through the extraction of heavy mineral sands, bauxite, phosphate, uranium and rare earth element deposits. The mining sector has suffered from comparative neglect on the part of government due to the perception that there were not many minerals in Malawi. Instead, interventions have tended to privilege the tobacco sector which was regarded as the most important export commodity.

The MGDS II has prioritized the development of the mining sector, due to its potential to contribute to economic diversification and development. During the period of implementation for the MGDS I, the contribution of mining to gross domestic product (GDP) rose from 3 percent to 10 percent, and the overall value of mineral exports rose from MK 43 million in 2006 to over MK 17.7 billion in 2010. The mining sector contributed over MK 2 billion to government revenue in 2010, and the sector currently employs over 21,000 people. The projected medium-term outcomes of the implementation of MGDS II include increased exploration and mining, increased employment generation and improved participation on the part of small and medium miners. A key strategy of the government in this regard is to facilitate the formation of mining cooperatives and associations for small-scale miners, with have the potential to contribute towards addressing problems of youth unemployment and poverty within rural populations.

The growth of the Malawian mining sector is constrained by factors including the high cost and sporadic supply of power; high transport costs; and a weak skills base. The weak skills base manifests in a lack of adequately trained human resources at all levels, including the supply of geologists, engineers, technicians, and artisans.

The legacy of relative neglect for the mining sector is reflected by the absence of in-country training in mining and mining related trades. Currently, Chancellor College offers a course in Geography and Earth Sciences, which has components in geology, but the program does not provide the full suite of skills required to work as a geologist in the mining sector. The Polytechnic offers engineering degrees in civil, mechanical, automobile, electrical and electronics, electronics and computer, electronics and telecommunications, energy and industrial engineering, but not mining. Malawi's technical colleges do not produce sufficient numbers of qualified artisans for the development of the sector. The gap in the supply of artisans to the economy in general was exacerbated by the discontinuation of the technician program at the Polytechnic; no alternative program has been put in place. Currently all of Malawi's geologists have been trained by the government outside the country, and in many instances trained personnel are poached from their jobs in government by mining companies due to the critical shortage of these skills in the mining sector more generally. The tertiary education system must respond effectively to the planned and anticipated growth of the mining sector.

The Department of Mines is in the process of negotiating with MZUNI and UNIMA for the introduction of a program in mining as part of a project funded by the World Bank and the European Union. However, the training of metallurgists has not been included in the proposed

box continues next page

Box 3.1 Mining in Malawi *(continued)*

program despite critical demand for these skills within the sector. The proposed WB-EU financed project will build capacity in selected institutions to deliver the program in partnership with overseas institutions, and through exchange programs with partner institutions. The objective of the project is to improve the efficiency, transparency and sustainability of mining sector management. The project will help the government acquire and disseminate geo-data, encourage the development of sustainable artisanal and small scale mining, increase the supply of Malawians trained at tertiary level to support the minerals sector, and improve the policy environment for mining-related infrastructure development. The project will support the introduction of degree programs and other tertiary level courses through UNIMA's Polytechnic and Chancellor College. The Polytechnic is in the process of designing a curriculum for a mining engineering degree program and Chancellor College is planning the introduction of a degree program in geology.

Small-scale mining in Malawi is limited to the extraction of limestone and the mining of gemstones and semi-precious stones which are primarily found in the North around Mzimba and in the South around Lower Shire and Chikwawa. An estimated 13,000 to 14,000 people are involved in small-scale mining activities in Malawi, and this sub-sector demonstrates significant potential for creating employment opportunities for youth. Work is conducted by individuals and cooperatives of individuals. Small-scale miners have received very little training in mining techniques and environmental protection. The Department of Mines, which should provide this training and monitor mining operations, has not been able to fulfill its role due to a lack of resources. There is almost equal participation in small-scale mining on the part of male and female workers, and youth and adult workers. In general, more adults are engaged in cooperative mining than youth and males tend to outnumber females in work relating to cutting and polishing. In order to mine and sell gemstones and semi-precious stones, miners must hold a Reserved Mineral License. Miners must find their own markets for both uncut rocks and gemstones. A poorly structured and regulated market has resulted in the general exploitation of miners who are often forced to sell at low prices to buyers and middleman. Training and the provision of equipment is necessary to enable the growth of the small-scale mining sector. Training institutions have a critical role to play in providing education and developing technologies to increase the productivity of small-scale miners.

MZUNI has created Faculty Committees in which the private sector participates in the review of curricula, and to facilitate feedback with regard to their quality and relevance. However, the university has not signed any MOUs with private sector organizations, which has constrained the development of linkages with industry.

Linkages between private institutions and industry are generally aligned with those evident in public institutions. The MAU works closely with companies and representative bodies in which it places its students for practical work experience. These bodies include the Auditors Association of Malawi, First Merchant

Bank, National Bank and FDH. The education departments in both public and private universities have received positive feedback from the Ministry of Education with regard to the quality of teachers being produced for deployment in the secondary school system. The institution has also received a request from the private sector to establish a degree program in Finance.

At CUNIMA, industry is engaged for the purposes of reviewing curricula for its Commerce program. Firms that provide work experience opportunities for students are invited to give feedback on the quality and relevance of the curriculum as demonstrated by students, and to participate in the curricula review. Due to the particularities of the education programs it offers, UNILIA relies on the Ministry of Education and the Primary Education Advisors (PEAs) to review curricula.

Collaboration between universities and the private sector takes place at the institution level and, in some cases, at the faculty level. However, there is no formal forum institutionalizing broader consultation between the higher education sub-sector at large, and the private sector. Interviews conducted with the Malawi Confederation of Chamber of Commerce and Industry (MCCCI) in support of this report indicated that the Chamber was unaware of any collaboration between institutions and private sector companies.

Box 3.2 Agricultural Development in Malawi

Agriculture remains the main driver of economic growth in Malawi. The farming of tobacco is the primary cash crop accounting for a large share of foreign exchange and economic growth. Economic diversification and improved performance in other sectors such as mining has led to a relative decline in the contribution of agriculture to GDP, from about 38 percent in 1994 to about 27 percent in 2010. Moreover, World Health Organization (WHO) restrictions with regard to the sale of tobacco will likely reduce the importance of this crop for economic growth in Malawi. Consequently Malawi should diversify its agricultural production and export base and provide new opportunities for small holder farmers whose livelihoods are currently dependent on tobacco.

Efforts to diversify the economy are taking two forms: diversification away from agriculture into other sectors (mining, tourism, service sector); and the diversification of agriculture production into new crops (wheat, cassava, macadamia nuts, fruits, pulses and vegetable commodities, cotton, soya, etc.), as well as through value adding activities such as irrigation, enhanced fisheries production, and the development of agro-processing.

The government has focused significant energy on moving away from the production and export of raw materials through the development of value added activities and the export of finished products in agriculture. Finished products fetch higher prices and create employment for Malawians, with positive effects for addressing poverty. Currently the performance

box continues next page

Box 3.2 Agricultural Development in Malawi *(continued)*

of the manufacturing sector in value addition is low. An important constraint to increasing agricultural productivity is the prevalence of traditional agricultural methods and the poor penetration of technology.

In support of the agricultural sector, higher education institutions should engage in research to advance interventions to diversify agricultural crops, improve agricultural production methods and improve productivity in livestock husbandry. Higher education institutions, working with the private sector, should engage in value chain analysis to determine the types of technology with the potential to catalyze production. Local technologies should be developed and deployed to assist small holder farmers to increase tillage and production. The use of short-courses should be explored to encourage technological adoption. Information made available for this study indicates that the Polytechnic and the Malawi Industrial Research and Development Center (MIRDC) have prototypes for technologies with the potential to significantly enhance value creation, but that a lack of capital has inhibited the diffusion of prototypes. To maximize their impact, higher education institutions should improve collaboration and synchronize activities to address the challenges inhibiting the growth of the agriculture sector.

Investment in research at the Bunda College of Agriculture has developed hybrid crops suited to Malawian conditions. The college organizes field days to introduce new varieties of crops and new agricultural methods designed to increase productivity. In spite of these successes, the biggest constraint faced by higher education institutions and the MIRDC is a lack of infrastructure and equipment, and associated funds. The sector is characterized by insufficient and ill-equipped laboratory space. The MIRDC is similarly encumbered by a shortage of space and the absence of dedicated facilities. The majority of equipment is obsolete and cannot be serviced due to a lack of spare parts. Staffing at Bunda is not a major constraint due to the implementation of a renewal strategy that has resulted in 60 percent of its staff being under the age of 40. Staffing shortages, however, are critical at the MIRDC. Poor staffing at senior levels is being addressed through a capacity building program. Lack of senior staff in the sector as a whole limits the relevance, quality and quantity of research output, and has undermined enrollment at the postgraduate level. Increasing postgraduate enrollment will require the building of capacity on the part of lecturers and the expansion and renewal of facilities at Bunda, the Polytechnic and MIRDC.

The growth of agro-processing is limited by the poor supply of raw materials due to low agricultural productivity arising from a general dependence on rain fed production and the utilization of poor farming techniques. Machinery procured to add value within the agricultural production chain remains idle due to the inadequate and inconsistent supply of raw materials, which serves as a significant disincentive for producers to invest in equipment. In the absence of local research and development, the majority of equipment and machinery is imported, and as a consequence limited access to foreign exchange constrains demand. The generation of investment to support agro-processing will be dependent on improvements in agricultural productivity. Institutions of higher learning can play an important role in this regard, with positive implications for the economic development of Malawi.

Alignment of Programs of Study with the Demands of the Workplace

Seventy eight percent of graduates surveyed by the TSTHEM considered their studies to be useful and applicable to their professional work. Seventeen percent of graduates regarded their university education as not very useful, with little applicability in the fulfillment of their professional tasks. The highest average score with regard to the utility of study was reported by graduates from the fields of law and ICT implying a close alignment between training and professional practice. Science graduates expressed dissatisfaction with a course of study perceived to be overly theoretical, with insufficient practical application in the workplace. The results of the survey indicate a positive association between study and employment; however there is need to increase enrollment in professional courses or introduce more professional courses to further push forward Malawi's development.

The majority of employers surveyed (74.4 percent) indicated that the average graduate required six months of on-the-job experience before they could carry out their tasks at an acceptable level. The lag in professional proficiency may be accounted for by poor work experience on the part of graduates, due to the absence of workplace partnerships and internship programs in the universities. Many employers highlighted differences in the quality of employees with the same academic degrees but coming from different institutions (Pfeiffer and Chiunda 2008). Harmonizing curricula and the provision of programs in the same field across colleges and universities would help to facilitate credit transfer and student mobility. The TSTHEM study highlighted the need to improve the alignment of knowledge and skills development in the tertiary education system with the needs of the labor market to boost low levels of external efficiency. RPED (2006) highlighted the critical shortage of skilled labor as a significant factor inhibiting economic growth and development. Due to the poor alignment of skills development with the needs of the private sector, many companies provide new employees with internal or external training to build the base of their skills.

In the past, universities were active in placing students within relevant companies and organizations to complement their education with practical experience. This practice familiarized students with the practical application of the content of their study, and acted to mitigate deficiencies associated with rote learning. The placement of students in complementary work-placement programs is becoming less common. In order to provide students with work experience, and for purpose of assessment, practical experience is integrated into programming for students enrolled in the fields of education, nursing and medicine. MZUNI, in addition to practical training for nursing and education students, attaches its library sciences and ICT students to relevant organizations. However, attachment programs have proven to be expensive and difficult to sustain as students require allowances for accommodation, sustenance and transport. Employers are not always willing to defray costs, and as a consequence the financial burden falls on students.

Criteria and Mechanisms for the Introduction and Review of Curricula

Curricula need to be reviewed regularly to ensure that they remain relevant to the shifting needs of the economy, and to ensure that they accurately respond to changes in technology. The MGDS articulates the need to improve curricula in universities to respond to national needs, with a focus on curricula review and assessment, and the training of academic staff to improve their knowledge and skills. In response to national imperatives, all institutions have engaged in curricula review, but this is not being undertaken in a systematic manner, and in some cases articulated criteria and procedures are not followed.

Curricula reviews at the UNIMA colleges are time-based and are meant to be undertaken every four to five years. A poor funding environment has constrained the introduction of demand-driven programs, and regular curricula review at most UNIMA colleges. Feedback indicated that the Senate has received progress reports and, where available, the reports of external examiners, in support of curricula review. Due to resource constraints, institutions can no longer afford to conduct tracer studies, and as a consequence interaction with the private sector with regard to curricula is facilitated through committees. The Polytechnic has conducted occasional satisfaction surveys to source the views of industry in this regard, although the application of this methodology is not uniform across the institution as a whole and surveys are irregular. KCN reported that it was in the process of conducting a tracer study at the time of data collection. KCN also facilitates stakeholder consultation improve the relevance and quality of curricula.

At MZUNI, curriculum review is time-based and the institution requires the review of curricula every four to five years. Industry is invited to participate in the reviews through committees formed for this purpose. Programs offered must conform to the Qualifications Framework of the university, which sets out requirements for the award of degrees, primarily through Credit Accumulation and Modular Schemes (CAMS). The Qualifications Framework enables degrees to be benchmarked to nationally and internationally recognized standards. The university's quality assurance system reportedly ensures that all programs are developed and delivered in conformity with the Framework and new courses are introduced on the basis of demand. The report on the Creation of a Second University also provided guidelines on which courses should be introduced.

Curricula at MAU are reviewed every two years by Baraton University, a private institution in Kenya, and new courses are introduced on the basis of demand. For example, the university reported that it had received a request to introduce programs in Agriculture and Finance, both of which are under consideration. At CUNIMA, curriculum review takes the form of a periodic rationalization of curricula to reduce duplication and increase efficiency in course delivery. At UNILIA, curriculum review is based on emerging issues in the respective fields of study, for example human immunodeficiency virus (HIV)/acquired immune deficiency syndrome (AIDS), and in response to changes in government policies. Curricula reviews have also been initiated in response to changes in the secondary education curriculum, specifically the introduction of life skills and the decision to make literature compulsory at the secondary level. UNILIA uses MZUNI and MoEST to review its curriculum every four to five years.

Research

The production of research is one of the principal functions of any university. The literature notes that the research output of African institutions is relatively low, and that the number of staff active in research is relatively poor, in comparison to other parts of the world (Hale 2010). While research output in Sub-Saharan Africa (SSA) has declined in recent years, Malawi's research output, relative to the size of its research community, is relatively substantial, in part a consequence of collaboration with UK academics, particularly in medicine (Hale 2010).

In a survey of Malawian research, UNESCO observed a variety of research output, including technical reports and journal articles, and found that the research produced has the potential to influence policy decisions and stimulate further research.[13] Researchers from COM routinely publish articles in international Open Access journals, with 156 articles published in BioMed Central and a further 70 articles published in the journals of the Public Library of Science (PLoS). The UNESCO report, however, noted that "most researchers in Malawi are not really aware of research and scientific outputs produced in the region… and that the results of research conducted in Malawi are locked up in the offices, libraries and resource centers of the country's higher education institutions and not used in important policy decisions." The survey of Malawian research output for this report was limited to information collated by UNESCO and Hale, and due to a lack of data it was not possible to quantify research output for each institution. None of the institutions who reported information for this study allocate faculty time exclusively for research. Moreover, suboptimal resources are allocated to research activities and individual members of staff are generally left to themselves to schedule research time, define projects within their areas of expertise, conduct research, and publish their results. An analysis of the expenditure patterns in the universities demonstrates that most institutions spend less than two percent of total expenditure on research, despite the fact that publication is influential in hiring and promotion decision-making. Institutional support for research activities will need to be strengthened in order to increase the research output of Malawian universities.

UNIMA maintains a policy, approved by its Senate in 2006, on research applicable in all its constituent colleges. The policy is implemented by the University Research and Publications Committee (URPC), a senate committee, and the college-based Research and Publications Committees (RPCs). These groups support and monitor all University approved research and related activities.

The goal of UNIMA's policy is:

> To be a stimulus and vehicle for the coordination, promotion, generation, creation of databases, strengthening and dissemination of knowledge, information and

technology through research for economic growth and development and the promotion of socio-cultural values.

The policy aims to establish a common mechanism to ensure consistency for planning, implementation and the monitoring of research processes across the university as a whole. The policy applies to all faculties, departments, centers, units and groups. It outlines all the processes in the research cycle from the identification of needs and prioritization, to the framing of the research project, proposal preparation and approval procedures; funding; project control and monitoring; the dissemination of research results; and the evaluation of research effectiveness. The framework is intended to promote relevance, efficiency and excellence across university research practices and the community at large (University of Malawi 2006).

Guiding principles for research at UNIMA include: its relevance to the needs of society; its contribution to excellence in research and service to society; proactivity in dealing with emerging issues in research and development; seeking, developing and advancing partnerships nationally, regionally and internationally; conducting research in conformity with ethical norms; encouraging research activities in postgraduate programs linked to the advancement of academic programs and the promotion of development; and defending and maintaining academic freedom and institutional autonomy in matters concerning research and development.

The policy advocates an increase in the public financial allocation to support research in the national budget, maintaining that this should be raised to at least one percent of the GDP. The policy moreover proposes that the university allocate at least five percent of its annual budget to research activities for both staff and students, encourages the development of linkages with industry to promote partnerships to improve the financing and relevance of research and development, encourages collaboration with foreign researchers, and the establishing of research chairs, to promote capacity building and financial resources.

In an effort to strengthen research management practices, oversight of research at UNIMA has been decentralized to the College Research and Publications Committees (CRPC) with mixed results. The policy is cognizant of weaknesses in the current structure supporting research and, when fully implemented, will attempt to address this through the establishment of the College Directorate of Research and Consultancy Services headed by a Director appointed by the council. The Director will be responsible for running the secretariat of the college Research and Publications Committee under the chairmanship of the Dean of Postgraduate Studies and Research.

The College Directorate will be responsible for bringing to the attention of the university, national priorities in research, will define the institutional research agenda in consultation with the faculties and research entities (without restricting research to national priorities alone), and shall review the research agenda every two years (University of Malawi 2006).

Research at UNIMA is conducted in the institutions as part of university activities and the teaching process. UNIMA also houses a number of full-time research centers such as the Center for Educational Research and Training (CERT), the Center for Social Research (CSR), the Center for Language Studies (CLS), and the Center for Agricultural Research and Development (CARD). The Polytechnic has developed its own research strategy and created a Water, Sanitation, Health, and Appropriate Technology Department (WASHTED) intended to support research.

In line with the pattern observed across the sector, MZUNI does not specifically allocate faculty hours for research. MZUNI has a research policy that was approved by its Senate in 2004. This policy created the post of Director of Research, accountable to the Vice Chancellor, who, in turn, chairs the Research and Publications Committee which is responsible for coordinating and overseeing the university's research and scholarly output. The Director works closely with the Research and Publications Committee to, *inter alia*: develop and recommend policies and procedures for research and scholarly publication; review research proposals for external or internal funding; administer the university's internal research budget; assist academic staff and academic-related library staff in the preparation of research proposals and the acquisition of research funding; review the output of externally-funded research projects to ensure compliance with donor requirements; represent the university, and liaise with current and potential donors, and research partners, and with external research organizations and agencies; and conduct other activities to encourage, facilitate and promote research and publication at MZUNI (MZUNI Research Policy). However, at the time of data collection, it was reported that the post of Director of Research had been vacant for over a year.

The duties of the MZUNI Research and Publications Committee are defined as: the preparation and submission of recommendations for the MZUNI research budget in line with the university's annual budget cycle; review and recommendation of proposals for internal research funding; the identification of needs with regard to research facilities, including equipment, and other resources; the recommendation and prioritization of expenditure for the acquisition or improvement of research facilities; to serve as a forum to identify and discuss research opportunities and challenges at MZUNI, and recommend appropriate responses; the conduct of periodic reviews of MZUNI research policies and procedures, and the recommendation of appropriate changes; and to advise and assist the Director of Research in the performance of their duties.

Research output in the private universities is generally very low. The absence of postgraduate programs and the small pool of staff with PhDs constrain research in the private sub-sector. To date, none of the private universities has implemented a research policy to guide research in their institutions. However research is promoted through alternative mechanisms: MAU has established a University Research Council to coordinate all research output, but none of the research initiatives had been completed at the time of data collection. In addition, each member of the academic staff at MAU is allocated MK 9,000 in seed money to support research, and is expected to source additional resources to augment these funds. CUNIMA also has a Research and Publications Committee, with a budget of MK 3 million to allocate in support of research activities. Each faculty is allocated MK 300,000 in seed money for research. The institution has initiated a number of research projects that are in various stages of completion. UNILIA is planning to introduce a Research Department to promote research in the institution; however the low number of staff with senior degrees could constrain research activities at the institution.

Universities face a number of challenges in their efforts to promote a culture of research: heavy teaching loads, a general lack of funding, and the low number of professors and PhD holders to supervise research constrain research output. Institutions with relatively higher numbers of senior staff capable of conducting and supervising research—such as Bunda, COM and Chancellor College—demonstrate more robust research output. Moreover, the relative scarcity of research grants, and a range of infrastructural or resource constraints, limit the amount of research institutions are able to undertake. Hale (2010) notes that a lack of a university-wide or departmental research culture linked to underfunding is tied to low or declining levels of research. In spite of these constraints, Bunda, MZUNI, Chancellor College and the COM, which has a number of collaborations with UK academics, continue to produce commendable research.

Sources of Research Funding

Public institutions receive funding to support research activities from government subventions. The National Institute for Higher Education has also funded research projects. Some institutions receive funding through donor-funded projects. For example the Polytechnic has benefited from funding from JICA, NUFU, USAID and the EU, and has received funding from local companies like Illovo for a project on adding vitamins to sugar and from Rap Processors on a Likhuni Phala project. The Polytechnic is also pursuing a research initiative with the Malawi Energy and Regulatory Authority (MERA) on biodiesel. MZUNI allocated MK 4 million to research in 2010/11 from its own resources through its RPC. The faculty of Environment Science, which had the largest number of research activities, received the largest allocation. MZUNI also received funding in support of a biogas project, funded through the British High Commission, a project conducting research in forestry, funded by Japan and DELPHI, and a fisheries project, funded by Sterling University.

The Polytechnic allocates 10 percent of its budget to research, through its RPC. The pool of funds dedicated to research is sourced from government allocations, student fees, funds generated by the institution, and donors. It also receives funding from private sector organizations such as Malawi Telecommunications Limited (MTL) and the Tea Estates. Scottish Power, a UK energy utility, donated a hybrid renewable energy unit, housed in a container, which works on solar and wind energy to power a hospital at the institution.

At private institutions the funding of research activities is sourced almost entirely from tuition fees. However, CUNIMA receives research funding from the Catholic Relief Services.

At UNIMA, funding for research and associated projects as a share of the institutional revenue increased from 22.1 percent (approximately MK 2.01 billion) in 2009 to 30.8 percent (approximately MK 3.7 billion) in 2010, with the largest share being allocated to COM. However, allocations to support research from the government and the university's own resources constituted only 0.71 percent of total budget (approximately MK 86 million).

Current Linkages with National and International Research Programs

Malawian institutions benefit from a number of international research initiatives. NORAD supports multi-disciplinary research at COM, KCN, Bunda and Chancellor, and supports training at the master's level and capacity building at Bunda.

Chancellor College benefits from established research partnerships with Michigan University (USA), the Universities of St. Andrews and Leeds University (U.K). Leeds University engages Chancellor College with regard to the delivery of a leadership program on climate change and development in the region, with further linkages to institutions in South Africa, Mozambique and Tanzania. The Forestry Department has developed local partnerships to support a climate change project. KCN is engaged in a research partnership with the University of Chicago focused on HIV/AIDS and circumcision.

The Faculty of Environmental Science at MZUNI benefits from more than 20 partnerships at both the national and international level, including Stenden University (DRENTHE), Netherlands; New Brunswick University, Canada; University of St. Andrews, Scotland; Kymenlaakson University of Applied Sciences, Finland; Development Partnerships in Higher Education (DelPHE), Scotland; ICRAF, Malawi Agroforestry Food Security Program (AFSP), Ireland; Longborough University, U. K; The Flame Tree Initiative, Arizona, USA; and UN-Habitat PSUP.

MZUNI's local linkages include: Northern Region Water Board; Shire River Basin Management Program; National Biodiversity Strategy (NBSAP); Millennium Challenge Account (MCA); Collaboration on Tourism, Parks and Wildlife; African Energy Policy Research Network–Kenya; Natural Resources College; Bunda College of Agriculture.

The Polytechnic has benefitted from partnerships with: University of Regina (Canada) funded by Canadian International Development Agency (CIDA); Strathclyde in the UK funded by Malawi Millennium Challenge; and the University of Leeds funded by the Department for International Development (DfID), U.K.; and Texas University. Information reported by MAU indicates that the university does not have any research linkages.

Conclusion

In the absence of a system-wide quality assurance system, it has been difficult to maintain and enhance the quality of the programs offered in both the public and private institutions of Malawi. Institutional efforts to sustain quality have tended to focus primarily on inputs, with comparatively little attention paid to outputs. Accurately assessing the relevance of programs is difficult in the absence regularly executed tracer and labor market studies. Due to funding constraints, institutions have not been able to conduct tracer studies to inform the content of programs and curricula. The 2008 Tracer Study of TEVET and Higher Education Completers in Malawi (TSTHEM) provided information on the quality and relevance of university graduate output, and relative demand for different fields of study.

The current context is marked by progressively increasing enrollment, in the absence of a concurrent and proportionate expansion of supporting infrastructure in support of quality education. The number of academic staff active in the system has changed only marginally during the period under review, resulting in rising student to lecturer ratios—although these trends vary across institutions and faculties. The number of staff holding senior degrees is low, with negative implications for institutional capacity capable of supporting postgraduate programming and research.

Public universities are engaged in a number of initiatives to address these challenges, in particular through staff development programs supported by government subventions. Consistent with the government's commitment to funding higher education there has been an improvement in the availability of learning and teaching materials in most public institutions. Progress in the adoption and expanded use of ICT has been slowed due to the low number of computers available for use in institutions, poorly managed networks and low bandwidth. These factors have constrained the ability of institutions to fully exploit the potential of ICT to complement and improve teaching and learning processes.

Quality enhancement mechanisms have not been rigorously implemented within institutions. Research output and community outreach is generally low, and collaboration with the private sector could be significantly enhanced. Graduate output is generally aligned with enrollment patterns, and rates of withdrawal from programs have been generally low. Graduate output from fields of study identified by the MGDS as critical for economic development (ICT, agriculture, science and technology) has been poor. Low enrollment in postgraduate programs is associated with low postgraduate output.

The challenging funding environment appears to be the primary constraint inhibiting efforts to enhance quality and relevance in both public and private universities. Inadequate funding has constrained the growth and rehabilitation of the existing stock of university infrastructure which was designed for a much smaller cohort of students. Pressure to increase enrollment, arising as a consequence of changes to enrollment policies, has placed further strain on overburdened infrastructure, facilities and teaching staff. Due to an absence of reliable data, it is not possible to accurately determine to what extent these challenges have affected the quality of higher education delivery in Malawi. A tracer study conducted in 2006 indicated that employers were generally happy with the quality of the graduates and the relevance of the programs, but this survey is nearly a decade old. Regular surveys of employment trends, and the views of employers, would help ensure that the higher education system is responsive to the development needs of the country, and shifting demand in the private sector. The development of stronger linkages, and partnerships, with the private sector, would also assist in this regard.

Research output has been low due to poor funding and the low number of qualified staff capable of initiating, guiding and sustaining research. These constraints are also reflected in the poor postgraduate output of institutions, and could be compromising the system's ability to respond to the development and innovation needs of country.

It is expected that the mandate of the newly established NCHE, to ensure quality, will help to address some of these challenges.

Programmatic Policy Options

Informed by the findings of this study, the policy options listed in table 3.3 are intended to assist the sector to address challenges negatively affecting the quality and relevance of higher education provision. Further study will be required to determine the relative cost effectiveness of policy options to inform a holistic quality assurance and enhancement strategy.

Table 3.3 Policy Options

Policy objective	Issue	Programmatic options to address supply/demand constraints:	Expected impact
Enhanced Quality	Presence of poorly qualified lecturers in the system	Expand current staff development programs to increase the number of staff with senior degrees and phase out staff associates and assistant lecturers.	Improved quality in the delivery of education programs and improved quality of research output.
		Provide incentives to attract high quality staff in areas of demonstrating significant shortages, such as the engineering and science.	
	Inadequate learning and teaching resources	Ring-fence resources for learning and teaching.	Increased quality in education programs and coverage.
		Strengthen ICT systems in the institutions through the procurement of computers and improved bandwidth.	

Table 3.3 Policy Options (continued)

Policy objective	Issue	Programmatic options to address supply/demand constraints:	Expected impact
	Lack of Internal Quality Enhancement Mechanism in the institutions	Set up a transparent staff appraisal system based on performance indicators linked to incentives. Gradually strengthen the external examiners system using local staff as far as possible in order to reduce cost. Provide support to the National Council for Higher Education so it can fully meet its mandate.	Improved quality in education programs. Effective and efficient national quality assurance system in place leading to improved quality in higher education institutions
	Absence of National Quality Assurance Framework	Establish external quality control and accreditation (National Quality Assurance Framework).	National Quality Assurance Framework in place
	Limited research and innovation	Expand research and ICT infrastructure to facilitate access to research journals and improve collaboration with national and regional research networks and initiatives. Ensure that Research and Publication Councils function effectively through the provision of resources and targets for research output.	Research output responsive to national development goals and agenda. Promote innovation and relevance in local research Increased research output and quality
Enhanced Relevance	Low number of graduates positioned to contribute to key growth areas identified in the MGDS	Conduct regular tracer studies with the involvement of the private sector. Reduce duplication of programs across institutions and create specialized institutions to optimize the use of scarce resources, including human resources.	Focused production of human resources relevant to the developmental needs of the country and improved collaboration between government, higher education institutions and the private sector. Improved relevance of education program and collaboration between higher education institutions and the private sector. Better utilization of scarce resources and improved responsiveness of education programs.
	Inadequate linkages with the private sector	Involve stakeholder representatives in the governance of institutions (e. g., University Council; departmental advisory committees) Establish partnerships between the private sector and institutions to increase relevance. e. g. a PPP policy as the case with UNIMA. Regularly update curricula with the active participation of the private sector.	Improved management in and performance of higher education institutions. Improved linkages between higher education institutions and the private sector leading to greater relevance of education programs and improved funding to higher education institutions. Improve quality of education programs and access.

Annexes for Chapter 3

Annex 3A.1 Staff by Institution and Qualification—2011

Institution	Undergraduate	Master	PhD	Total
Bunda	31	104	23	158
COM	29	42	40	111
KCN	12	42	5	59
Polytechnic	63	118	19	200
MZUNI	30	86	20	136
MAU	3	10	3	16
CUNIMA	11	31	4	46
UNILIA	5	15	0	20

Source: Higher Education Institutions.

Annex 3A.2 Staff by Institution and Designation—2011

Institution	Associate Lecturer	Assistant Lecturer	Lecturer	Senior Lecturer	Associate Professor	Professor	Total
Bunda	31		80	24	13	10	158
COM	29		45	21	10	6	111
KCN	12		32	10	5	0	59
Polytechnic	14	49	107	28	1	1	200
MZUNI	31		81	16	6	2	136
MAU			7	3	0	2	12
CUNIMA	5		29	7	3	2	46
UNILIA	5		15	0	0	0	20

Source: Higher Education Institutions.

Annex 3A.3 Staffing by Qualification at COM—2008–11

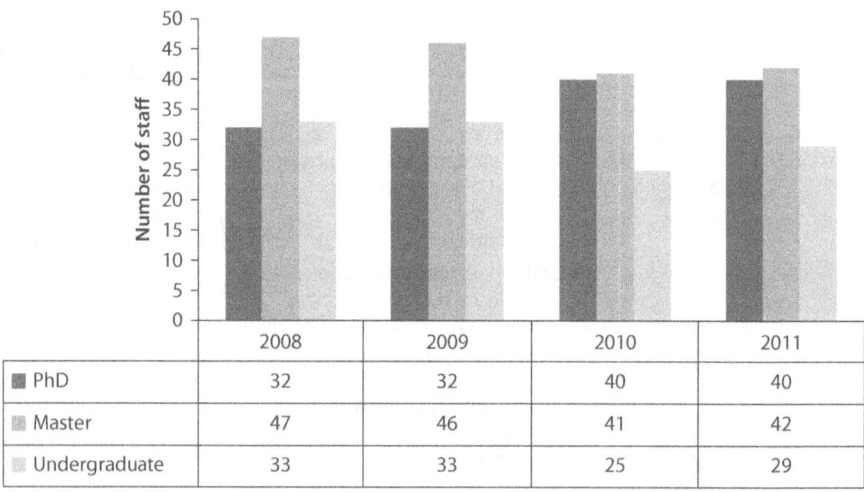

	2008	2009	2010	2011
PhD	32	32	40	40
Master	47	46	41	42
Undergraduate	33	33	25	29

Source: College of Medicine: UNIMA.

Annex 3A.4 Staffing by Qualification at MAU—2008–11

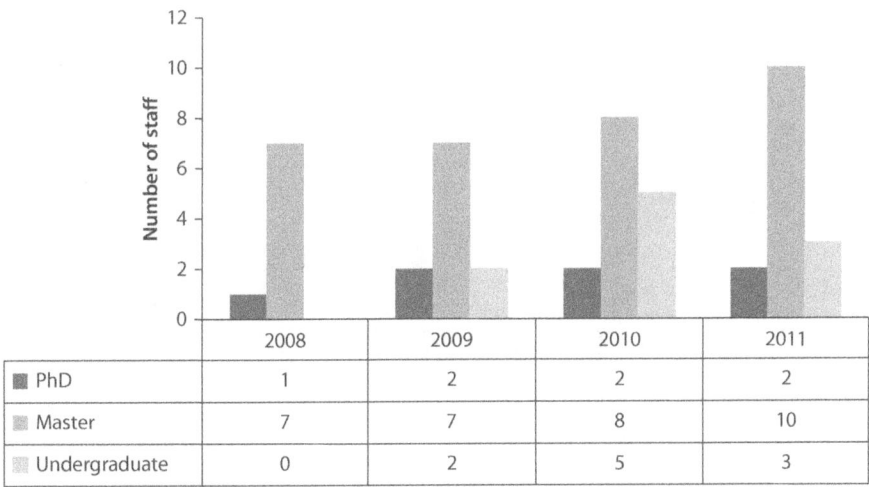

	2008	2009	2010	2011
PhD	1	2	2	2
Master	7	7	8	10
Undergraduate	0	2	5	3

Source: Malawi Adventist University.

Annex 3A.5 Staffing by Qualification at CUNIMA—2008–11

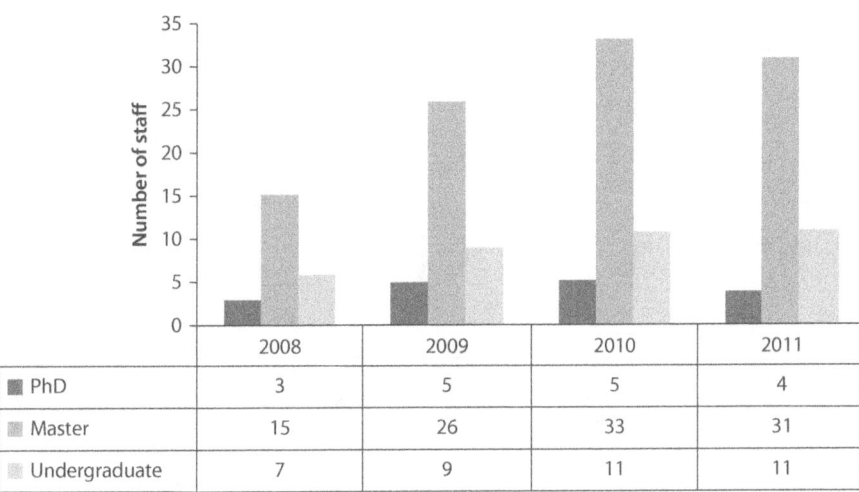

	2008	2009	2010	2011
PhD	3	5	5	4
Master	15	26	33	31
Undergraduate	7	9	11	11

Source: Catholic University of Malawi.

Annex 3A.6 Staffing by Qualification at the Polytechnic—2008–11

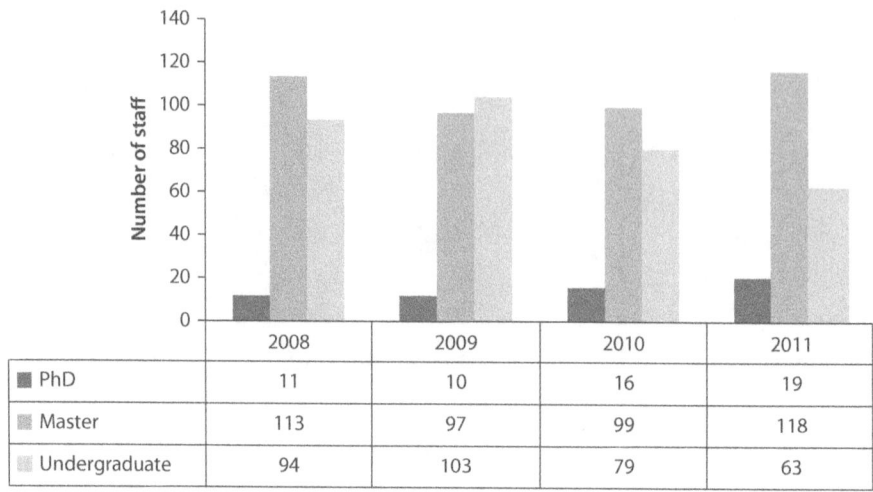

	2008	2009	2010	2011
PhD	11	10	16	19
Master	113	97	99	118
Undergraduate	94	103	79	63

Source: Malawi Polytechnic: UNIMA.

Annex 3A.7 Number of Staff on Staff Development Programs—2011

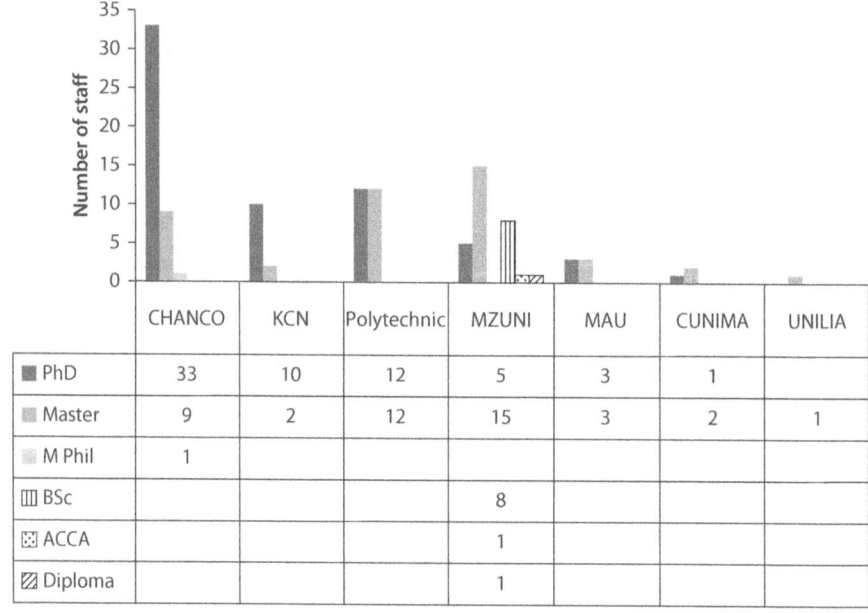

	CHANCO	KCN	Polytechnic	MZUNI	MAU	CUNIMA	UNILIA
PhD	33	10	12	5	3	1	
Master	9	2	12	15	3	2	1
M Phil	1						
BSc				8			
ACCA				1			
Diploma				1			

Source: Higher Education Institutions.

Annex 3A.8 Percentage of Female Graduates—2008–11

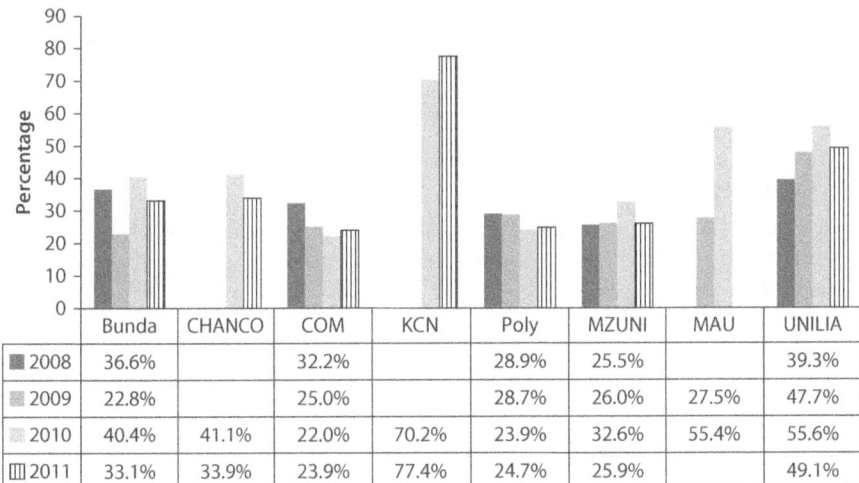

	Bunda	CHANCO	COM	KCN	Poly	MZUNI	MAU	UNILIA
2008	36.6%		32.2%		28.9%	25.5%		39.3%
2009	22.8%		25.0%		28.7%	26.0%	27.5%	47.7%
2010	40.4%	41.1%	22.0%	70.2%	23.9%	32.6%	55.4%	55.6%
2011	33.1%	33.9%	23.9%	77.4%	24.7%	25.9%		49.1%

Source: Higher Education Institutions.

Notes

1. This is the only recent tracer study that has been conducted in Malawi.
2. An establishment is the number of posts that are created for an institution or department that can be filled in order to carry out the mandate of the institution or department. Establishments are approved based on a functional review and the availability of resources to pay for the positions in the establishment. When funds are inadequate, some establishment posts are frozen and left unfilled.
3. Tracer study of TEVET and Higher Education Completers in Malawi-Final report: Dietmar Pfeiffer and Gerald Chiunda pp. 20.
4. In 2006, the percentage of staff with first degrees ranged between 11.1 percent and 41.2 percent.
5. Annual pay increments are not performance related.
6. UNIMA's stated objective of achieving an SLR of 25:1 will not be implemented at COM or KCN due to the particularities of medical training.
7. The data sets for 2010 are complete. In 2008 information for Chancellor College, MAU and KCN was missing, and in 2009 data from Chancellor College and KCN was not forthcoming. Moreover, 2010 data for MAU is not available.
8. See figure 3.8.
9. Data from CUNIMA was not available.
10. Table 7.10 in World Bank (2010b) presents cumulative university graduate outputs from 2003 to 2007.

11. The growth sectors highlighted by the MGDS are: Agriculture and Food Security; Transport Infrastructure; Energy, Industrial Development, Mining and Tourism; Education, Science and Technology; Public Health, Sanitation, Malaria, HIV and AIDS Management; Integrated Rural Development; Green Belt Irrigation and Water Development; Child Development, Youth Development and Empowerment; and Climate Change, Natural Resources and Environmental Management.
12. The survey captured data on graduates from all existing universities, however this was not disaggregated by institution but by field of study.
13. UNESCO, Global Open Access Portal, Malawi http://www.unesco.org/new/en/communication-and-information/portals-and-platforms/goap/access-by-region/africa/malawi/

CHAPTER 4

The Financing of Higher Education

Introduction

This chapter reports on the findings of the study with regard to the mobilization, allocation and utilization of resources in both public and private institutions of higher education, and findings related to institutional unit costs and student financing.

Findings of the Study

Resource Mobilization

In a context characterized by constrained resources, the rapid knowledge expansion, and scientific and technological advancement, it is difficult for universities in developing countries to respond to the changing societal demands. In many countries, associated challenges are exacerbated due to the dependence of the higher education sub-sector on government funding. In Malawi public funding constitutes approximately 80 percent of total expenditure in the public higher education sub-sector. There are three primary sources of income for universities in Malawi: government subventions for public universities, tuition fees, and income flowing from grants, research activities and externally funded projects. The Malawian government plans to increase the number of public universities to expand access to, and accommodate increasing demand for, higher education. With the exception of tuition fees which are set by government, public universities have been unable to augment government allocations with a diversity of funding sources. The planned increase in the number of public universities, and the further expansion of enrollment in higher education, will increasingly strain the financing of public funding for public higher education. Public universities need to find new ways of mobilizing resources to boost revenues and reduce their dependence on government funding.

Government Subventions to Public Universities

The main source of finance in support of capital and recurrent expenditure in Malawian public institutions takes the form of subventions from government.

The total subvention for public universities and the University of Livingstonia (UNILIA)[1] increased from MK 5.89 billion in 2007/08 to MK 7.46 billion in 2009/10[2] as illustrated in figure 4.1. The share of public funding for higher education as a proportion of total public funding for education fell from 23.8 percent in 2007/08 to 21.8 percent in 2009/10, followed by an increase to 25.8 percent in 2011. The share of the government's education budget allocated to higher education is relatively high compared to other sub-Saharan African countries as demonstrated in annex 4A.1. There has been a marginal decrease in the contribution of government subventions to university budgets due to improved income generation from other sources. In 2009/10, Projects, Grants and Research accounted for the following portion of institutional budgets: 37.8 percent at Bunda, 63.1 percent at COM, 55.5 percent at KCN, 23.1 percent at Chancellor College, and 11.1 percent at the Polytechnic.

The contribution of fees to total institutional budgets in the public sub-sector has remained relatively low; from a low of 4 percent at Bunda to a high of 17.4 percent at the Polytechnic. The contribution of tuition fees as a proportion of institutional budgets has fallen at all UNIMA colleges in the period under review, with the exception of the Polytechnic where it increased from 13.4 percent in 2008 to 17.4 percent in 2009/10. The share of tuition fees in total institutional budgets has fallen despite an increase in enrollment in part because fees, set by government, have remained relatively static. The contribution associated with government subventions to the budget of Chancellor College grew year-on-year by 39.8 percent in 2009 due to allocations to support the rehabilitation of facilities. The Chancellor College subvention grew by a further 2.8 percent in 2010.

Figure 4.1 Trends in Subventions to Public Universities—2008–11

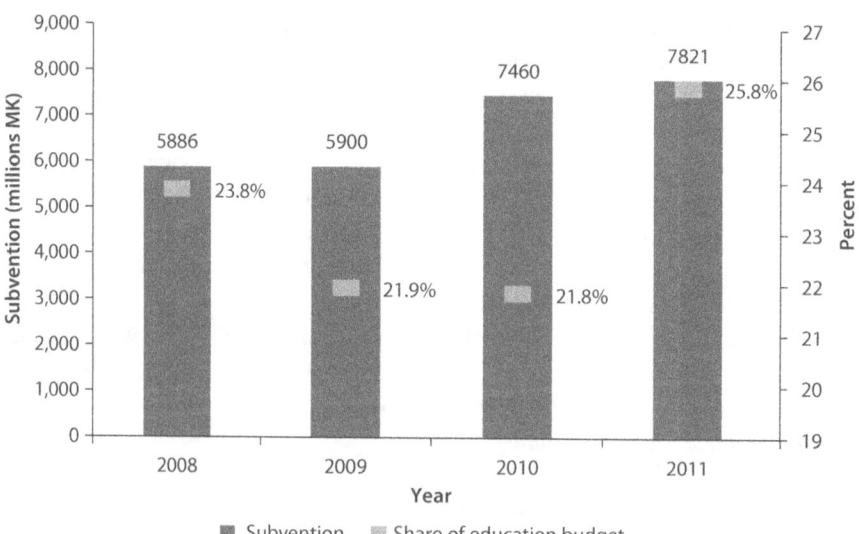

Source: Draft Estimates of Expenditure on Recurrent and Capital Budget for Financial Year 2009/10 and 2010/211.

The Financing of Higher Education

The fall in the share of subventions to the budgets of UNIMA institutions, in a context of sustained government support and rising enrollment, is associated with improved resource generation from other sources. The increase in locally generated resources is associated with improved and more transparent management of research and consultancy income, through polices and structures that promote accountable stewardship of resources. UNIMA has included a provision in its research policy that requires 10 percent of the total budget of any research or consultancy to be paid to the institution to cover overhead costs (however not all donors will support overhead costs). As detailed in the previous chapter, UNIMA has also intensified efforts to coordinate donor-funded research and consultancies across the institutions of the university. To incentive the generation of income, UNIMA departments that raise additional income are allowed to retain a percentage generated income. Departmental staff that bring in additional funds are also rewarded with a percentage of the financing.

To varying degrees, the colleges of UNIMA are slowly reducing their dependence on government allocations to support university activities. MZUNI is an exception among public institutions in this regard, and the share of subventions as a proportion of the university's budget increased from 82.5 percent in 2008 to 92.3 percent in 2009, although there was a subsequent drop to 83.8 percent in 2010.

Institutional sources of income for the period 2008 to 2010 are illustrated in table 4.1. Residential students at UNIMA pay a combined tuition and accommodation fee of MK 25,000 per year, while those at MZUNI pay MK 55,000 per year. The non-residential and mature students enrolled in the public institutions

Table 4.1 Sources of Income by Institution—2008–10

Institution	Source	2008 thousands MK	2009 thousands MK	2010 thousands MK
Bunda	Subvention	716,166	1,141,993	942,647
	Fees	72,300	69,682	96,744
	Research	26,746	409,788	739,126
	Other	61,911	123,751	178,024
	% derived from Subvention	81.6	65.4	48.2
Chancellor	Subvention	1,191,829	1,587,257	1,803,231
	Fees	142,218	134,853	279,872
	Research	0	769,161	679,328
	Other	64,371	123,860	176,543
	% derived from Subvention	85.2	60.7	61.4
COM	Subvention	721,521	860,451	947,729
	Fees	66,882	188,199	128,326
	Research	0	1,719,952	2,717,529
	Other	327,096	92,619	519,980
	% derived from Subvention	64.7	30.1	22.0

table continues next page

Table 4.1 Sources of Income by Institution—2008–10 *(continued)*

Institution	Source	2008 thousands MK	2009 thousands MK	2010 thousands MK
KCN	Subvention	513,027	744,677	837,422
	Fees	52,925	51,653	72,777
	Research	0	393,406	1,222,983
	Other	43,731	65,453	76,155
	% derived from Subvention	84.1	59.3	37.9
Polytechnic	Subvention	1,070,288	1,487,083	1,468,430
	Fees	177,703	359,142	333,791
	Research	0	146,917	234,456
	Other	77,538	60,514	67,511
	% derived from Subvention	80.7	72.4	69.8
MZUNI	Subvention	656,515	947,061	950,000
	Fees	98,451	64,856	119,650
	Research	0	0	0
	Other	40,446	14,660	63,817
	% derived from Subvention	82.5	92.3	83.8

Source: Higher Education Institutions.

paid substantially more than residential students amounting to MK 100,000 at UNIMA, and MK 150,000 at MZUNI, during this period. Fees levied on residential and non-residential students are now aligned under a new policy. In all instances, these fees are much lower than the unit cost associated with university education in Malawi, demonstrating the effects of the government subsidy for tuition, accommodation and subsistence. New admissions policies have also resulted in non-residential students receiving a subsistence allowance of MK 33, 000 per month.

The share of sources of income, as a proportion of total institutional budgets in the public sub-sector is illustrated in annex 4A.2, showing that, with the exception of COM, the contribution on the part of government subventions has fallen, but remains the single largest source of income. The overall contribution of subvention for public institutions fell from 78.6 percent in 2007/08 to 47.1 percent in 2009/10.

Projects, Grants and Research

Income generated through projects and research grants does not contribute to the general operational budgets. These monies are ring-fenced to support costs associated with the research and project to which they have been allocated, except in instances where 10 percent of the income is forwarded to university coffers in support of overhead costs. Project funds that are not spent are held as deferred income to be utilized in the future. As a consequence, public institutions continue to primarily rely on government subventions to support operational budgets.

Attempts on the part of universities to mobilize additional sources of income have demonstrated varying degrees of success, in part tied to variance in the capacity of public institutions to mobilize resources. At Bunda, for example, income generated through projects, grants and research contributed only 3 percent to the total income in 2008, but rose to 38 percent in 2010.

At Chancellor College, income generated through projects, grants and research contributed 29.6 and 23 percent to institutional income in 2009 and 2010 respectively. Income generated through projects at COM accounted for 63 percent of the total income. COM received an additional 12 percent from other sources of revenue, for example through the hiring out its sports complex and mortuary fees.

At the Polytechnic, income from projects and research increased from 7.2 percent of total income in 2009 to 11.1 percent in 2010, while the share contributed by government subventions decreased from 80.7 percent to 69.8 percent over the same period. "Other" income contributed only 3.2 percent in 2010.

Tuition Fees
Fees levied on students account for the lowest share of total income at public institutions, ranging from 4.9 percent of income at Bunda to a high of 17.4 percent at Polytechnic. The share of fees as a proportion of total income has fallen at UNIMA colleges in the period under review, with the exception of the Polytechnic where it increased from 13.4 percent in 2007/08 to 15.9 percent in 2009/10. The decline in the contribution of fees is primarily a consequence of an inability of universities to independently raise fees, which have remained static in line with government prescriptions. Fees at Bunda contributed an average of 5.7 percent of the university budget over the three-year period, despite a corresponding increase in enrollment of approximately 13 percent between 2008 and 2010. At the same time, the contribution of fees to total income at Bunda dropped from 8.2 percent in 2008 to 4.9 percent in 2010. At Chancellor College, the contribution of the fees to the total budget fell from 10.2 percent in 2008 to 9.5 percent in 2010. At MZUNI, the contribution of fees to the university budget decreased from 12.4 percent in 2008 to 10.6 percent in 2010. At the Polytechnic the portion of income derived from fees increased from 13.4 percent to 15.9 percent in the period under review. The data shows that in a context of static fees, and increased resource generation on the part of institutions, the percentage contribution of tuition fees to total income has fallen in most public institutions, and is now relatively negligible at Bunda (4.9 percent), COM (3 percent) and KCN (3.3 percent).

Tuition fees constitute the primary source of income for private institutions, as illustrated in figure 4.2. In the absence of a government subsidy, fees in private institutions are much higher than at public institutions, and range between MK 200,000 and MK 360,000.

Support from the authority responsible for MAU accounted for 2.2 percent of the university's income in 2010 while CUNIMA received no support at all

Figure 4.2 Percentage Distribution of Sources of Income in Private Universities—2008–10

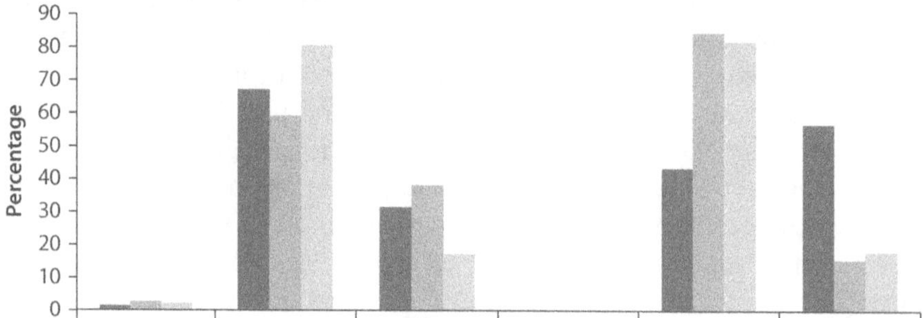

	MAU			CUNIMA		
	Subvention	Fees	Other income	Subvention	Fees	Other income
2008	1.4%	67.2%	31.4%	0.0%	43.3%	56.7%
2009	2.6%	59.2%	38.1%	0.0%	84.5%	15.5%
2010	2.2%	80.6%	17.2%	0.0%	82.0%	18.0%

Source: Private Higher Education Institutions.

from its responsible authority. At MAU the contribution of tuition fees to university income was 80.6 percent in 2010, up from 59.2 percent in 2009, while other income decreased to 17.2 percent in 2010 from 38.1 percent in 2009. At CUNIMA, fees contributed over 80 percent of total income in 2009 and 2010, up from 43.3 percent in 2008 as a result of the fall in other income. Other income in the private sub-sector primarily takes the form of private donations to support the process of establishing institutions. Private institutions have not received any public resources, with the exception of UNILIA, which received MK 70 million for the construction of a female hostel.

Analysis of Tuition Fee Regimes

The planned expansion of higher education will require the substantial expansion of the sector's current resource base, as well as the further diversification of sources of finance. An under exploited resource in this regard is tuition. Malawi's policy of cost sharing requires students to contribute towards the cost of their education. Public universities are autonomous, and in theory should be in a position to determine fees paid by students following the "consideration of any recommendation or report ... from the Senate."[3] However, in practice fee increases require approval from Government and have remained unchanged since 2005. Fees at the colleges of UNIMA are MK 25,000 per year, while at MZUNI fees are levied at MK 55,000 per year.[4] The universities have submitted a number of proposals to government to increase fees, but none have been approved. In the absence of a fee increase, government has increased its subventions to universities, but these have been inadequate to meet capital and recurrent budgetary needs.

Fees in public institutions are well below the unit cost associated with higher education provision, underlining large public subsidy allocated to the sector. In practice the subsidy takes two primary forms: Firstly, through the effective subsidization of low fees, and secondly through subsistence support to students, either in the form of subsidized accommodation, or through the provision of allowances to non-residential students. Fees have been kept low for equity reasons, on the assumption that if the fees are increased then students from poorer families will not be able to access higher education. However, household data from the recent IHS3 (2012) demonstrates that 81.9 percent of current enrollment in higher education is accounted for by students drawn from the richest quintile of households, and only 1.5 percent of students come from the poorest quintile of households. In this context, low fees subsidized by government regressively benefits students from comparatively well-to-do households. In a context of rising enrollment, it is unlikely that current levels of public support to the sector will be sustainable, or that the government will be able to mobilize the resources required for the planned expansion of higher education.

A review of regional university tuition fees (table 4.2) shows that fees paid by students in the Malawian public higher education system are relatively low. Moreover, a number of comparator universities charge different fees for different programs and courses. For example, at the University of Cape Town annual fees for in the faculty of commerce range from USD 3,750 to USD 4,680 per year, and in engineering fees range from USD 3,620 to USD 5,240. Annual fees at Makerere University, in Kampala, range from USD 325 for a BSc in Agriculture Management to USD 633 for a BSc in Speech and Language Therapy.

Other public universities follow the same model as Malawi in which all students are charged the same fee regardless of their program of study. This is the case at the University of Namibia, which charges USD 540 per semester with a

Table 4.2 Comparison of Annual Tuition Fees for Universities in the SADC Region

	Agriculture	Arts	Business	Science	Engineering	Medical	GDP per Capita (USD 2011)
Botswana		2,519	2,519	3,332	3,332	3,672	9,481
Kenya (Kenyatta)	1,924	1,455			1,924	5,376	851
Malawi	150–330	150–330	150–330	150–330	150–330	150–1,800	351
Namibia	1,075	1,075	1,075	1,075		1,075	5,828
South Africa (UCT)			5,784	4,665	5,224	5,846	8,066
Tanzania		635	825	952			553
Uganda (Makerere)	930	550		695	1,427	1,070	477
Zambia		1,157–2,244		1,418–2,772		1,444–2,660	1,414
Zimbabwe (NUST)			700	800	800	800	741

registration fee of USD 113, although these fees are much higher than those charged in Malawi.

At the University of Zambia, fees differ by program and change by year of study. The highest fees are levied on first year students, with fees progressively decreasing by year of study. In Category A programs (Arts degree programs) fees range from USD 1,154 in the first year to USD 590 in the fifth year; in Category B programs (Sciences) fees range from USD 1,425 in the first year to USD 730 in the fifth year; and in Category C (Medicine) the fees range from USD 1,638 in the first year to USD 743 in the seventh year. The differentiation of fees per program takes into account the fact that some programs cost more than others to deliver, and as a consequence students are required to pay more for these courses.

Malawi has the lowest fee regime of the regional countries surveyed, and consideration should be given to increasing the fees to make the cost sharing policy more effective. There is also a need to consider implementing a differentiated fee structure that takes into account the cost of programs, based on an analysis of unit costs by faculty.[5]

It is important to take into account the ability of students to pay fees when considering changes in fees. Table 4.3 compares the tuition fees as a percent of gross domestic product (GDP) per capita in comparator countries. The data demonstrates that tuition fees in Malawi are lowest in USD terms, but moreover, that tuition fees in Malawi as a percentage of GDP per capita are among the lowest in the region. There is a concurrent need to strengthen the loan scheme to ensure that financially disadvantaged students can access loans and to improve loan recovery.

Due to the fact that fees constitute the primary source of income for private institutions, fees in the private sub-sector are significantly higher than those levied by public institutions. Fees in private universities range between MK 200,000 and MK 360,000. The disjuncture between fees charged in private and public

Table 4.3 Comparison of Tuition Fees for Universities in the SADC Region as a Percent of GDP per Capita

	Agriculture (%)	Arts (%)	Business (%)	Science (%)	Engineering (%)	Medical (%)	GDP per Capita (USD 2011)
Botswana		26.6	27.0	35.0	35.0	39.0	9,481
Kenya (Kenyatta)	226.2						851
Malawi	42.7 – 94.0	42.7 – 94.0	42.7 – 94.0	42.7 – 94.0	42.7 – 94.0	42.7 – 94.0	351
Namibia	18.4	18.4	18.4	18.4	0.0	18.4	5,828
South Africa (UCT)			71.7	57.8	64.8	72.5	8,066
Tanzania		114.8	149.1	172.1			553
Uganda (Makerere)	195.0	115.3	0.0	145.7	299.2	224.3	477
Zambia		81.6 – 158.7		81.4 – 196.1		101.8 – 188.1	1,414
Zimbabwe (NUST)			94.5	108.0	108.0	108.0	741

universities suggests that there is scope to increase fees in public institutions without affecting equity, especially in light of the existing loan scheme established to facilitate access for those who would otherwise be unable to afford fees. Given current enrollment of approximately 12,000, if fees for public universities were set at the lower end of the private universities' fee structure, this would generate an additional MK 2.4 billion in revenue for public universities, equivalent to 32 percent of the total subvention to the public institutions in 2010. Annex 4A.4 compares the distribution of revenue for universities in the SADC countries, demonstrating that, as a proportion of total revenue, Malawi has the second lowest contribution from student fees (7.7 percent), after Mozambique (1.3 percent). Malawian public higher education receives the highest government subsidy, equivalent to 91.3 percent of revenue in the public education system, compared to 88.5 percent for Mozambique. The DRC has the lowest public subsidy for higher education derived from government subsidies (33.3 percent) followed by Mauritius (39.5 percent). These two countries also demonstrate the highest share of income derived from fees: 48.3 percent for DRC and 58.5 percent for Mauritius.

Development Partners
Funding from development partners constitutes an additional source of revenue for universities. Internationally, transfers from development partners in support of higher education average USD 600 million per annum, and approximately 26 percent of this funding supports African universities and research centers (*World Bank 2010a*).

Figure 4.3 shows the distribution of direct foreign aid to higher education in selected sub-Saharan African countries for the period 2001 to 2006, measured in millions of constant 2006 USD. Of the countries shown, South Africa received the most (USD 17.4 million), and Swaziland the least (USD 0.1 million). While Malawi's absolute share was relatively small at USD 0.5 million, in terms of support per student Malawi received USD 105, compared to Kenya and Ethiopia where funding is equivalent to USD 45 per student. In absolute terms, support to the Malawian higher education is among the smallest, and more needs should be done to attract donor funding to higher education. Higher education in Malawi has benefited from the World Bank supported Education Sector Support Project (ESSUP), in which Chancellor College, the Polytechnic and MZUNI benefited from infrastructure, learning and teaching materials, and the training of staff at the postgraduate level. The current Project to Improve Education Quality in Malawi (PIEQM), supported by the Education Pooled Fund, will provide support to higher education in areas that support the development of secondary teachers; however, no specific budget for higher education is included in the project. Malawi will also benefit from the African Development Bank's (AfDB) Support to Higher Education, Science and Technology (HEST) Project, a five year project that commenced in 2012. The project's components aim to develop ICT for Skills Development and

Figure 4.3 Direct Aid to Higher Education in Selected African Countries, Annual Average Commitments—2001–06

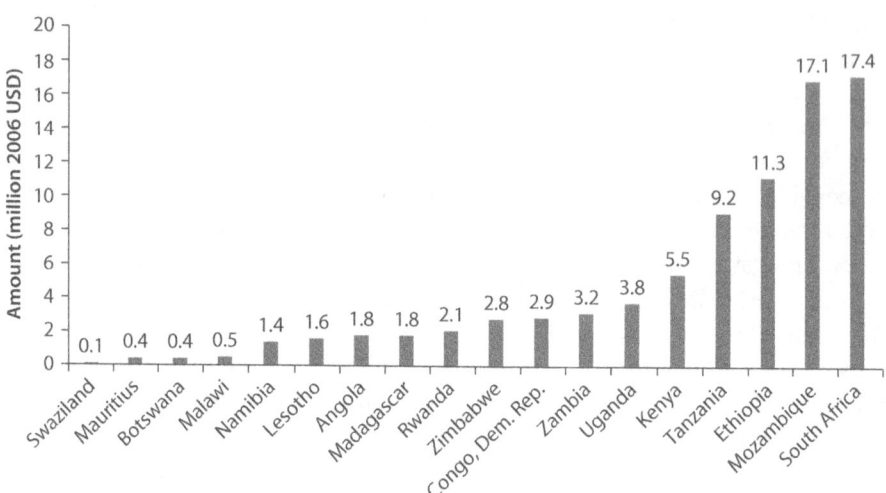

Source: Current Funding Policies and Practices in Financing Higher Education in Africa. World Bank.

Employability by providing institutional and human capacity development, improved connectivity, networked computing facilities and ODL equipment, and the provision of ICT related services in implementing agencies, including selected higher education institutions.[6] Project goals also include the promotion of access through the rehabilitation and construction of infrastructure in selected higher education institutions; improvements to the quality and relevance of higher education; the provision of training to staff in beneficiary institutions; improved links with the productive sector; and the updating of curricula. Total funding to be provided under this project is AU 29.45 million, of which the Government of Malawi will contribute AU 2.95 million in counterpart funds.[7]

Partnerships with the Private Sector
In the context of an enabling regulatory framework, public private partnerships (PPPs) have the potential to generate significant resources for universities. PPPs have demonstrated results in improving service delivery to students (such as meals, housing and transportation), and add value and relevance in the context of collaborative research projects.

Institutions can also partner with the private sector to secure sponsorship for activities and events, and in the provision of performance awards to students. The private sector and professional bodies can also be engaged to support demand driven programs and short courses delivered by universities. The private sector and professional bodies can also play an important role in awarding scholarships to students. Examples of existing collaboration in this regard include the

National Bank merit awards program which rewards outstanding students at UNIMA with annual prizes. There is also scope for universities to pursue projects with the private sector premised on corporate social responsibility. For example, at MAU, the National Building Society (NBS) and Standard Bank have sponsored sports days and the Reserve Bank of Malawi has provided computers to the institution.

Public-private arrangements can be used to augment public funds to cover investment costs, and to improve the quality and efficiency of education delivery. Greater private sector engagement with the management of higher education has been demonstrated to improve efficiency in areas such as marketing, finance, and human resource development, and can contribute to skills development and the employability of graduates (Irandoust and Kromadit 2010).

Alumni Associations
Universities, particularly in America, have strong alumni associations that assist institutions in mobilizing resources. Alumni associations are gaining popularity as universities receive less money from governments and increasingly depend on networking initiatives for funding purposes. Resources are sometimes raised through gifts alumni make to institutions and through the sale of university artifacts. Alumni can also assist in securing research projects and consultancies for the universities. While the development of alumni networks and associations in Africa is becoming more popular, including in Malawi, more can be done to further these relationship and bodies in support of fundraising.

The websites of both UNIMA and MZUNI indicate the existence of alumni associations, but these have not been very active. Other universities and institutions have created alumni networks on LinkedIn and Facebook. A review of social media networks, suggests that they are used primarily for sharing information, rather than in support of fundraising for institutions. In general universities have not benefited from the existence of alumni associations and networks in terms of resource mobilization.

Other Income
Malawian universities generate additional income through, *inter alia*, rent recovery from staff; administrative and overheads costs from projects and consultancy fees; payments for conference facilities, the staging of conferences and workshops; catering; book sales; the renting of sports facilities; facility hiring fees; interest from bank balances; and dividends from medical schemes. From the information available for this study, it was not possible to quantify the contribution of these sources of income to total income.

Resource Allocation

Resource allocation in public universities occurs at both the national and local level in the universities.

Public universities receive government funds in the form of a subvention which covers approximately 80 percent operational costs. In practice the Ministry of Finance uses the previous year's funding allocation as a bench mark for an incremental increase, taking into account anticipated salaries, utilities, student catering as well as funds for procurement of books and other necessities. Subventions also factor in a five percent increase to account for inflation. Development budgets are considered separately, and are evaluated on the basis of need and the availability of funds. (Source: Ministry of Finance)

The budget preparation process at UNIMA commences at the college level. Colleges formulate master budgets (recurrent and development) which are premised on departmental budgets and a budget projecting institution-wide needs and expenditure. A consolidated draft budget is then submitted to UNIMA's central office for further evaluation before submission to the government. Government subventions are usually lower than the amounts requested in draft budgets as demonstrated in figure 4.4. Public universities then cut out various line items to accommodate committed funds. Figure 4.4 demonstrates how subventions and additional income routinely fail to meet the targets set in draft budgets, creating funding gaps that can lead to budget deficits. It is not clear why budget ceilings are provided after institutions have already prepared draft budgets. This results in significant systemic inefficiency as universities and colleges invest significant time in readjusting their budgets. The current system of aligning allocations with historical precedent does not incentivize the improved utilization of allocated resources, and the

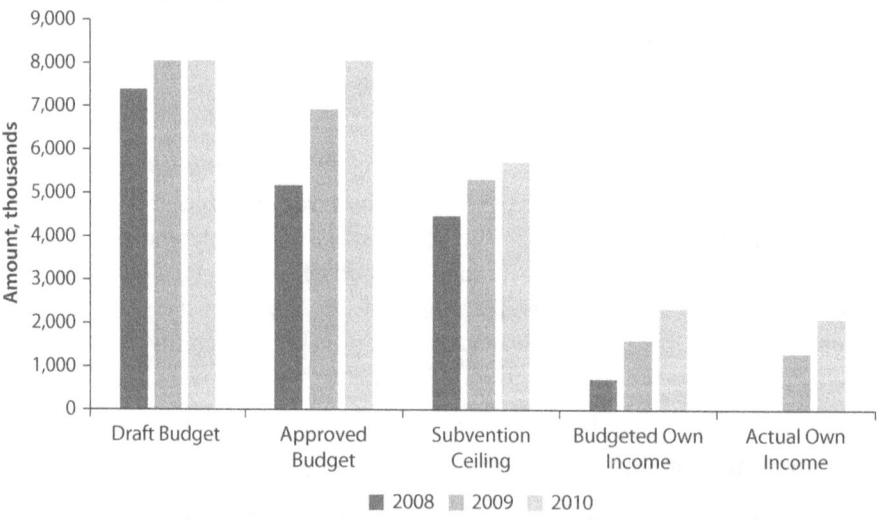

Figure 4.4 Funding Gaps in Subvention, and Internally Generated Income

Source: University of Malawi.

absence of performance indicators leads widespread inefficiencies in the utilization of resources.

Public funding of higher education in Malawi would benefit from the blending of "historical-based budgeting approaches" and "formula-based funding" methodologies. Formula based funding integrates incentives and performance measures to reward colleges that meet performance criteria with additional funding. This method has been demonstrated to improve the internal efficiency of institutions, and encourages improved performance in a context characterized by limited resources. Incentives and awards can also be aligned to leverage institutions to more effectively support the developmental needs of the country.

In general the funding of universities conforms to two broad models, or a hybrid thereof: input-based methodologies benchmark funding in line with inputs such as staff salaries, unit costs, and student enrollments. A much rarer approach to higher education budgeting incorporates measures of output into the formula. Commonly used indicators include rates of student repetition, trends in the number of minorities, women, or regionally disadvantaged students in enrollment, and research productivity. Funding can also be earmarked, wherein it is effectively ring-fenced to target particular activities.

Performance contracts take the form of contractual agreements between institutions and governments wherein funding is linked to the achievement of agreed upon performance criteria.[8] Table 4.4 demonstrates differences in the funding models utilized in the region. South Africa, for example, uses a combination of three funding methodologies, while Mozambique and Tanzania use a combination of two. There is merit in Malawi weighing the costs and benefits of different funding methodologies to inform a new policy for public funding with the potential to improve budget allocations and the performance of the

Table 4.4 Methods of Allocating the Higher Education Budget in Select African Countries

Operating budget				Investment budget	
Historically based budgets	Input based budget	Formula funding	Performance contracts	Earmarked funding	Competitive funds
Angola	Ghana	South Africa	Mali	South Africa	Ethiopia
Congo, Dem. Rep of	Kenya		Mauritania		Mozambique
Lesotho	Mozambique		Senegal		South Africa
Madagascar	Tanzania				Tanzania
Malawi	Rwanda				
Namibia	Uganda				
Swaziland	Mauritius				
Zambia					
Zimbabwe					

Source: Based on Table 3.1 of World Bank (2010a).

sector. There is a concurrent need to review the current system wherein budget ceilings are provided by treasury only after institutions have prepared their draft budget. The current system results in frustration and significant inefficiency.

Allocation at the institutional level, in both public and private institutions, is premised on the input model with a focus on the staff complements of departments and enrollment. KCN premises departmental allocations on their strategic plan and departmental staff compliments, due to salaries accounting for the largest share of the budget.

MZUNI incorporates several criteria in weighing departmental allocation decisions, including: student numbers, relative staff complements and particular needs relating to the department's discipline (the sciences in general are allocated larger budgets).

In general, institutional allocation methods are poorly defined, and, in practice, a variety of factors influence decision-making. This is commonly observed in contexts characterized by resource constraints and the need to share resources.

Resource Utilization

Trends in Recurrent Expenditure

Tables 4.5 to 4.8 capture the breakdown of expenditure in selected categories for UNIMA, MZUNI, MAU and UNILIA.[9] The data shows differences in the pat-

Table 4.5 Expenditure Trends for UNIMA— 2008–10

Expenditure category	2008 (%)	2009 (%)	2010 (%)	Total (%)
Emoluments	50	35	27	34
Benefits	16	11	9	11
Emoluments + benefits	**67**	**46**	**36**	**46**
Utilities	3	2	1	2
Student provision/allowances	6	5	6	6
Teaching materials/equipment	1	1	1	1
Books and periodicals	0	1	0	0
Travel subsistence	1	1	1	1
Vehicle maintenance/fuels & oils	3	2	1	2
Repair houses, buildings, equipment	2	5	2	3
Lease financing & assets purchase	5	1	0	1
Cleaning materials/rates & sanitation/kitchen equipment	1	1	1	1
Training and staff development	1	1	1	1
Research & publication/conferences & workshops	1	1	1	1
Common services (represents general administration)	3	2	4	3
Projects & research expenses	0	22	31	21
Other	8	11	16	12
Total expenditure	**100**	**100**	**100**	**100**

Source: University of Malawi.

Table 4.6 Expenditure Trends at MZUNI—2008–10

Expenditure category	2008 (%)	2009 (%)	2010 (%)	Total (%)
Emoluments	64.0	63.9	66.0	64.7
Benefits	1.6	1.4	1.4	1.4
Emoluments + benefits	**65.6**	**65.3**	**67.4**	**66.1**
Utilities	4.9	4.2	4.3	4.3
Student provision/allowances	7.7	7.0	6.4	6.9
Teaching materials/equipment	2.4	2.1	2.4	2.3
Books and periodicals	0.3	0.0	2.2	0.9
Travel subsistence	5.2	4.7	4.7	4.8
Vehicle maintenance/fuels & oils	2.6	2.6	2.9	2.7
Repair houses, buildings, equipment	0.9	0.9	0.7	0.8
Lease financing & assets purchase	2.6	3.3	2.2	2.7
Cleaning materials/rates & sanitation/kitchen equipment	1.5	1.8	1.5	1.6
Training and staff development	2.7	2.6	1.1	2.0
Research & publication/conferences & workshops	0.0	0.0	0.0	0.0
Common services (represents general administration)	3.6	5.5	5.3	4.9
Other	0.0	0.0	0.0	0.0
Total	**100.0**	**100.0**	**100.0**	**100.0**

Source: Mzuzu University.

Table 4.7 Expenditure Trends at MAU—2009–10

Expenditure category	2009 (%)	2010 (%)	Total (%)
Emoluments	7.6	10.1	9.0
Benefits	4.5	13.2	9.4
Emoluments + benefits	**12.1**	**23.3**	**18.3**
Utilities	0.1	0.9	0.5
Student provision/allowances	n/a	n/a	n/a
Teaching materials/equipment	1.2	2.3	1.8
Books and periodicals	3.2	1.4	2.2
Travel subsistence	0.2	0.8	0.5
Vehicle maintenance/fuels & oils	26.9	1.9	13.0
Repair houses, buildings, equipment	25.1	45.0	36.2
Lease financing & assets purchase	10.1	5.5	7.5
Cleaning materials/rates & sanitation/kitchen equipment	3.0	3.2	3.1
Training and staff development	1.0	2.0	1.6
Research & publications/conferences & workshops	1.0	0.7	0.8
Common services (represents general administration)	16.1	13.0	14.4
Other	0.0	0.0	0.0
Total	**100.0**	**100.0**	**100.0**

Source: Malawi Adventist University; data for 2008 was not provided.

Table 4.8 Expenditure Trends at UNILIA—2008–10

Expenditure category	2008 (%)	2009 (%)	2010 (%)	Total (%)
Emoluments	31.7	34.7	29.7	31.7
Utilities	4.5	3.5	3.5	3.8
Student provision/allowances	0.0	0.0	0.0	0.0
Food	18.3	22.2	35.9	27.0
Teaching practice	16.4	6.9	6.6	9.5
Books and periodicals	1.2	1.6	1.1	1.3
Travel subsistence	1.9	2.6	1.5	1.9
Vehicle maintenance	13.0	13.8	13.1	13.3
Repair houses, buildings, equipment	5.6	8.8	3.2	5.5
Lease	0.0	0.0	0.0	0.0
Cleaning materials	2.9	0.9	0.3	1.2
Training and staff development	0.0	0.0	0.0	0.0
Research publications	4.5	1.3	0.6	1.9
General administration	0.0	0.0	0.0	0.0
Others	0.1	3.5	4.4	2.9
Total	**100.0**	**100.0**	**100.0**	**100.0**

Source: University of Livingstonia.
Note: Teacher Practice referred to in the table relates to the time trainee teachers spend practicing teaching in schools as part of their program

tern of expenditure across the four institutions, which could reflect differences in management structures and practices, the diversity of programs offered, and differences in the ages of institutions. At UNIMA, MZUNI and UNILIA, expenditure associated with salaries and staff benefits accounts for the largest share of recurrent expenditure. At MAU these items represent the second largest expenditure item after "Repair houses, building and equipment," which accounted for up to 45.0 percent on this category (2010). The large share of expenditure allocated to infrastructure is likely a consequence of the fact that MAU was, at this time, still comparatively new, and still in the process of finishing and equipping campus infrastructure.

Expenditure on staff salaries (emoluments) and benefits varies across the two public institutions. At UNIMA, expenditure in this regard trended downward in the period under review, and spending on "project and research expenses" rose steeply. At MZUNI, salaries and benefits consumed a large and consistent share of recurrent expenditure, averaging 66.4 percent between 2008 and 2010.[10] The data demonstrates shifting expenditure priorities across institutions, except at MZUNI where the top five expenditure line items remained unchanged in the observed period.

Expenditure on Core Activities at Public Universities: 2008–10

Actual expenditure on core university activities increased each year in the observed period (as shown for UNIMA in figure 4.4). Increased spending is aligned with increases in government allocations to meet the needs of public institutions. However, despite improved budget allocations, actual expenditure surpasses budgeted expenses, and institutions have become more indebted during the period of review. On average, salaries and benefits accounted for approximately 46 percent of recurrent expenditure at UNIMA and 66 percent at MZUNI. The next highest component of recurrent expenditure relates to students' provisions and allowances, which account for 6 percent to 7 percent of recurrent expenditure in the two public universities.

Surplus/Deficits in Public Institutions
Figure 4.5 captures trends in funding and other sources of income against expenditure between 2008 and 2010 at UNIMA and MZUNI. Surpluses and deficits were calculated by subtracting expenditure from income, inclusive of government subventions, tuition fees and other sources of income. Large fluctuations in the economic fortunes of colleges are evident in year on year swings from surplus to deficit. Bunda demonstrates a deficit of MK 153 million in 2008, then a surplus of MK 231 million in 2009, followed by another deficit of MK 117 million in 2010. Chancellor College had a surplus of MK 38 million in 2010, following deficits in the previous two years.

The books of COM demonstrate a surplus of MK 47 million in 2008 followed by deficits of MK 14 million and MK 63 million in 2009 and 2010 respectively. Similar fluctuations in surpluses and deficits are evident at KCN

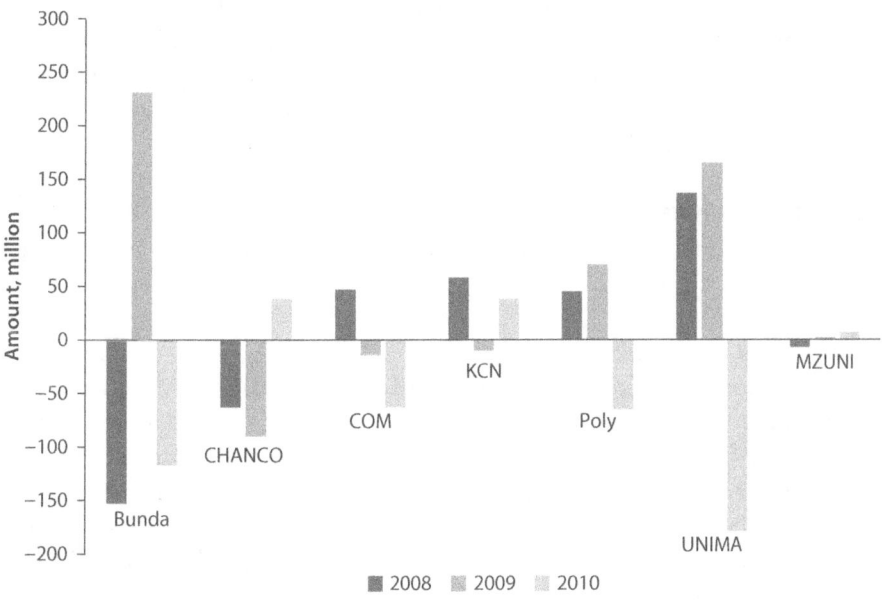

Figure 4.5 Surplus/Deficit in Public Institutions—2008–10

Source: Higher Education Institutions.

and the Polytechnic. UNIMA as a whole had surpluses of MK 137 million and MK 165 million in 2008 and 2009 respectively, followed by a deficit of MK 178 million in 2010. MZUNI was relatively stable, with lower surpluses and deficits compared to UNIMA. The institution incurred a deficit of MK 7 million in 2008, followed by surpluses of MK 2.4 million in 2009 and MK 7 million in 2010.

The magnitude of deficit spending in the public sector underlines the inadequacy of current public funding. In a context of rising enrollment, and plans to build more universities, these levels of indebtedness will be unsustainable. Without interventions to improve and diversify the income of public universities, the quality of education delivered is likely to be compromised.

Debt Levels

Information provided by institutions demonstrates outstanding Pay as You Earn (PAYE) and TEVET levy payments on the part of public institutions to the Malawi Revenue Authority (MRA). These debts are substantial and together amount to approximately MK 140 million. In some instances, universities were unable to service PAYE commitments due to poor disbursement of funds from government to universities, or the failure to transfer funds, which forced universities to divert monies to cover essential expenditure. All public institutions indicated that they were owed unpaid tuition fees by the government, and for some institutions outstanding payments amounted to MK 9 million. In this context, some students who have not paid fees are allowed to continue to receive services from the institution on the understanding that government will eventually pay the arrears.

None of the institutions surveyed owed suppliers money beyond the regular 90-day invoicing period. None of the private institutions had incurred debt, but some were owed money by students in the form of outstanding fees. In instances where fees are left unpaid after the completion of academic programs, certificates are withheld until the outstanding fees are paid.

Unit Costs Analysis

Unit cost analysis provides insight into expenditure trends and the priorities that institutions set for expenditure.

Unit Costs at the Institution Level

Figure 4.6 illustrates unit costs which have been calculated using total actual expenditure, as provided by institutions. Unit costs do not include costs incurred by students for travel, books and other education related expenses, and, as a result, unit costs do not reflect the full cost of providing education to a student. Building in these costs would be difficult as they vary by type of student and their personal situations. Costs incurred by students were estimated at around 11 percent of national expenditure.[11]

The Financing of Higher Education

Figure 4.6 Unit Costs by Institution—2008–10

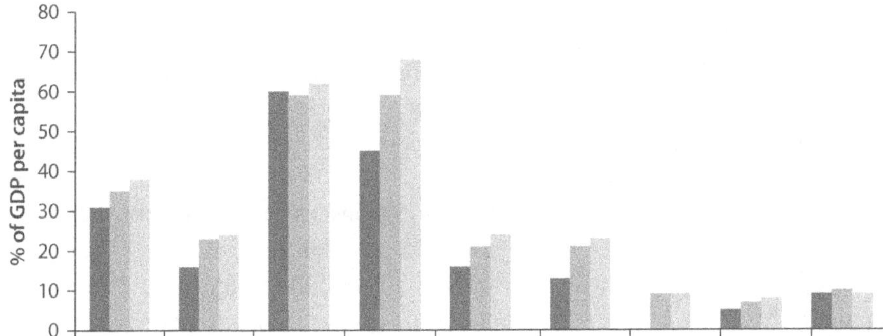

	Bunda	Chancellor	COM	KCN	Polytechnic	MZUNI	MAU	CUNIMA	UNILIA
2008	31	16	60	45	16	13		5	9
2009	35	23	59	59	21	21	9	7	10
2010	38	24	62	68	24	23	9	8	9

(% of GDP per capita)

Source: Higher Education Institutions.

Figure 4.6 compares the unit cost of education across the surveyed institutions in terms of GDP per capita to enable comparison across countries.[12] Public universities have unit costs that are much higher than private universities, which may be tied to the higher SLRs prevalent in the private sub-sector, and the more efficient use of staff (or larger classes). Another possible reason for the lower unit cost demonstrated in private institutions could relate to the programming of these institutions, which do not require investments in expensive equipment, materials and consumables compared to some courses offered at COM and KCN. Unit costs for private institutions demonstrate little change over the period surveyed, and are closely aligned with the tuition fees paid by the students.

Unit costs at UNIMA are higher than those at MZUNI, with unit costs trending upwards at both institutions through the period under review. There is variability in the unit costs of the individual UNIMA colleges, with COM and KCN demonstrating the highest costs across the UNIMA system. Rising unit costs in the public sector should be closely monitored. Increases could be associated with a general increase in the cost of living, but this does not seem to have affected private institutions to the same extent.

Unit costs at KCN rose rapidly from 45 percent of GDP per capita in 2008, to 68 percent in 2010, with the latter year demonstrating the highest unit cost for any institution in the observed period. At COM unit costs remained high, near 60 percent of GDP per capita, throughout the period of review. Chancellor College and the Polytechnic both trended upwards off a comparatively low base from 16 percent of GDP per capita in 2008, to 24 percent in 2010. Bunda College had the third largest unit costs after COM and KCN – with unit costs rising from 31 percent of GDP per capita in 2008 to 38 percent in 2010. High unit costs at COM and KCN are associated with the nature of the programs they offer and relatively low enrollment. Bunda, COM and KCN also demonstrated low SLRs, with negative implications for unit costs.

Throughout the public sub-sector, unit costs are inversely proportional to enrollment; although this trend does not apply to private colleges. This may be a consequence of the nature of the programs offered in these institutions and the imperative to keep unit costs aligned with student fees. Lower unit costs in private institutions suggest that private institutions use their available resources more efficiently due to the more pronounced requirement to stay on budget. It is noted that private institutions also had higher SLRs than those exhibited in public institutions, implying larger class sizes and/or more efficient use of teaching staff.

Public universities should work to counter the trend of rising unit costs, which in some cases increased by up to 50 percent in three years, through the identification of areas in which they can reduce spending, or improve efficiency. Due to large changes in unit costs in the public institutions, the national unit cost increased from 24 percent of GDP per capita in 2008 to 30 in 2010. Using all available data, there has been a significant increase in unit costs associated with Malawian higher education, and that the magnitude of this increase gathered momentum in the period under review. One would usually associated increases in enrollment with decreases in unit costs, but this has not occurred in this instance. Further study is required to identify and address the key drivers of rising unit costs in the public sub-sector.

Unit Cost by Expenditure Category

An analysis of unit costs by expenditure category enables analysis with regard to how much is spent on each student in that category and allows for comparison of expenditure across institutions. Expenditure is analyzed according to the following expenditure categories: Emoluments, Student Provision/Allowances, Teaching Materials/Equipment and Common Services.

The results of the analysis are shown in tables 4.9 to 4.12. A comparison of tables demonstrates that unit costs for Emoluments and Benefits at UNIMA and

Table 4.9 Unit Cost Expenditure by Selected Expenditure Categories—UNIMA

Expenditure category	2008	2009	2010	Total
Emoluments + benefit	586,102	601,256	604,483	597,838
Utilities	26,210	20,759	23,844	23,516
Student provision/allowances	55,852	70,035	98,093	75,773
Teaching materials/equipment	6,894	6,913	8,496	7,472
Books and periodicals	1,396	8,942	2,750	4,456
Cleaning materials/rates & sanitation/kitchen equipment	4,941	7,102	8,820	7,064
Common services (general administration)	22,455	28,865	60,435	38,201

Source: University of Malawi.

Table 4.10 Unit Cost Expenditure by Selected Expenditure Categories—MZUNI

Expenditure category	2008	2009	2010	Total
Emoluments + benefit	316,595	506,952	591,312	458,203
Utilities	23,762	32,348	35,684	30,008
Student provision/allowances	37,160	54,317	53,926	47,516
Teaching materials/equipment	11,678	16,435	19,998	15,655
Books and periodicals	1,520	0	18,297	6,102
Cleaning materials/rates & sanitation/kitchen equipment	7,448	13,972	12,584	11,012
Common services (represents general administration)	17,202	42,741	46,683	33,980

Source: Mzuzu University.

Table 4.11 Unit Cost Expenditure by Selected Expenditure Categories—MAU

Expenditure category	2009	2010	Total
Emoluments + benefit	43,797	103,760	74,109
Utilities	283	3,872	2,097
Student provision/allowances	n/a	n/a	n/a
Teaching materials/equipment	4,518	10,231	7,406
Books and periodicals	11,775	6,365	9,040
Cleaning materials/rates & sanitation/kitchen equipment	10,847	14,104	12,493
Common services (represents general administration)	58,550	57,675	58,108

Source: Malawi Adventist University.

Table 4.12 Unit Cost Expenditure by Selected Expenditure Categories—UNILIA

Expenditure category	2008	2009	2010	Total
Emoluments + benefit	106,282	95,430	109,838	103,966
Utilities	14,952	9,676	12,989	12,416
Student provision/allowances	0	0	0	0
Books and periodicals	4,050	4,287	4,055	4,132
Travel and subsistence	6,361	7,212	5,546	6,338
Cleaning materials/rates & sanitation/kitchen equipment	9,692	2,463	1,047	3,943
Common services (represents general administration)	0	0	0	0

Source: University of Livingstonia.

MZUNI increased in the period under review, with UNIMA surpassing MZUNI in expenditure per student. UNIMA averaged MK 597,838 in expenditure on Emoluments and Benefits per student compared to the MZUNI average of MK 458,203 per student. This is consistent with the fact that UNIMA had an average SLR of 8:1 compared to MZUNI's of 11:1. The rate of increase, however, was higher at MZUNI compared to UNIMA, perhaps aligned with changes in the SLR for MZUNI which decreased from 14:1 to 10:1 during this period, implying that lower SLRs result in greater inefficiency in the use of resources. Cost per student in this category of expenditure more than doubled at MAU, from MK

43,797 in 2009 to MK 103,760 in 2010, with an average of MK 74,109 in the period under review. This is likely a consequence of the introduction of new allowances at MAU which none of the other universities provide. At UNILIA, costs associated with salaries and allowances fluctuated slightly around the observed average of MK 103,966.

The data demonstrates much lower costs per student for emoluments and benefits in private institutions compared to the public institutions. This is partly explained by differences in SLRs across the two sub-sectors, as well as the comparatively large numbers of adjunct staff present in private institutions. It is also possible the salary scales for private institutions are lower than those for public institutions. Data was not available to compare Malawi's unit cost performance against other countries in the region.

Student Provisions was the second largest expenditure category, with UNILIA having the highest average of MK 88,700 per student.[13] At all institutions, the cost per student increased consistently in line with the cost of living. Of note is the fact that the unit cost of Student Provisions for UNIMA, averaging MK 75,733, was approximately one-third of the MK 25,000 tuition fees paid by the students. At MZUNI, the 2010 unit cost for Student Provisions at MK 53,926 is almost equally aligned with tuition fees of MK 55,000. These outcomes demonstrate the extent of government's subsidization of public higher education. The two public institutions also demonstrate large costs per student for utilities compared to private institutions, probably due to comparative class sizes, larger operations, and comparatively large numbers of residential students in the public sub-sector. The unit cost of utilities averaged MK 23,516 per student at UNIMA, with an upward trend from MK 23,762 in 2008 to MK 35,684 in 2010. UNIMA should investigate this trend, as it may represent an area in which the university can extract cost savings. For example, during field visits to the institution, lights were left on in many unused buildings, and at one college security lights, which consume a lot of power, were left on all day when they were not needed.

Unit costs for utilities in private institutions averaged MK 12,416 per student at UNILIA and MK 2,097 at MAU. At MAU the unit cost for cleaning materials, averaging MK 12,493, was the largest observed in any institution. Unit costs for common services was higher in public institutions and averaged MK 58,108 at MAU. Costs per student related to common services increased from MK 22,455 in 2008 to MK 60,435 in 2010 at UNIMA, and from MK 17,202 to MK 46,683 at MZUNI over the same period.

There is a need to examine ways of reducing the cost of common services in light of the fact that teaching and learning materials, and books and periodicals, had the lowest unit cost at all institutions. MZUNI had a higher unit cost for teaching materials, which averaged MK 15,655 through the period of review, rising from MK 11,678 in 2008 to MK 19,998 in 2010. The average cost of teaching materials at UNIMA was approximately half of MZUNI's at MK 7,472. The generally low amounts being spent per student in these categories of expenditure requires further review to ensure that it is in line with the universities' mandate to provide quality education.

Consideration should be given to the total privatization of student services, to reduce associated costs and generate savings. A recent study suggested that had Chancellor College privatized its catering service, as opposed to outsourcing it, the institution could have saved MK 289,315,000, equivalent to 10 percent of its total income in 2010.[14]

It is interesting to note that although the unit cost for teaching materials and equipment was among the lowest in the public institutions, institutions rated the availability of teaching materials, as well as books and periodicals as at least satisfactory. This is probably due to the fact that institutions are now able to access journals and periodicals online, and that the government ring-fenced resources for teaching materials which has probably helped to improve the availability of these resources in public institutions.

Annexes 4A.5 to 4A.9 illustrate unit cost analyses for expenditure categories at the constituent colleges of UNIMA. The annexes demonstrate that COM had the highest costs per student for emoluments and benefits, which reached a high point of MK 1,113,735 in 2009. High unit costs at COM are consistent with low SLRs in this institution. Bunda had the second highest unit cost for emoluments, followed by KCN. The unit costs for emoluments and benefits are lowest at Chancellor College and the Polytechnic, the two institutions with the highest enrollment. Unit costs for student provisions at Bunda more than doubled from MK 56,144 in 2008 to MK 123,783 in 2010, while at COM it increased from MK 135,644 in 2008 to MK 181,046 in 2010. KCN demonstrated the highest unit cost for student provisions, reaching MK 213,405 in 2010. Chancellor College and the Polytechnic spend less on student provisions per student than the other three UNIMA colleges. Unit costs of teaching materials are comparatively low at all institutions except for KCN which MK 182,837 per student on this line item in 2008, but very little in subsequent years. KCN should monitor large unit costs incurred for common services in 2009 and 2010, which were not aligned with increases in enrollment.

In general, the three colleges with the lowest enrollment had the highest unit costs in almost all categories analyzed. Differences in the relative cost of living across institutions does not warrant the degree of variance in costs incurred with regard to students provisions. Colleges should interrogate these numbers to identify areas for cost savings. For example, both COM and the Polytechnic are both located in Blantyre, yet their unit cost in 2010 was almost MK 100,000 per student.

In summary, the analysis shows that a large proportion of expenditure in the two public institutions and at UNILIA is spent on emoluments. The next largest expenditure per student is student provision/allowances and amounts spent on this item are much lower than the total fees paid by the students for both tuition and living costs in public institutions. Amounts spent per student on teaching materials and books and periodicals are among the lowest of all the categories.

The amounts spent on common services (administration) are much higher than on quality-related inputs such as teaching materials and books and periodicals. There is need for the universities to formulate strategies to reduce expenditure in non-core activities and improve expenditure on learning and teaching materials, as well as books and periodicals. Universities should also work to improve the allocation of resources for research and publications, which currently receive very small allocations.

Faculty Unit Costs

Analysis of unit costs presented in this report started at the institution level, which combined all the constituent colleges of UNIMA into one institution, and then moved to an analysis of each constituent UNIMA college using selected expenditure categories. Significant differences in the unit costs were noted in both cases. Differences may be accounted for due to the nature of programs offered in institutions, the use of staff, and other inefficiencies that could not be identified in this report.

It is instructive to carry out further analysis at the faculty level to observe differences in unit costs. The unit cost calculation by faculty is crude and only gives a rough estimate of this indicator. Faculty unit costs were calculated by dividing the budget allocation of each faculty by the number of students enrolled in that faculty. Staff emoluments were excluded from budget allocations, to enable an analysis of operational costs associated with teaching, research, and community outreach activities. The unit costs are shown in table 4.13.

The table shows that unit costs vary by faculty. Commerce demonstrates the lowest unit cost of any faculty at MK 91,930 followed by Education at MK

Table 4.13 Unit Cost by Faculty for UNIMA Colleges

Faculty	Allocation (MK)	Enrollment	Unit Cost (MK)
Faculty of Medicine	664,913,063	733	907,112
Faculty of Agriculture	359,696,653	544	661,207
Faculty of Environmental Studies	196,536,547	322	610,362
Faculty of Sciences	389,892,639	677	575,912
Faculty of Engineering	230,539,955	412	559,563
Faculty of Nursing	285,380,234	536	532,426
Faculty of Law	65,236,039	134	486,836
Faculty of Education and Media Studies	190,922,867	478	399,420
Faculty of Applied Sciences	208,725,821	582	358,635
Faculty of Development Studies	157,205,515	476	330,264
Faculty of Social Science	202,856,476	627	323,535
Faculty of Humanities	236,292,927	910	259,663
Faculty of Built Environment	84,924,252	398	213,378
Faculty of Education	134,228,433	1,039	129,190
Faculty of Commerce	57,915,812	630	91,930

Source: Higher Education Institutions.

129,190. As expected, Medicine had the highest unit cost of MK 907,112 followed by Agriculture with MK 661,207 and Environmental Studies with MK 610,362. The differences in the unit cost by faculty clearly shows that some programs are more expensive than others, and could provide a justification for the introduction of differentiated tuition fees, as is the practice in many other countries. Data from Chancellor College shows that there is some correlation between unit costs and enrollment in the faculties as illustrated in annex 4A.10.

Student Financing

Student financing is one of the biggest challenges constraining the provision of quality higher education in Africa, due to the comparatively high cost of higher education and the inability of students to service associated costs. As a result, many governments subsidize higher education in an effort to expand access and improve equity. In this regard, many countries have established loan schemes to improve the ability of students to service costs associated with higher education. Loans schemes are successful to the extent that they are properly targeted, loan recovery is executed effectively and within a reasonable timeframe, interest is charged to cover the cost of recovery, and debtor information is efficiently managed to facilitate loan recovery. The effectiveness of accompanying legislation, and the regulation thereof, plays an important enabling role in the loan recovery process.

Malawi's student loan scheme was introduced in 1994 as part of a broader set of interventions to promote cost-sharing between the government and students, and to improve access for comparatively poor students who would otherwise have been excluded due to an inability to pay tuition fees. The Malawian model, like many others in the world, is premised on a mortgage type loan linked to a fixed rate of payment over a given time period. Other countries use income contingent systems, in which repayment is linked to a percentage of the salary of borrowers, following their employment, which is maintained until the loan is repaid (World Bank 2010b).

The scheme was, however, established without adequately defined mechanisms for the recovery of loans, which were extended to borrowers' interest free. In 2005, the Public University Student Loan Trust (PUSLT) was established to disburse loans, and more effectively recover loans, including those that had been disbursed prior to the establishment of the PUSLT.

However, loan recovery on the part of the PUSLT remained poor, and the scheme was transferred to the Malawi Savings Bank (MSB) in 2010. The MSB was entrusted with the recovery of loans going back to 2001. MSB dispensed loans to enrolled students between 2010 and 2012, but pulled out of the scheme in 2013. Responsibility for loan disbursement is now vested with the MoEST.

The MSB has not yet commenced its loan recovery program, but is reportedly preparing to commence operations and has recruited staff from the former PUSLT to assist in this regard. The MSB will only locate debtors who benefited from loans after 2001, suggesting that loans disbursed before this date have been written off. The MoEST is in the process of drafting legislation to facilitate the recovery process. The proposed policy will require the cooperation of employers to dock debtors' salaries to finance repayment.

Students enrolled at UNIMA are eligible for a loan of MK 25,000 to cover tuition and an additional loan of MK 30,000 to fund textbooks and writing materials.[15] Beneficiaries at MZUNI are eligible to borrow MK 55,000 for tuition and an additional loan of MK 30,000 for stationary. Since the transfer of loan disbursement from PUSLT to the MSB, students can now borrow additional monies to support insurance (MK 680) and an arrangement fee (MK 856.08). Beneficiaries are granted a one-year grace period following graduation, after which they are expected to commence the repayment of their loans over a period of four years, regardless of their employment status.

Not all beneficiaries take out loans for both tuition and stationary, and students who take out loans to cover tuition, do not always take out the full amount. The cumulative value of loans disbursed since 2001 is close to MK 1.346 billion, comprised of MK 993 million in tuition loans and MK 353 million in stationary loans. Malawian students in private universities are not currently eligible for loans under the scheme.

Figure 4.7 shows the total number of beneficiaries and the value of loan disbursements for each year between 2006 and 2010. The figure shows that the number of beneficiaries increased steadily until 2009, before falling off sharply in 2010. At its peak in 2009, the 4,483 loan beneficiaries represented a little over half of total public enrollment.

Data provided by MSB is not disaggregated by gender, district, or household income. Authorities should ensure that these indicators are included going forward to inform analysis of the extent to which the scheme is effectively targeting needy students. Moreover, data provided by PUSLT and MSB does not specify the number of students who applied for the loans, so it is not possible to determine the percentage of applicants who receive loans.

Figure 4.7 Beneficiaries and Loans disbursed—2006–10

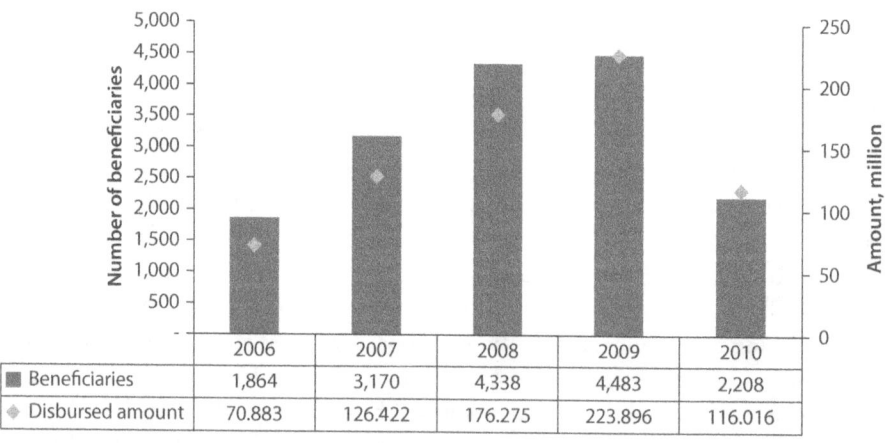

	2006	2007	2008	2009	2010
Beneficiaries	1,864	3,170	4,338	4,483	2,208
Disbursed amount	70.883	126.422	176.275	223.896	116.016

Source: Malawi Savings Bank.

The drop in the number of beneficiaries coincides with the transfer of disbursement responsibilities from PULST to MSB in 2010, which may suggest the application of a more rigorous screening process. The main criterion used to inform disbursement decisions, is the applicant's parental income. In 2012, it was reported that 800 loan applicants (constituting 59.6 percent of total enrollment) at Bunda College had their applications for loans turned down. (*Daily Times*, January 17, 2012).

UNIMA students who receive the full support from the loan scheme owe MK 226,144 by the time they graduate. Payment of this loan over a four-year period will entail a monthly payment of MK 4,711. Students at MZUNI who receive full support from the loan scheme will owe a total of MK 346,144, requiring a monthly payment of MK 7,211 over a four-year period. The government should assess the burden of repayment on graduates over the course of four years. Increasing the repayment period to at least twice the amount of time students are enrolled in study could reduce the monthly repayment burden, and in the longer term result in improved loan recovery.

Under the previous admissions policy, parallel students supported tuition and subsistence costs at rates much higher those of residential students, and supported these costs entirely from their own resources. The discontinuation of the policy applying to parallel students will affect universities in two ways: Each non-residential at UNIMA student will pay MK 25,000 compared to the MK 100,000 previously paid by parallel students - a decline of MK 75,000 per student. At MZUNI non-residential students now pay MK 55,000 compared to tuition of MK 150,000 previously paid by parallel students - a decline of MK 95,000 per student. Moreover, government now supports non-residential students through a stipend of MK 33,000 per month. The number of non-residential students at UNIMA increased from 1,777 in 2008 to 2,529 in 2011 as shown in figure 4.8. The UNIMA colleges lost revenue of MK 638 million over the same

Figure 4.8 Number of Nonresidential Students by Institution—2008–11

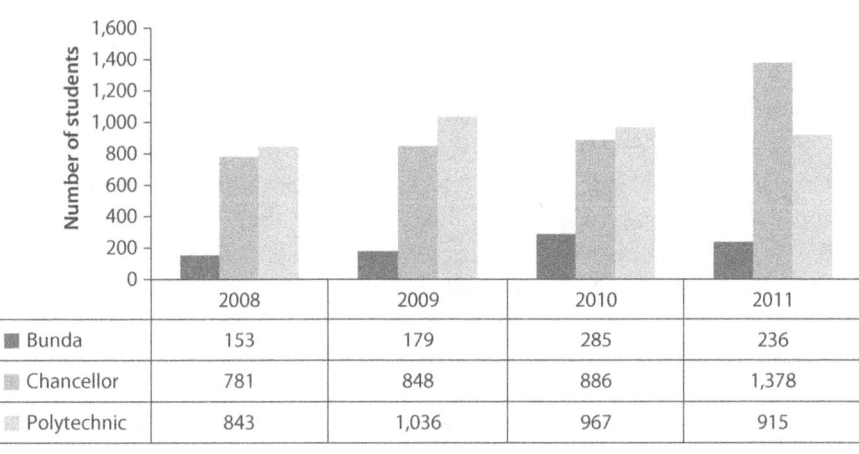

	2008	2009	2010	2011
Bunda	153	179	285	236
Chancellor	781	848	886	1,378
Polytechnic	843	1,036	967	915

Source: Higher Education Institutions.

four-year period. The government, on the other hand, accrued an additional financial obligation of MK 2.3 billion in subsistence support to these students. MZUNI had 752 non-residential students in 2010; the change in tuition policy resulted in a decline of MK 71.4 million in tuition payments, and committed government to subsistence payments totaling MK 198.5 million.

Costs Associated with the Projected Growth of Public Higher Education

It is the government's stated intention to increase enrollment in higher education through a further increase in the number of students admitted to existing institutions, and the establishment of new institutions. These objectives will require a substantial increase in the allocation of public resources in support of higher education to fund, *inter alia*, expanded infrastructure, the procurement of equipment, staff recruitment, and the significant costs associated with constructing and capacitating new public universities.

UNIMA is projected to expand enrollment up to 15,000 by 2016, and enrollment at MZUNI could rise to 5,000. In the absence of a national plan to expand enrollment, each institution must independently determine its growth path premised on its resource envelope. Access to higher education has become increasingly politicized, and public institutions are under a great deal of pressure to increase the size of their student bodies.

With total enrollment in existing public institutions projected to reach 20,000 by 2016, the funding of public higher education is likely to become more constrained, with potentially negative implications for the quality of education delivered. To prevent the erosion of the quality of service provision, expanded enrollment will need to be complemented by adequate, predictable and sustainable financial support from the government.

Conclusion

Although government subventions remain the largest source of revenue for public higher education institutions, alternative sources of finance are slowly beginning to assume a greater share of total institutional revenue. The largest source of locally generated income accrues through projects and research. Tuition fees continue to contribute very little to total revenue due to the effective freeze on fees on the part of government, and due to the fact that fees are poorly correlated with the actual costs of public higher education. Private institutions rely on almost entirely on tuition fees to finance their operations, which is reflected in the comparatively high fees levied in the private sub-sector.

To support the expected expansion of higher education in Malawi, universities will need to further diversify their sources of income. More can be done to deepen existing relationships and partnerships, and to court more development partners to support the higher education sub-sector. Effectively capacitated public private partnerships can also be leveraged to effectively support higher education.

Patterns of expenditure in the public higher education system have remained relatively unchanged, with the largest share of expenditure allocated in support of salaries (emoluments) and student provisions. Quality related inputs, such as books, periodicals and equipment, continue to receive relatively low priority, particularly in public institutions. Expenditure continues to exceed income in the public subsector, resulting in institutional deficits in the 2009 and 2010 financial years.

Unit costs vary by institution and by faculty, with COM and KCN demonstrating the highest unit costs. Generally, unit costs in public institutions are much higher than those in private institutions whose costs tend to be closely aligned with the fees paid by students. Unit costs tend to be higher in institutions with low SLRs. The variation in unit costs by institution and program suggests that there is merit in reviewing tuition fees in line with unit costs associated with specific programs of study, instead of the current practice of charging uniform fees regardless of the program of study.

Unit cost by category of expenditure demonstrates variance in the amounts different institutions allocate per student for type of service. This suggests inefficiencies in the expenditure patterns of some institutions, and will require monitoring and further study to identify cost savings, and optimize efficiency.

The provision of student loans has been taken over by MoEST. The changeover from the MSB remains too recent to enable an accurate evaluation of efficiency. While data is limited, it appears that the assessment of applications has become more rigorous, resulting in a drop in the number of loans extended to students. The main criterion used for awarding the loans is income of parents or guardians.

The government should improve efficiency in the budget processes through the timely communication of resource ceilings, and review the methods used to determine allocations to institutions. It is likely that significant efficiency and performance improvements can be induced through the introduction of performance incentives linked to measurable indicators, and the introduction of output measurements to inform a new formula for the funding of higher education institutions.

Programmatic Policy Options

Informed by the findings of this study, the policy options listed in table 4.14 are intended to assist the sector to address challenges in the financing of higher education in Malawi. Further study will be required to determine the relative cost effectiveness and feasibility of policy options to inform holistic solutions to optimize the financing of institutions in a context characterized by significant resource constraints.

Table 4.14 Policy Options

Policy objective	Issues	Programmatic options to address supply/demand constraints:	Expected impact
Finance	Insufficient funding and regressive financing of higher education to the detriment of equity.	**Mobilization** Introduce fees that differentiate fees by course and year of study in line with the actual cost of the program of study. (See annex 4A.11 for fee options.) Provide short courses and continuous learning to cater for more clients in order to increase revenue through tuition fees. (See annex 4A.12 for an estimate of fees that can be raised by offering short term courses.)	Increased revenue available to the institutions and a reduction of the dependence on government subventions and improved cost sharing. Increased revenue, promotion of lifelong learning and improved and efficient use of facilities.
		Allocation Review budget allocation procedures and recommend adjustments for greater equity (e.g. unit cost budgeting) and institutional performance. Review institutional financial regulations and assess the existing degree of budget flexibility.	Improved budget allocation, increased accountability of public resources allocated to public institutions and improved performance of institutions. Better, flexible and more responsive systems.
		Utilization Empower the National Council for Higher Education to offer financial incentives for quality improvements and to apply sanctions for poor performance.	Improved leadership resulting in improved performance and accountability of institutions. Improved quality assurance systems and improved quality in delivery of programs and research. Better utilization of resources and improved efficiency in the delivery of programs and research.
		Privatize non-core activities as part of PPPs.	Increased collaboration between institutions of higher learning and the private sector, leading to increased funding to the higher education sub-sector.
	Weak local income generation	Provide incentives to encourage departments and faculties to engage in income generating activities. Create transparent mechanisms for accounting for all income generated in the institutions.	Increased funding and collaboration between higher education institutions and business. Improved revenue generation at the local level. Increased research activities in the departments and faculties. Increased revenue arising from better accountability of locally generated resources.

table continues next page

Table 4.14 Policy Options *(continued)*

Policy objective	Issues	Programmatic options to address supply/demand constraints:	Expected impact
	Budget allocation method is weak on performance incentives	Review current budget allocation system at both national and institutional level and use different models in line with the intended outcomes, e.g. performance contract, competitive funding, and funding formulas that promote more effective use of scarce resources etc.	Improved budget allocation, increased accountability of public resources allocated to public institutions and improved performance of institutions.
			Improved responsiveness and relevance of higher education programs.
		Adopt different government funding models where institutions/programs with greater social returns are allocated more than those with higher private returns.	
	Inefficient student loan scheme	Review and improve student financing assistance programs to ensure equity in enrollments and introduce bursaries and scholarships.	More effective targeting of student funding and improved use of funding to address national skill needs and research programs aligned with national development priorities.
	Forward financial planning for higher education is poor	Review job entry requirements for senior administrative staff to improve quality of staff.	Improved quality arising from recruitment of staff with appropriate qualifications.
			Improved leadership resulting in improved performance of higher education institutions.
		Link University strategic plans to national development plans.	Improved quality in the delivery of education programs.
			Improved relevance of programs and improved role of higher education institutions in national development.

Annexes for Chapter 4

Annex 4A.1 Expenditure on Higher Education as a proportion of Total Educational Expenditure—2006–09

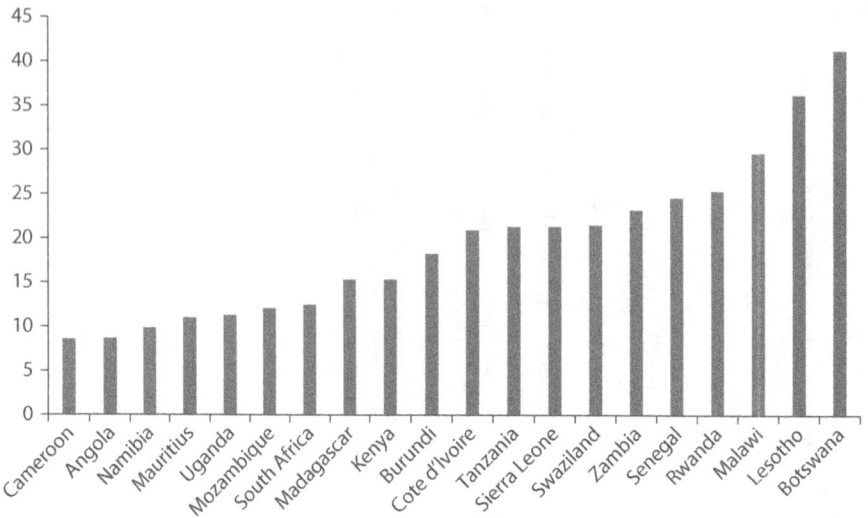

Source: Edstats SAA Indicators; Angola-2006; Namibia-2008; Kenya-2006; Cote d'Ivoire-2007; Tanzania-2008; Swaziland-2008; Lesotho-2008.

Annex 4A.2 Percentage Distribution of Sources of Income by Public Institution—2008–10

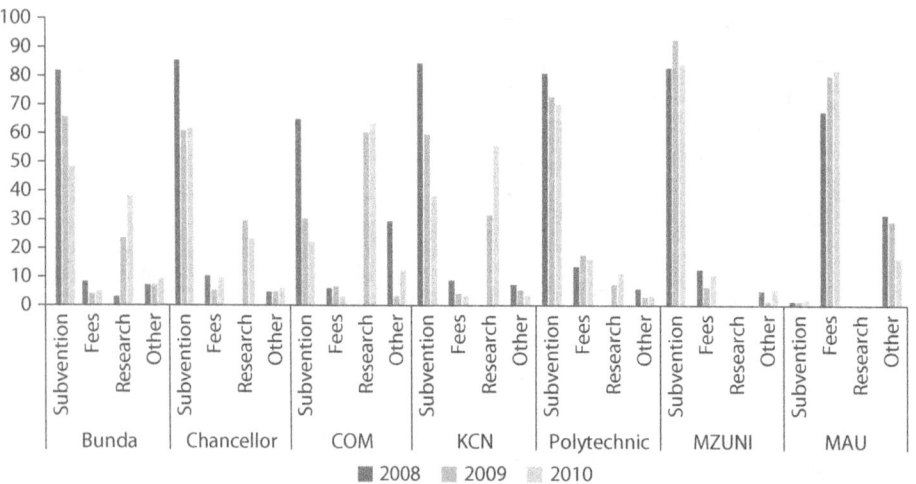

Source: Higher Education Institutions.

Annex 4A.3 Percentage Distribution of Income less Revenue from Projects and Research Grants—UNIMA: 2008–10

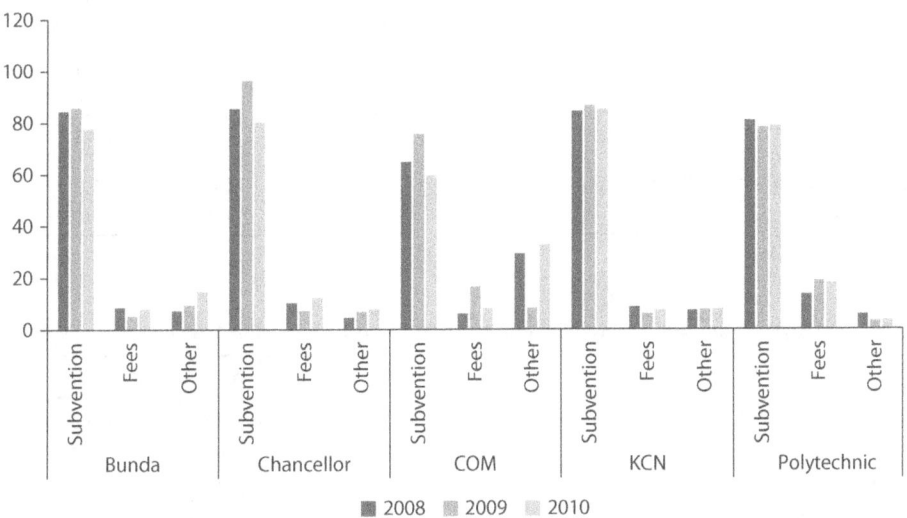

Source: Higher Education Institutions.

Annex 4A.4 Percent Contribution of Sources of Income in SADC Countries

Country	Sources of funding (%)				
	Student fees	Government subsidy	donations	loans	others
Angola	No data	No data	No data	No data	No data
Botswana	26.0	74.0	0.0	0.0	0.0
Congo, Dem. Rep.	48.3	33.3	4.5	0.0	0.0
Lesotho	No data	No data	No data	No data	No data
Madagascar	19.6	75.4	0.2	0.2	3.8
Malawi	7.7	91.3	0.5	0.0	0.5
Mauritius	58.5	39.5	0.0	0.0	2.0
Mozambique	1.3	88.5	0.5	0.0	10.8
Namibia	21.0	62.0	13.0	0.0	4.0
South Africa	29.3	46.0	2.6	3.4	13.9
Swaziland	20.0	66.0	0.0	0.0	0.0
Tanzania	18.9	62.6	14.1	0.6	3.0
Zambia	31.5	62.0	0.0	0.0	6.5
Zimbabwe	12.4	82.4	0.2	1.3	4.2
Regional average	24.6	65.3	3.0	0.5	4.1

Source: Annex 4A.4: Sources of higher education funding as reported by higher education institutions in Leadership Challenges for Higher Education in Southern Africa: SARUA Leadership Dialogue Series— Vol. 1 Number 1 2009.

Annex 4A.5 Unit Cost Expenditure by Selected Expenditure Categories: Bunda College

Expenditure	2008	2009	2010
Emoluments + benefits	897,345	856,997	986,206
Utilities	49,296	34,260	39,421
Student provision/allowances	56,144	86,476	123,783
Teaching materials/equipment	11,935	19,801	22,780
Books and periodicals	27	6,449	216
Cleaning materials/rates & sanitation/kitchen equipment	3,984	3,848	12,197
Common services (general administration)	45,214	8,170	9,586

Source: Higher Education Institutions.

Annex 4A.6 Unit Cost Expenditure by Selected Expenditure Categories: Chancellor College

Expenditure	2008	2009	2010
Emoluments + benefits	438,174	466,312	418,220
Utilities	25,809	17,741	17,859
Student provision/allowances	37,164	52,816	73,403
Teaching materials/equipment	4,565	5,678	5,264
Books and periodicals	132	4,900	423
Cleaning materials/rates & sanitation/kitchen equipment	448	606	732
Common services (represents general administration)	3,602	566	42,642

Source: Higher Education Institutions.

Annex 4A.7 Unit Cost Expenditure by Selected Expenditure Categories: College of Medicine

Expenditure	2008	2009	2010
Emoluments + benefits	1,092,451	1,113,735	998,280
Utilities	58,556	44,619	49,766
Student provision/allowances	135,644	174,648	181,046
Teaching materials/equipment	24,344	5,372	17,123
Books and periodicals	7,044	56,889	27,090
Cleaning materials/rates & sanitation/kitchen equipment	10,933	13,444	37,076
Common services (represents general administration)	23,987	20,089	36,055

Source: Higher Education Institutions.

Annex 4A.8 Unit Cost Expenditure by Selected Expenditure Categories: Kamuzu College of Nursing

Expenditure	2008	2009	2010
Emoluments + benefits	799,192	827,588	747,564
Utilities	17,386	30,230	29,465
Student provision/allowances	161,816	178,647	213,405
Teaching materials/equipment	182,837	30,560	19,098
Books and periodicals	12,772	30,125	2,514
Cleaning materials/rates & sanitation/kitchen equipment	36,891	39,426	19,159
Common services (represents general administration)	5,525	255,843	176,222

Source: Higher Education Institutions

Annex 4A.9 Unit Cost Expenditure by Selected Expenditure Categories: Polytechnic

Expenditure	2008	2009	2010
Emoluments + benefits	417,053	444,445	485,219
Utilities	12,286	11,890	17,018
Student provision/allowances	40,122	46,299	83,794
Teaching materials/equipment	2,596	2,467	5,676
Books and periodicals	0	99	116
Cleaning materials/rates & sanitation/kitchen equipment	641	5,743	8,673
Common services (represents general administration)	4,138	2,079	6,061

Source: Higher Education Institutions.

Annex 4A.10 Relationship between Student Numbers and Unit Costs: Chancellor College—2011

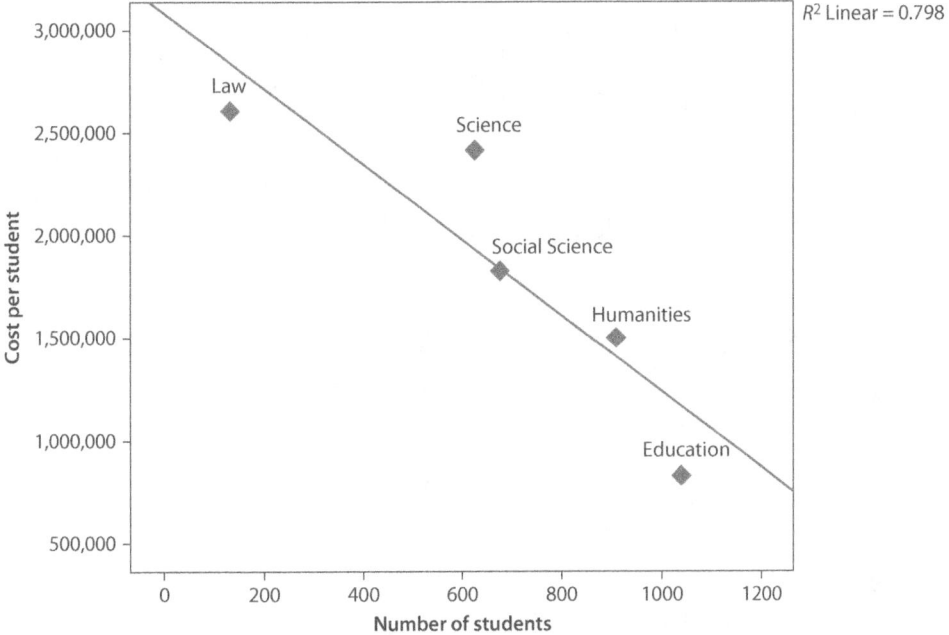

Source: Higher Education Institutions.

Annex 4A.11 Modeling of Tuition Fee Options to Increase Revenues

	Enrollment	Unit cost	Estimated tuition fees	30% of Unit Cost	Tuition fee option 50% of unit cost	70% of unit cost	@ 30% unit cost	Additional income @ 50% unit cost	@ 70% unit cost
Medicine	733	907,112	55,000	272,134	453,556	634,978	159,158,929	292,141,548	425,124,167
Agriculture	544	661,207	55,000	198,362	330,604	462,845	77,988,982	149,928,304	221,867,626
Environmental Studies	322	610,362	55,000	183,109	305,181	427,253	41,250,969	80,558,282	119,865,595
Sciences	677	575,912	55,000	172,774	287,956	403,138	79,732,727	157,711,212	235,689,697
Engineering	412	559,563	55,000	167,869	279,782	391,694	46,501,987	92,609,978	138,717,969
Nursing	536	532,426	55,000	159,728	266,213	372,698	56,134,101	113,210,168	170,286,235
Law	134	486,836	55,000	146,051	243,418	340,785	12,200,807	25,248,012	38,295,217
Education and Media Studies	478	399,420	55,000	119,826	199,710	279,594	30,986,828	69,171,380	107,355,932
Applied Science	582	358,635	55,000	107,591	179,318	251,045	30,607,671	72,352,785	114,097,899
Developmental Studies	476	330,264	55,000	99,079	165,132	231,185	20,981,699	52,422,832	83,863,965
Social Science	627	323,535	55,000	97,061	161,768	226,475	26,371,934	66,943,223	107,514,512
Humanities	910	259,663	55,000	77,899	129,832	181,764	20,837,999	68,096,665	115,355,331
Build Environment	398	213,378	55,000	64,013	106,689	149,365	3,587,333	20,572,222	37,557,111
Education	1039	129,190	55,000	38,757	64,595	90,433	−16,876,477	9,969,205	36,814,887
Commerce	630	91,930	55,000	27,579	45,965	64,351	−17,275,230	−5,692,050	5,891,130
Total							572,190,259	1,265,243,766	1,958,297,272

Annex 4A.12 Forecast Revenue from the Introduction of Short Courses

		Tuition options (MK)			
		20,000	40,000	50,000	75,000
Number of short courses	Number of students	Income	Income	Income	Income
10	100	20,000,000	41,000,000	50,000,000	75,000,000
20	150	60,000,000	120,000,000	150,000,000	225,000,000
30	200	120,000,000	240,000,000	300,000,000	450,000,000
40	250	200,000,000	400,000,000	400,000,000	750,000,000

Annex 4A.13 Detailed Expenditure Trends for Malawian Higher Education Institutions

At UNIMA, emoluments and benefits decreased from 67 percent of the total budget in 2008 to 36 percent in 2010, and averaged 46 percent over the period of review. The reduction in the proportion of expenditure allocated to emolument and benefits was accompanied by an increase in the proportion of expenditure on Project and Research expenses, which increased from zero in 2008 to 31 percent in 2010. This development is linked to increased income generated from project grants and research during this period, and is a significant development in light of the fact that in the World Bank (2010b), allocations to this category in 2007 amounted to only 0.4 percent. The share of expenditure allocated to student provisions and allowances remained consistent, between 5 percent and 6 percent, over the period of review.

Expenditure data for UNIMA also captures spending by the University Office (UO). Expenditure on the part of the UO as a proportion of total UNIMA expenditure increased from 1.4 percent in 2008 to 6.6 percent in 2010. In 2010, the UO incurred significant expenditure in support of emoluments and benefits (23.1 percent), projects and research (33.5 percent) and general administration (33.6 percent). This may imply the duplication of functions on the part of the UO and the constituent colleges.[a]

Data for MZUNI demonstrates that emoluments and benefits remained the largest expenditure item, above 60 percent of the total budget and averaging 66.4 percent over the period under review. The next three items among the top five expenditures items were student provisions, which accounted for 7 percent of expenditure, which is slightly higher than UNIMA; travel and subsistence allowances at around 5 percent of expenditure; and common services which accounted for approximately 5 percent of expenditure. Spending on books and periodicals, teaching and learning materials and equipment have remained a low priority, representing approximately one percent and two percent of average annual expenditure respectively.

As a proportion of total expenditure, MAU allocated less on emoluments and benefits than universities in the public sector, with this category of spending averaging 22.6 percent between 2008 and 2010. However, MAU allocated proportionately higher shares of expenditure to vehicles and maintenance (30.7 percent in 2008) and the repair of houses and buildings (59.4 percent in 2010), although these items may reflect the relative youth of the institution, and ongoing costs associated with its establishment. The third largest expenditure line item, in contrast to the public institutions, was common services which accounted for 18.4 percent of expenditure in 2009 and 17.1 percent in 2010, followed by lease financing at 11.5 percent in 2009 and 7.2 percent in 2010.

Patterns of expenditure at UNILIA demonstrate a different pattern of allocation: Expenditure on student provisions and allowances was the highest of all institutions, accounting for 35.9 percent of expenditure, while the share of expenditure consumed by emoluments was 29.7 percent in 2010. Costs incurred in support of vehicle maintenance are also relatively high at UNILIA, accounting for approximately 13 percent of total expenditure. This may be a consequence of the poor road infrastructure in the vicinity of the campus. Costs associated with the repair of buildings accounted for 5.6 percent of total expenditure in 2008 and 8.8 percent in 2009.

a. This issue is further discussed under the Chapter of Governance and Management.

Notes

1. In 2009/10 UNILIA was allocated MK 70 million for the construction of a girls' hostel and the purchase of a bus.
2. The allocation for 2011 was MK 7. 821 billion and was 25. 8 percent of the total public education budget.
3. Paragraph 10.1 in University of Malawi Act (2008) and Paragraph 10.1 of the Mzuzu University Act apply.
4. Exchange Rate USD 1= MK 165.
5. See the section of Faculty Unit Costs.
6. The project will provide support to Chancellor College, Malawi Polytechnic, Mzuzu University, (Lilongwe, Nasawa, Salima, and Soche Technical Colleges)
7. 1 AU = UAS 1. 5859 = MK 334. 617 (2011)
8. World Bank 2010a.
9. These are recurrent expenditures as opposed to capital expenses.
10. For more detail on expenditure trends in public and private institutions, see Annexes 4A.5 to 4A.9.
11. See World Bank 2010a, page 58.
12. GDP per Capita was estimated at MK 36,506.
13. MAU did not provide data for "student provision/ allowance.
14. Figure was extracted from "The Impact of Out-Sourcing of Non-Academic Services on Financial Resources," a paper presented at the 2011 Joint Sector Review by Prof C. F. Kamlongera.
15. Data on loan beneficiaries is not disaggregated by gender, limiting this analysis.

CHAPTER 5

Governance and Management in Malawi Universities

Introduction

This chapter describes the management structures of, and system of accountability in, higher education institutions in Malawi. The analysis highlights challenges inhibiting the effective functioning of these systems, and recommends way in which they may be addressed.

Governance in this context refers to the structures and relationships that exist between the government/responsible authority, the university council, the university management, and other stakeholders. Governance refers also to the structures through which the policies and objectives that direct an institution are determined, and how performance is monitored.

Management in this context refers to the organization and coordination of activities at an institution, in accordance with articulated policies. Systems in this regard would involve the planning, controlling, and directing of institutional resources to achieve policy and operational objectives.

Current Status of Higher Education Institutions in Malawi

Universities in Malawi fall into two primary sub-sectors: public universities, which were established by government through Acts of Parliament, and private universities, accredited by government, which were established through university charters. The MoEST is responsible for drafting bills to establish public universities. Entities that establish private universities are tasked with the articulation of the university charter and obtaining approval from government.[1] MoEST does not exercise direct control over public universities, as these are statutory organizations. However the Department of Higher Education within MoEST liaises closely with universities, and serves as the link between the universities and the government on matters of policy. As subsidized organizations, public universities obtain funding directly from the Ministry of Finance and are accountable for the resources they receive from the state.

MoEST is responsible for developing the vision and mission of higher education and the strategic direction of tertiary education in general. Each individual institution is responsible for developing its own strategic plan in alignment with the MGDS and the National Education Sector Plan (NESP), 2009–17.

Public Universities

The public universities of UNIMA and MZUNI were established by Acts of Parliament which clearly delineate institutional governance and management structures. UNIMA is a federal institution composed on five individual colleges. Due to the similar nature of their provenance, UNIMA and MZUNI demonstrate significant similarities in the manner in which they are structured, although there are some notable differences. The UNIMA Act provided for the establishment of the constituent colleges, and their respective governance and management structures. As a consequence UNIMA's constituent colleges have College Academic Boards in addition to a Senate, which is tasked with oversight of issues pertaining to academic quality. Similarly, the charters of the private universities demonstrate some similarities and differences in structure of governance and management systems.

Each institution of higher learning has a governing body which formulates the institution's strategic direction. In theory, each institution should be free to manage their own affairs and be held responsible and accountable for their performance (Fielden 2008). University governance is generally guided by principles of autonomy and accountability that limit external interference. In practice, however, the government, through the responsible ministry (education) and its participation in university councils, has a direct impact on the governance of public universities. The government's influence on the management of private institutions takes alternative forms.

Traditionally, the management of universities is coordinated through a system of committees, comprised of representatives of the university, government and other stakeholders, under the leadership of the Vice Chancellor. This system is applied in Malawi's public universities.

Council/Board of Governors

The universities of UNIMA and MZUNI are governed by councils, which are responsible for the management and administration of the university, including their property and revenues. Council's exercise general control and supervision over all the affairs of the universities, including their relations with the public.[2] Each private university is governed by a board of trustees, which assumes a role equivalent to that played by councils in the public sub-sector. Councils establish, where needed, the colleges, and other academic divisions of each university, and oversee the assignment of faculties, schools or academic sections to specified colleges. Councils moreover determine the terms of service and conditions of employment for all staff in the institution, including salary scales and rates of payment, and fees charged to students. Public university employees are not civil servants, since universities are regarded as statutory commissions. In carrying out these functions the council receives recommendations from the senate and, in some instances, from the Vice Chancellor.

The council has four main committees, which provide recommendations on governance issues. These are as follows:

Finance Committee
The Finance Committee is comprised by a subset of members of council and is chaired by the Vice Chancellor. It assists the university council in fulfilling its oversight responsibility with regard to financial management, the financial reporting process, systems of internal control, external audit functions, the monitoring of compliance with relevant laws and regulations and compliance with the code of conduct guided by the committee's charter. The Finance Committee makes recommendations to the full council on, *inter alia*, matters relating to investment and the management of the university funds; the annual budget for academic and research activities, which is prepared by the senate in consultation with the finance officer; the control of expenditure from budgetary allocations through financial regulations and other pertinent criteria; the preparation and presentation of the annual accounts of the university; and on any other matter which the council may delegate to it.

Audit Committee
The Audit Committee assists the university council in fulfilling its oversight responsibility for the financial reporting process, systems of internal control, external and internal audit processes, and the processes for monitoring compliance with laws and regulations and the code of conduct. The council may delegate to the committee any of its executive functions with regard to audit matters, subject to the general policy, control and guidance of the council.

The responsibilities of the internal auditor are to evaluate and improve the effectiveness of risk management, control, and governance processes in the university, in order to assist members of management and the council to discharge their oversight responsibilities effectively. The university's internal auditor reports administratively to the university registrar and functionally to the council through the Audit Committee. Legislation requires the appointment of a deputy university internal auditor, senior assistant university internal auditor, and assistant internal auditors to assist the university internal auditor in the performance of his/her duties.

In addition to the system of internal audit, public universities are required to comply with the provisions of the Public Finance Management Act (No. 7 of 2003), the Public Audit Act (No. 6 of 2003), the Public Procurement Act (No. 8 of 2003) and any other applicable laws. The acts require that public universities be audited at the end of each financial year by an external auditor or external auditors appointed by the council. The Procurement Act requires that public institutions follow the provisions of the Act in their procurement processes.

These systems of control ensure that public institutions are held accountable for the public funding they receive through government subventions.

Appointments and Disciplinary Committee

At UNIMA, the Appointments and Disciplinary Committee deals with matters relating to: salary scales; incremental promotions within scales; promotions from one scale to another; renewal and extension of contracts of appointment; and the granting of allowances to staff. The Appointment and Disciplinary Committee scrutinizes the dossiers of applicants for appointment to the post of full professor and then forwards its recommendation to the council.

At the college level, the Appointments and Disciplinary Committee assigns functions to sub-committees called the College Appointments and Disciplinary Committees. At MZUNI, these functions are carried out by the Academic and Senior Administrative Staff Appointments and Promotions Committee of the University Council.

Senate

The functions and powers of the senate include, *inter alia*: making recommendations to council on matters affecting the academic policy of the university; reviewing the work of the university and reporting this to the council; and making recommendations to the council with regard to fees charged to students of the university. In both the UNIMA and MZUNI Acts, the senate is required to play an important role in the work of the council, as the latter relies a great deal on the recommendations of the senate in areas of policy and governance. While the council includes members from outside of the university community, the membership of senate is limited to people who are involved in the day-to-day functions and activities of the universities.

A key function of the senate is to ensure accountability with regard to the academic affairs of the university. The senate is required to review the academic organization and development of the university with reference to the effectiveness of the university's work in relation to its mission and objectives. One of the senate's roles in ensuring that quality is maintained in teaching programs is to appoint internal and external examiners and academic consultants for degree and diploma examinations.

The senate also ensures the maintenance and enhancement of the quality of teaching by controlling all matters relating to content, methods of teaching and methods of assessment through examination or otherwise for the award of degrees, diplomas, certificates and other academic distinctions. It is also responsible for the consideration of the performance of students in examinations and decisions pertaining to which students shall pass, be referred, repeat or not be re-registered (based on the recommendation of the College Academic Board in the case of UNIMA constituent colleges).

The senate determines and controls the terms and conditions under which any research, outreach and consultancy or any other activity may be conducted or carried out in the university or by members of staff, or under the sponsorship of, or in collaboration with, the university or with members of its staff.

The faculties, centers and institutes of the university are established by the council on the recommendations of the senate. For UNIMA, the faculties are created within individual colleges, and each UNIMA college has an academic board which is responsible for the academic affairs of the college. In addition to the faculties, UNIMA colleges also have various departments within faculties. Since MZUNI is a singular university, the faculties are created under the senate.

University Officers
Chancellor
The Chancellor is the nominal head of the institution. For the two public universities, the Chancellor is the State President. For private universities, the Chancellor is selected from among members of the entity that established the institutions, which in the case of Malawi is the relevant church. For instance, at MAU, the Chancellor is from Baraton University in Kenya and at CUNIMA the Chancellor is the Bishop of the Catholic Church in Malawi.

Vice Chancellor
The Vice Chancellor at public universities is appointed by the council following the recommendation of a special committee set up for that purpose. He or she is the university's principal academic and administrative officer. The appointment is subject to the approval of the Chancellor and the post is held for four years. The Vice Chancellor is literally appointed by the Chancellor.

Other Officers
The university's main administrative officers are each appointed by the council: the deputy Vice Chancellor is approved by the Chancellor and assists the Vice Chancellor in his or her duties; the Registrar is the chief administrative office of the university and works under the authority of the Vice Chancellor; the librarian is the principal officer in charge of the library and also works under the authority of the Vice Chancellor; the finance officer is the principal finance manager and treasurer of the university and is accountable to the registrar.

MZUNI appoints additional administrative officers: a director of investment who, as the name implies, is in charge of investing the university's funds and is appointed by the council; and a director of research who is responsible for research activities in the university. Both these officers report to the Vice Chancellor.

The next level of officers is constituted by the deans. There is one dean for each faculty and school, as well as for postgraduate studies, and a dean of students. At UNIMA, deans are elected from within, and by, the full-time academic staff of the faculty or school concerned. Deans were initially supposed to hold office for two years, but the senate has determined to extend appointments to a four-year term. At MZUNI, deans are appointed by the council from among the senior academic staff of the faculty, and hold office for three years or as determined by the senate. UNIMA is in the process of amending its Act to introduce the appointment of executive deans, to replace the current system of elected deans. Executive deans will be appointed by the Vice Chancellor for a period of four years. The change to appointed executive deans with four-year tenure in place of elected two-year elected deans is intended to mitigate challenges associated with the politicization of dean appointments through the process of elections, and to contribute to the professionalization of the position, with positive implications for efficiency and accountability.

Deans are entrusted with: the overall coordination of all matters relating to the welfare of the students within their faculty, school or postgraduate program; and to carry out duties in connection with students' studies, attendance at lectures, welfare, and other academic matters as determined by the senate. Deans are also responsible for the selection of persons registered as students for study or research assigned to the faculty in which he/she is dean.

Private Universities

MAU is governed by a council of thirteen members. The councils memberships is meant to be composed of two-thirds of membership selected from the laity and one-third from the clergy. In practice, this is not always observed, with the clergy comprising more than a third of the council. The Vice Chancellor is appointed by the council after an interview process. He/she is supported in his/her duties by the registrar and finance officer.

CUNIMA has a council and a Vice Chancellor assisted by three Deputy Vice Chancellors of Administration; Finance; and Academics. The Registrar reports to the Deputy Vice Chancellor of administration while the Finance officer reports to the Deputy Vice Chancellor of Finance. The deans report to the Deputy Vice Chancellor of Academics. Below the Vice Chancellor are the Director of Research and Publications; the librarian; and the Director of Investment and Purchasing.

UNILIA has only the College of Education, which is headed by the College Principal, supported by a Deputy College Principal. Below the Deputy College Principal are: the dean of studies who is supported by the deputy dean of studies; the dean of students who also has a deputy; the college finance officer supported by a deputy, who is in turn is supported by the chief accountant; the college registrar is supported by a deputy registrar who is in turn supported by an academic registrar and an administrative registrar; and a college librarian supported by a deputy.

In the absence of agreed performance indicators, it has not been possible to determine whether the differences in organizational structures in public and private universities impact the performance of institutions in such areas as completion rates and rates of employment for graduates. Differences between public and private institutions were noted with regard to higher SLR in the private sub-sector, which may be associated with better and more efficient use of staff in private universities. This is something that the newly appointed NCHE should study further. It has also not been possible to determine the level of autonomy of the institutions based on governance and management structures. An autonomy scorecard,[3] as administered in European universities, could shed some light on the level of autonomy that universities in Malawi enjoy.

National Council for Higher Education

In 2011, the National Council for Higher Education (NCHE) Bill was approved by Parliament and assented to by the State President making it law. The NCHE has now been appointed in accordance with the provisions of the Act. According to the Act, the council's main functions are to regulate higher education institutions through: the promotion and coordination of education provided by higher education institutions; the registration of such institutions; the selection of students into public universities; the design and recommendation of institutional quality assurance systems for higher education; and the provision of guidance on terms and conditions for the awarding of grants and scholarships to students at public higher education institutions. The council is made up of six persons with high professional standing in higher education, appointed by the minister. The council includes two Vice Chancellors who represent public universities; one Vice Chancellor to represent private universities; the chief executive officer of the council; and the following ex-officio members: the secretary for education (or representative); the secretary for finance (or representative); the comptroller of statutory cooperation (or representative); and the secretary for human resource management and development (or representative).

An important function of the NCHE will be the registration and accreditation of institutions of higher education. The first phase will entail the registration of institutions using prescribed criteria and standards. The second phase will involve the evaluation of institutional performance in every academic cycle for the purposes of accreditation. The council will issue accreditation certificates to institutions that fulfill quality assurance standards set by the minister on the recommendation of the council. In this respect, the NCHE will contribute to ensuring that higher education institutions maintain the standards for which they were awarded their registration and accreditation.

The NCHE will have the power to advise the minister to revoke the charter of a private university if the council establishes that the institution has failed to carry out its objectives; has breached its charter in any material respect; is not carrying out its functions properly; and/or that it is in the general interest of higher education in Malawi for the charter to be revoked. It is still too early to judge how the council will perform and what its impact will be, but it is destined to play a critical role in quality assurance and enhancement in the higher education institutions in Malawi.

There will be need for a further clarification of the role of the NCHE vis-à-vis the roles of the University Councils also established by Acts of Parliament and the roles of the Senates that assume the lead for ensuring standards of quality and the relevance of programs in the universities. The relationship between MoEST as the parent Ministry, the Ministry of Finance as the funder of programs, and the NCHE also needs to be clearly understood in order to ensure a holistic program to promote performance and accountability in the public universities.

Challenges of Governance and Management in Higher Education

Many new challenges have arisen for the higher education sub-sector in Malawi following the establishment of a number of private universities in the absence of clear policy direction from MoEST. Proprietors of these universities have used the National Education Sector Plan (NESP) as a springboard for their establishment, but, NESP lacks indicators to measure the performance of these higher education institutions.

Governance in Higher Education
Autonomy in Higher Education Institutions

According to Fägerlind and Strömqvist (2004), autonomy concerns the relative ability of a higher education institution to govern itself without outside control. Outside control refers to leverage from entities outside the formal university institutions and the university community itself. Part II (4) of the MZUNI Act (and similarly for UNIMA) creates the university and designates the Head of State as the Chancellor of the university. Technically, the Chancellor is a member of the university. The Chancellor also appoints the chairman of the university council, which is the governing body of the institution, and the chairperson is required to keep the Chancellor fully informed on matters concerning the general conduct of the affairs of the university.

This therefore creates a delicate balance between the state and the public universities when it comes to matters of autonomy. What autonomous rights can institutions claim when directions are given by the state, whose head is simultaneously their Chancellor? A review of both the UNIMA and the MZUNI Acts shows they do not specifically grant these two institutions autonomy as defined by Fägerlind and Strömqvist (2010). The university council is referred to as a "body corporate" with certain responsibilities relating to giving direction to the institution, but it does not operate as an autonomous body.

The membership of the council itself, which includes a chairperson appointed by the country's President, ex-officio members such as the secretaries of education, and the treasury, may not necessarily be interpreted as state interference but be seen as a way of steering the institutions in a direction that is consistent with government's general policy direction and development agenda. The debate on the relative autonomy and academic freedom of the universities is current in other countries. For instance, in 2006, the Council for Higher Education (CHE) in South Africa commissioned a study on "Academic Freedom, Institutional Autonomy and the Corporatized University in Contemporary South Africa". A report on this study notes that the reliance of public universities in Africa on public funding has left them and their staff vulnerable to pressure from government. The report notes that state financing of the higher education systems enhances the power of state bureaucrats, with the potential to violate university autonomy as well as the freedom of individual academics. It also notes instances in which autonomy and academic freedom are under threat from institutional bureaucrats within the universities, which includes the councils and those in administrative hierarchies including Vice Chancellors who undermine the atmosphere of collegial governance in the universities. It further notes that university research agendas are no longer determined by the academics themselves, but by those prepared to buy (fund) their research and, in particular, the private sector. By and large, in post-colonial Africa, universities have been seen to be anti-state when they have criticized the excesses of government and, in many instances, these criticisms have led to interference in the affairs of universities.

In 2008, the European Commission (Directorate-General for Education and Culture) provided financial support to the Eurydice European Unit to produce a report on "Higher Education Governance in Europe—Policies, structures, funding and academic staff", focusing on the autonomy of universities in Europe. The report highlights the balance between autonomy and accountability in higher education. Although higher education institutions in Europe are legally autonomous entities, the regulatory framework allows governments and the public to hold them accountable for the services they provide and the funds they receive. The report notes that universities' internal governance structures are defined by legislation, which defines the institutional governance bodies and their respective rights, duties and responsibilities. The procedures for election or appointment to institutional governance bodies are specified in institutions' constitutions or statutes.[4] In Malawi this takes the form of the establishing Acts of public institutions, and their associated Statutes and Regulations. Both the South African and EU reports emphasize how institutional reliance on state funding can undermine their level of autonomy and academic freedom. This is clearly the case in Malawi where institutions are even more dependent on government subventions than institutions in Europe.

The extent to which public universities can assert autonomy from the state from which it derives the largest percentage of its budget, will remain a pressing issue. Husén (1991) argues that the relationship between public universities and the state is delicate, and the discussion thereof must make the distinction between "dependency" and "intervention". Events that led to the closure of Chancellor College in 2010/11, after a lecturer was questioned by the police about what he had taught in a lecture, brought to the fore the potential for tensions to arise between higher education institutions and the state in issues of governance. Undue tension creates environment unconducive for public universities to fulfill their mandates, undermining growth and their ability to become strong and responsive institutions. Tensions are bound to surface from time to time, and, as a consequence, these tensions must be managed for the good of the students who are the direct beneficiaries of higher education and for the growth of higher education.

The Acts establishing higher education institutions and the relevant statutes governing them give both public and private universities complete autonomy in a number of areas. This includes the appointment of staff - apart from those in senior management, where approval of the Chancellor is required. Institutions also enjoy autonomy in the use of resources that are provided from the state, subject to audit requirements that affect all statutory organizations that receive public support. Universities also have complete autonomy in the selection of students and in the programs that they offer. Nonetheless, as indicated above, situations arise on occasion that threaten academic freedom and impinge on academic autonomy.

Other issues contribute to tensions between institutions and the state. The imposition of the "quota system," designed to promote more equitable distribution of students by region and district, has been regarded by the institutions as interference on the part of government in the selection of students. The government in practice also sets tuition fees, even though this function is clearly indicated in the Act as falling under the purview of each university's council. This has been a challenge for the institutions since the fees mandated by government are inadequate to meet the costs of higher education provision, even with enrollment subventions. The university is mandated to run income-generating programs to subsidize the subvention from the government. However, cost sharing with the government is currently very low, leaving the government as the main provider of funding for operations at the public institutions.

At UNIMA, the recruitment of staff and lecturers has been decentralized to the constituent colleges. The University Office recruits senior administrative staff and academic lecturers at the level of associate professor and full professor. The recruitment process is based on a set of prescribed procedures. However, there are many anomalies associated with recruitment processes, raising the need for a monitoring mechanism to ensure that recruitment processes are aligned with agreed upon protocols.

The decentralization of staff recruitment should be complemented by the decentralization of capacity and accountability. In general policy is poorly implemented due to a lack of knowledge regarding policies, and weak capacity to implement them. Clear guidelines and accountability mechanisms are needed for decentralization to work efficiently.

Private universities have the freedom to determine their own goals and set priorities, choose leaders, employ and dismiss staff, determine their rates of growth through enrollment, manage their resources and save generated funds. The provisions of MZUNI's Act similarly assert these freedoms. However, for the constituent colleges of UNIMA some of these decisions are made at a centralized level by the university council and senate. It is anticipated that the NCHE will facilitate improved interaction between the government and the universities and will assist in mitigating tensions between universities and the state with regard to issues of autonomy and academic freedom.

Public universities are financed by public resources and should be accountable for these resources. Accountability should function in two ways: First, there should be accountability in terms of the use to which the resources are put — this is usually achieved through audit and management reports. Secondly, universities should be accountable with regard to delivering on their mandate to produce the human resources required to support the country's socioeconomic development, and in performing research aligned to the country's developmental challenges. To what extent the universities are responding and contributing to the goals, objectives and targets set in the MGDS—and their overall usefulness to society—is a topic for further discussion.

Public universities are audited annually by an external auditor appointed by the university council, as provided for in the Act. MZUNI has fallen behind with its audits and there is a need to ensure that audit reports for MZUNI are produced as stipulated in the Act. UNIMAs finances have been consistently audited on an annual basis.

Limited Membership of Council and Boards

The membership of the Councils in public universities is limited with respect to the representation of professionals and the skills mix of its members. The membership of the university council comprises the following: the chairperson of the council, appointed by the country's president; Vice Chancellor; principals of the colleges; the Secretary for MoEST (or designated representative), ex-officio; the secretary to the treasury (or designated representative), ex-officio; two members appointed by the Chancellor; four members appointed by the senate from among its members; one member elected by the University of Malawi Ex-students Association; one member appointed by the council from a panel of three persons distinguished in university affairs in Malawi, nominated by the Vice-Chancellor; one female member and one male member elected by the University of Malawi Students Union; and such other members, not exceeding four, as the council may co-opt. The composition of MZUNI's council is more or less the same as that for UNIMA, except that its membership also includes a member of the senate from UNIMA and the chairman of the board of trustees of the Mzuzu University Trust.

An examination of the membership of the councils shows that it is limited to members of the academia community and the government. Councils are not required to include representatives of the private sector. This is despite the fact that the private sector is an important consumer of higher education output, and is recognized as a potential source of finance in support of higher education through proposed public private partnerships (PPPs). Moreover, Councils are not required to include special interest groups like women, those living with disabilities, and members of the trade unions, which represent important stakeholders in the provision and consumption of higher education. Consideration should be given to requiring the inclusion of representatives of these groups as members, without leaving it to the council to choose whom to co-opt.

Membership of the councils of private universities is also generally limited to the university personnel, church leadership and lay church members. Universities could benefit from improved governance and management practices by the inclusion of people from the private sector in their councils. In addition to providing financing, private sector members of the council can encourage improved management and business practices. Participation of the private sector in the councils will also go some way in promoting PPPs, which have the potential of providing the additional resources and could facilitate the attachment of both staff and students in the private sector as part of their training programs.

Effectiveness of Council Sub-Committees

The management of universities relies to a large extent on the committees and sub-committees of the council and senate. These entities may be permanent or established to achieve specific tasks as and when the need arises. There is a general over-reliance on committees for decision-making in the Malawian university system. Information from the institutions suggests that various committees have not been very effective. Due to a lack of funding, committees do not meet regularly, with the consequence that when they do meet agendas are overburdened, and decisions tend to be rushed. Effectiveness is also hindered by the relatively high turnover of deans, whose participation is limited by their four-year tenure. Associated costs for institutional memory, and efficiency, are heightened by poor handover practices through the process of transitioning from one dean to another.

Lack of Critical Positions in the Universities

It has been noted that higher education institutions in Malawi do not have offices designated to fulfill functions consistent with the aspirations of a modern university. The registrar's office tends to be tasked to deal with tasks that have not been clearly assigned through the institution's structure. The university Acts describe the registrar as the "chief administrative officer," who, because of the lack of other essential positions in the structure of the university, is encumbered by other functions that are not administrative in nature. This study identified some of the offices that could be established in order to promote improved performance and responsiveness on the part of institutions. These are: strategic planning officer, fund-raising officer, the public relations officer, and the marketing officer. Clear job specifications and job descriptions for each position will clarify the roles and responsibilities of officers and promote accountability.

Strategic Planning Officer

Strategic planning is an important function critical for the effective development of short-term, medium-term and long-term plans to articulate institutional visions and mandates. However, there is no dedicated officer in any of the universities specifically assigned to perform this function. Instead, Planning

Committees are responsible for the development of strategic plans. At the UNIMA colleges, the committee works in coordination with college registrars and the pro-Vice Chancellor.

Fundraising Officer
It was noted in the financing chapter that resources generated by the universities are relatively low in comparison to the proportion of income derived from government subventions and tuition fees. As the demands on government resources increase, its ability to continue to support an expanding higher education system will be limited. This makes it essential for universities to take active steps to fundraise for themselves through the creation of the post of fundraising officer who will work closely with the marketing officers.

Public Relations Officer
None of Malawi's universities or colleges has a dedicated person entrusted with public relations. As a consequence, the office of the registrar is typically tasked with coordinating public relations activities, resulting in the overloading the registrar. As a result, registrars are passive and/or defensive in dealing with issues involving the university. Moreover, registrars may not have undergone any formal training in public relations and are therefore not adequately equipped for the work. Given that the universities operate in an increasing complex environment and are expected to be part of the development process, need to actively engage with a host of stakeholders, and should be accountable for resources provided by the taxpayers, there is need to create a public relations office responsible for developing and implementing a public relations plan for each institution.

Marketing Officer
Currently no university in Malawi employs an officer to coordinate marketing activities and provide professional advice. In an increasingly competitive and constrained resource environment, universities need to market themselves and the services they provide if they are to generate additional resources to fulfill their missions. Marketing assists in attracting students and the private sector for purposes of investment and raising additional resources through PPPs, research, project grants and consultancies. There is a need to centralize these activities in one office instead of leaving them to individual faculties to handle.

Currently, marketing activities are handled by the registrar's offices. Marketing efforts on the part of universities is relatively ineffective as registrars are not trained in marketing and this should not be a focus of their work. Public universities are inherently advantaged due to high demand for their programs due to affordable fees, strong reputations and a diverse range of programs on offer, and may not need to market to the same extent as the private universities. But there is certainly more that needs to be done to woo the private sector and other stakeholders to boost universities' resources. The private universities such as

CUNIMA, MAU and UNILIA need more marketing to navigate comparatively intense competition in the private sub-sector, and to create a source of competitive advantage.

The University Office of UNIMA

UNIMA is composed of five constituent colleges under a central University Office (UO). The UO is primarily tasked with the administration and oversight of the colleges. Its structures are duplicated at each constituent college, which in turn provide oversight of these functions at the college level. UO expenditure as a percentage of total UNIMA expenditure increased from 1.4 percent in 2008 to 6.6 percent in 2010. In 2010, the largest components of expenditure at UNIMA were Emoluments and Benefits (which accounted for 23.1 percent of total expenditure), Projects and Research expenses (33.5 percent), and General Administration (33.6 percent). The Malawi Institute of Management in 1996 recommended the decentralization of a number of functions from the UO to the constituent colleges, and this reform has been on-going but is yet to be completed. The current strategic plan recognizes the need to continue the process of decentralization, but it is not clear what role the UO perform once the process of decentralization is completed. It will be useful at this stage to review whether the continued existence of this office can be justified. This should be done against the background of the government's efforts to combine tertiary education institutions of similar function to form free standing universities, as is the case with Lilongwe University of Agriculture and Natural Resources (LUANAR).

The UNIMA structure is seen inefficient due to the fact that some UO functions are duplicated in individual colleges. Costs incurred in support of duplicated functions could be allocated to colleges for other important activities. Moreover, the duplication of functions in the same hierarchy undermines accountability and clear lines of responsibility, with adverse effects for institutional performance. Significant expenses are incurred through travel costs. This is a consequence of all college principals being members of the UNIMA Council and the fact that most of the deans of the colleges are members of the senate and various sub-committees of the senate. Council and committee members must travel to Zomba for meetings and other activities where their presence is required. The centralized decision-making process inevitably leads to unnecessary delays, as meetings have to be scheduled when members are available. There is need to carefully examine what value the UO adds to the operations of the colleges through its oversight in relation to its related costs.

Management in Higher Education

Lack of Skills in Planning, Leadership, Implementation, Entrepreneurship Decision-Making and Resource Utilization

Information provided by institutions for this study, indicates that personnel holding management positions generally do not receive training or orientation with regard to their responsibilities. The posts of Vice Chancellor and Deputy Vice

Chancellor are occupied by lecturers who have been promoted into these positions. As a result, they do not have significant expertise in management and administration. At UNIMA, this pattern of promotion to management applies to the principals of the constituent colleges. Principals are not trained as managers, as they are drawn from the community of academic members of staff. On appointment, the senior management of universities and colleges should be given training in the management of higher education institutions, to equip them with the tools required to effectively manage their institutions.

There is no real training for the position of register and appointees typically learn their skills on the job, with support from short courses like those arranged by the Galilee College in Israel. The UO has started an orientation program to provide training in management skills, financing, planning, and procedures and processes for registrars. Systems are also being put in place to ensure that appointees to management posts are provided with all relevant policy documents and regulations to assist them in executing their responsibilities. With the proposed creation of executive deans, there is need to prepare guidelines and clear responsibilities, as well as provide training, since the new deans will be expected to do more and be more accountable to the administration.

In many instances there are no operational guidelines and manuals for key areas of university operations. In this context there is an over-reliance on institutional memory and precedent to determine how things should be done. These practices undermine the efficient delivery of services in the institutions. The process of decentralizing the functions of the UO to the constituent colleges has contributed to these problems due to the absence of guidelines and terms of references to inform decentralized functions.

Lack of Identification of Institutional Competitive Advantage
Until recently, there have been no attempts to identify the competitive advantage of each institution, to assist institutions in the development of study programs. Some of the new programs introduced in universities duplicates what is already being offered in other institutions. Institutions should diversify into new areas based on the needs of growth sectors of the economy as indicated in the MGDS. The proposed establishment of the LUANAR is a step in the right direction. More needs to be done in this regard, through the delinking of the constituent colleges of UNIMA to make them into individual universities, each with a unique focus. The planned merger of the COM and the College of Health Sciences, and the proposed establishment of the University of Marine Biology and of the University of Science and Technology are further steps in the right direction. The transformation of the constituent colleges of UNIMA into fully-fledged universities will also enable faster decision-making in the management of these universities.

Undefined Methods for Resource Allocation
In most universities, budget allocations are premised on staffing levels in the faculty, student numbers and equivalent ratios, with weighting based on the

complexity/cost of the program. These budget allocations are not informed by a clear formula. The budgets presented by the university are activity-based, but funding is given in accordance with enrollment, and in line with other priorities in the national budget. Many governance and management activities cannot be adequately performed due to lack of financial support.

Staffing
There is little evidence of overstaffing in Malawian universities. However problems arise due to a high number of staff doing comparatively little or redundant work. Inefficiencies in this regard, result in high operational costs. In order to improve efficiency, some universities like UNIMA and CUNIMA have outsourced a number of non-academic functions such as catering, maintenance, security and cleaning services.

The size of the academic staff in most universities is either below the required number or merely adequate, and as reflected in SLRs. Information suggests that universities engage part-time lecturers when there are shortages of staff, particularly in specialized fields like medicine, law and engineering. The system of part-time staff recruitment is practiced at UNIMA, MZUNI, MAU and CUNIMA.

Timely Recruitment of Staff and Succession Planning
Efficient and timely recruitment and replacement of staff is a persistent challenge in the public higher education system. Academic and non-academic posts are often left vacant for considerable periods of time. This problem is more acute in specialized fields such as the sciences, law, engineering, medicine due to the relative scarcity of qualified people available to fill these positions.

Delays in the staffing of non-academic posts is acute, apparently due a lack of appreciation on the part of management for the importance of non-academic staff, perhaps because their contribution is indirect and less visible. Delays in the replacement of staff can be attributed to an overly bureaucratic recruitment system which requires approval by the appointment committee of the senate. Public universities such as UNIMA and MZUNI are legally required to advertise vacancies in the media. The process of advertising, interviewing and final selection is time consuming; resulting in delays at the expense of efficient service delivery.

Lack of Staff Appraisal System
Public universities currently do not have a performance appraisal system for top management and academic staff. While the senate is responsible for ensuring quality in the conduct of university academic mandates, information from the institutions shows that there is no formalized system to assess staff performance in the three focus areas (discussed in chapter 3) of Teaching, Research and Community Outreach. There is also no mechanism for the evaluation of administrative staff, although there have been cases where students have demonstrated against the performance of administrative staff in public institutions, and also in one private university.

Staff Retention Incentives
Research shows that members of staff work effectively when they are well motivated. Incentives generally take two forms: those that apply to all staff and those that are provided as a reward for exceptional performance based on results achieved (merit awards). Data obtained from higher education institutions show that there are no established incentive mechanisms for staff in public universities, except in the form of promotion and merit awards. MAU, however, has a comprehensive incentive system for staff. However, these incentives are not performance related but are utilized by MAU to attract and retain staff. The introduction of incentives can play an important role in motivating staff, improving staff retention, and boosting performance with positive implications for efficiency and service delivery.

Lack of Adequate Support for Staff Welfare
There are well-established staff welfare committees in the public university subsector, primarily in the form of labor unions. Public universities do not financially support social welfare committees, rendering them largely ineffective, with negative implications for staff motivation. Private universities have no unions and the staff welfare committees are funded through monthly contributions from members of staff. Public universities should study the model offered in private universities for possible duplication.

Lack of Leadership Skills among Student Union Leaders
All universities have student representative unions/councils which run the affairs of the student body. However, most student unions fail to operate effectively due to lack of training, poor finances and poor capacity to raise funds. Elected students' representatives are only offered a one day orientation program on leadership and management. Training of student representatives is inadequate considering the complexity of tasks required of the students' representative councils and the role played by student representatives on university councils.

Universities should facilitate training for students' representative council members in leadership, community service, conflict mediation, and advocacy, to empower their work as student leaders, and to benefit them in later life.

Although it is unpopular with university administrations, one of the means by which student governments could be strengthened is to allow leaders to take time off from school to pursue leadership training.

Inadequate Management Information Systems
Most universities in Malawi have improved their information management systems for the maintenance of student records, however further improvements can be made. A significant challenge encountered in the preparation of this study related to difficulties in obtaining information from higher education institutions, despite the existence of computerized management information systems. In some institutions, the format for data relating to enrollment and staffing has changed from year to year, and is inconsistent.

UNIMA has established a committee to introduce a university-wide ICT system. The university plans to introduce online enrollment in line with the model implemented at COM, where students can access their examination results online. The Research and Consultancies Committee plans to create a database of all lecturers in order to match their skills to consultancies awarded to the colleges. The AfDB has proposed a project to, *inter alia*, increase access to and the use of ICT through improved facilities and services at Chancellor College and the Polytechnic. The other UNIMA colleges are not included in this project and other strategies will need to be devised to ensure that these colleges benefit from an inclusive and comprehensive management information system.

Improved management information systems will not only provide timely and accurate data on enrollment, but will help to strengthen capacity and informational resources for strategic planning and policy analysis at the national and institutional levels. NCHE should assume an important role in the development of improved systems at the national level, and improved data will help the NCHE to deliver on its mandate to strengthen M&E systems in the long run.

Outsourcing of Non-Academic Services
Substantial progress has been made in the outsourcing of non-academic services in public universities and colleges relating to cleaning, grounds maintenance, security, and student catering. An analysis (annex 5A.1) of the outcomes associated with outsourcing at Chancellor College demonstrates mixed results with improved cash flow offset by increased expenditure of MK 48.4 million. Additional benefits include a reduction in staff retrenchments; a reduction in applications for advances and funeral expenses; fewer demonstrations by students; improved use of utilities; and a reduction in the cost of perishable items, emoluments, and pensions. A close analysis of the expenditure pattern after outsourcing shows increased catering costs—from MK 130 million to MK 289 million. The total privatization of this function is one potential solution, as demonstrated by CUNIMA where students pay for the meals directly to the contractor without the involvement of the College Administration. The resulting savings could be used to support other quality related inputs such as books and periodicals, and equipment.

Conclusion

Public universities were established by Acts of parliament that lay out the governance and management structures of the institutions. Similarly, private universities have been established by charters and are accredited by Malawi's Registration and Accreditation Committee. The UNIMA and MZUNI Acts were approved some time ago, and aspects of this legislation may now inhibit the ability of universities to respond to the increasingly complex environment in which they operate. The proposed amendments to the UNIMA Act are a step in the right direction, but need to go further. New administrative structures should be established to enable the institution to move alleviate its financial dependence on the state. The proposed appointment of deans through an interview process should lead to the improved management of faculties. There is a need to create structures to more effectively facilitate interaction between universities and the private sector to increase revenues and the relevance of programs. Vice Chancellors should provide strong leadership in their institutions and spend a substantial amount of their time on tasks associated with the expansion of international partnerships, the mobilizing resources, and marketing to translate strategic plans/visions into action and desired outcomes.

The lack of an interface between the government, universities and the private sector will continue to undermine the ability of universities to respond to the country's current and future needs. There is need to review the composition of the councils in public universities, which tend to be inward looking and dominated by academics and government officials, with little representation from the private sector and civil society groups. Balanced representation will improve the capacity of councils to raise additional resources through PPPs, introduce new approaches to the way universities are organized and run, and enhance the alignment of university programming with the needs of the economy and society at large.

Tensions relating to autonomy and academic freedom are common in systems of higher education, internationally. However, in the Malawian context greater autonomy should granted to public institutions, and the role of government should be reduced with regard to its influence on the governance and management of the public universities.

The role of the UO at UNIMA needs to be reviewed in the light of progress in implementing the government's education decentralization policy. There is need to explore the privatization of non-academic services to promote financial savings and improved administrative efficiency. Privatization of these functions will reduce the burden imposed on the university administrations, freeing up more time to deal with core academic functions.

The creation of the NCHE is welcomed as an important step towards the improving the quality and relevance of higher education institutions. It is important that the council is fully capacitated and financed to enable it to effectively implement its mandate.

Programmatic Policy Options

Informed by the findings of this study, the policy options listed in table 5.1 are intended to assist the sector to address challenges negatively affecting the governance and management of higher education. Further study will be required to determine the relative cost effectiveness and the feasibility of policy options to inform holistic governance and management strategies.

Table 5.1 Policy Options

Policy objective	Issue	Programmatic options to address supply/demand constraints	Expected impact
Governance and Management	Perceived loss of autonomy and academic freedom	Revise the composition of university council to bring in other stakeholders outside government, including the private sector and civil society. Delink constituent colleges to create autonomy of current colleges from the UO.	Improved management of higher education institutions, increased autonomy, and reduction of management costs.
	Lack of national policies and documents like human resources to map skill requirements for public and private sector	Adopt an integrated human resource development planning which links the HRD strategy to other national development strategies. Establish a framework to promoting improved interaction between government, the private sector and the universities.	Improved levels of human capital in line with the country's needs.
	Lack of skills in planning, leadership, implementation, entrepreneurship and decision-making	Build capacity of professional and administrative staff through appropriate training.	Improved management of institutions and more efficient and effective utilization of resources.
	Lack of computerized Management Information Systems in the university system.	Establish computerized management information systems.	Improved management of higher education institutions.
	Unclear criteria for promotion to leadership positions in the public institutions.	Ensure merit-based appointment to top leadership positions in institutions, using clearly articulated and appropriate criteria	Improved management of higher education institutions.

Annex for Chapter 5

Annex 5A.1 A Comparison of Estimated Expenditures for 2007/08 and 2010/11 for Outsourced Services

Expenditure Category	2007/08	2010/11
Salaries	100,785,071	
Actual Maintenance	33,944,105	
Outsourced Maintenance		37,690,000
Security Services		34,524,000
Cleaning Services		35,340,000
Student Feeding		
Salaries	32,458,860	
Cost of Foodstuffs	97,821,840	
Outsourced Students' Catering		289,315,000
Estimated Annual Pension		
Contributions	43,304,278	
Estimated Annual Medical		
Contributions	5,196,513	
Estimated Annual TEVET Levy	1,332,439	
Estimated Annual Duty Allowances	19,986,590	
Estimated Annual Leave Grants	986,005	
Estimated Annual Terminal Benefits	12,697,007	
Total	348,512,707	396,869,000
Gain/Loss		−48,356,293

Notes

1. For church-based universities, this will be the Diocese under which the university falls and for private universities this would be a group of investors who often constitute the Board of the university.
2. University of Malawi Act (2008) and Mzuzu University Act (1997).
3. The score uses certain indicators to determine Organizational; Staffing; Financial; and Academic Autonomy.
4. Eurydice European Unit (2008).

References

Adams, J. C. 1994. "Appraising Classroom Teaching in Higher Education: An Alternative Approach." *Quality Assurance in Education* 2 (2): 15–17. MCB University Press.

Archbald, R. B., and D. H. Feldman. 2006. "Explaining Increases in Higher Education Costs." Working Paper Number 46, College of William and Mary Department of Economics, Williamsburg, VA.

Baldwin, R. G., and M. V. Krotseng. 1985. "Incentives in the Academy: Issues and Options." In *Incentives for Faculty Vitality: New Direction for Higher Education*, edited by R. G. Baldwin, No 51, 5–20. San Francisco, CA: Jossey-Bass.

Bentley, K., A. Habib, and S. Morrow. 2006. "Academic Freedom, Institutional Autonomy and the Corporatised University in Contemporary South Africa." HEIAAF (Series No. 3, November 2006), The Council on Higher Education, Pretoria.

Bloom, D., D. Canning, and K. Chan. 2006. *Higher Education and Economic Development in Africa*. Human Development Sector, Africa Region. Washington, DC: The World Bank.

Davoodi, H. R., E. R. Tiongson, and S. S. Asawanuchit. 2003. "How Useful Are Benefit Incidence Analyses of Public Education and Health Spending?" IMF Working Paper (WP/03/227), International Monetary Fund, Washington, DC.

Edward, C. 1984. *Performance Appraisal—A Working Guide*. London: The Industrial Society.

Eurydice European Unit. 2008. *Higher Education Governance in Europe: Policies, Structures, Funding and Academic Staff*. Brussels: Eurydice.

Fägerlind, I., and G. Strömqvist.2004. *Reforming Higher Education in the Nordic Countries: Studies of Change in Denmark, Finland, Iceland, Norway and Sweden*. Paris: International Institute for Educational Planning.

Government of Malawi. 1997. *Mzuzu University Act* No. 12.

———. 1998. *University of Malawi Act* (1974). Incorporating the Amended Act of 1998.

———. 2006. "Malawi Growth and Development Strategy: From Poverty to Prosperity 2006–2011." Available from http://www.malawi.gov.mw/Publications/MGDS%20November%202006%20-%20MEPD.pdf.

———. 2012. "Malawi Growth and Development Strategy II." Available from http://www.gafspfund.org/sites/gafspfund.org/files/MGDS%20II%20final%20document%20january%202012.pdf.

Hale, J. 2010. *Growing Knowledge: Access to Research in East and Southern African Universities*. London: The Association of Commonwealth Universities.

Husen, T. 1991 "The Idea of the University: Changing Roles, Current Crisis and Future Challenges." *Prospects* 21 (2): 171–88.

Irandoust, S., and V. Kromadit. 2010. "The Time is Now for Public-Private Partnerships in Higher Learning." *The Nation*, June 4. Thailand. Available from http://www.nationmultimedia.com/home/2010/06/04/opinion/The-time-is-now-for-public-private-partnerships-in-30130834.html.

Johnston, D. B. 2006. *Financing Higher Education: Cost Sharing in International Perspective*. Boston, MA: Center for International Higher Education.

Kamlongera, C. F. 2011. "The Impact of Out-Sourcing of Non-Academic Services on Financial Resources." Unpublished paper presented at the 2011 Joint Sector Review.

Levental, G. S. 1976. "The Distribution of Rewards and Resources in Groups and Organizations." In *Advances in Experimental Social Psychology*, edited by L. Berkowitz and E. Hatfield, 91–131. New York: Academic Press.

Materu, P. 2007. "Higher Education Quality Assurance in Sub-Saharan Africa: Status, Challenges, Opportunities and Promising Practices." World Bank Working Paper No. 124, World Bank, Washington, DC.

Materu, P., P. Obanya, and P. Righetti. 2011. "The Rise, Fall, and Reemergence of the University of Ibadan, Nigeria." In *The Road to Academic Excellence: The making of World-Class Research University*, edited by P. G. Altbach and J. Salmi. Directions in Development. Washington, DC: World Bank.

Ministry of Education, Science and Technology. 2011. "Education Sector Performance Report. Lilongwe, Malawi."

Morris, L., P. Stanton, and S. Young. 2007. *Performance Management in Higher Education: The Great Divide*. Melbourne, Australia: La Trobe University.

Pfeiffer, D., and G. Chiunda. 2008. "Tracer Study of TEVET and Higher Education Completers in Malawi—Final Report." GTZ/World Bank, Lilongwe.

The Quality Assurance Agency for Higher Education. 2010. *Assuring Quality and Standards in Higher Education*. Gloucester UK: South Gate House.

Regional Programme on Enterprise Development. 2006. *Malawi Investment Climate Assessment*. Africa Private Sector Group. Washington, DC: The World Bank.

Richardson Jr., R. C., K. R. Bracco, P. M. Callan, and J. E. Finney. 1998. *Higher Education Governance: Balancing Institutional and Market Influences*. San Jose, CA: The National Center for Public Policy and Higher Education.

Salmi, J. 2009. *The Challenges of Establishing World Class Universities*. Human Development. Washington, DC: World Bank.

SARUA. 2009. "Leadership Challenges For Higher Education in Southern Africa." In *SARUA Leadership Dialogue Series* 1 (1). South Africa.

Scot, G. 2003. "Effective Change Management in Higher Education." *Educause Review* (November/December): 64–80. Boulder, CO: Educause. Available from https://net.educause.edu/ir/library/pdf/ERM0363.pdf.

Scribbin, K., and F. Walton. 1987. *Staff Appraisal in Further and Higher Education: A Study in Performance Review and Development*. Bristol: Further Education Staff College.

Smith, T. C. 2005. "Comprehensive Paper Presented in Partial Fulfillment of the Requirements of the Degree of Doctor of Philosophy." School of Education Capella University, Minneapolis, MI. Available from http://home.surewest.net/tcsmith/papers/Ted%20Smith%20Comp%20Paper%204.pdf.

UCU. 2010. "UCU Policy Briefing: Student:Teacher Ratios in Higher and Further Education." Available from http://www.ucu.org.uk/media/pdf/q/6/ucupolicybrief_ssratios_may10.pdf.

UNESCO Institute for Statistics, UIS. Stat

University of Malawi. 2006. "University of Malawi Policy on Research and Consultancy."

World Bank. 2009. *Accelerating Catch-up: Tertiary Education for Growth in Sub-Sahara Africa*. Directions in Development. Washington, DC. Available from http://siteresources.worldbank.org/INTAFRICA/Resources/e-book_ACU.pdf [accessed 2013].

———. 2010a. *Financing Higher Education in Africa*. Directions in Development. Washington, DC: World Bank. Available from http://documents.worldbank.org/curated/en/2010/01/12228311/financing-higher-education-africa.

———. 2010b. "The Education System in Malawi." Africa Education Country Status Report, World Bank Working Paper No. 182, World Bank, Washington, DC.

ECO-AUDIT

Environmental Benefits Statement

The World Bank Group is committed to reducing its environmental footprint. In support of this commitment, the Publishing and Knowledge Division leverages electronic publishing options and print-on-demand technology, which is located in regional hubs worldwide. Together, these initiatives enable print runs to be lowered and shipping distances decreased, resulting in reduced paper consumption, chemical use, greenhouse gas emissions, and waste.

The Publishing and Knowledge Division follows the recommended standards for paper use set by the Green Press Initiative. The majority of our books are printed on Forest Stewardship Council (FSC)–certified paper, with nearly all containing 50–100 percent recycled content. The recycled fiber in our book paper is either unbleached or bleached using totally chlorine free (TCF), processed chlorine free (PCF), or enhanced elemental chlorine free (EECF) processes.

More information about the Bank's environmental philosophy can be found at http://crinfo.worldbank.org/wbcrinfo/node/4.

www.ingramcontent.com/pod-product-compliance
Lightning Source LLC
Chambersburg PA
CBHW060315240426
43661CB00059B/2767